Save Your Florida Home ... NOW!

Save Your Florida Home... NOW!

Or Walk Away With
No Debt, Better Credit and
Money in Your Pocket

Charles W. Price, Esq.

LIABILITY DISCLAIMER

The material contained in this manual is general in nature and is not intended as specific advice on any particular matter. The author and publisher expressly disclaim any and all liability to any persons whatsoever in respect of anything done by any such person in reliance, whether in whole or in part, on this book. While the author is engaged in rendering legal services, the author and publisher are not engaged in rendering accounting, career, or financial services. Any services, references, and/or websites that may be mentioned or referred to in this manual are provided for information purposes only. Please take appropriate legal and/or professional advice before acting on any information in this manual.

ISBN: 978-0-615-38136-7

CONTACT INFO

www.SaveYourFloridaHomeNow.com

PRICE LAW FIRM
ATTORNEYS AT LAW

Price Law Firm, PLC
390 Maitland Avenue, Suite 1000
Altamonte Springs, FL 32701
407-834-0090
866-381-9243
www.CPriceLawFirm.com

Table of Contents

Acknowledgments

The author gratefully acknowledges the following people for their support and creative contributions:

My wife, Suzi, my biggest supporter and cheerleader, who edited my manuscript and picked up the slack for our family while I wrote this book. (Sorry. You can't have her contact information. She's all mine!)

My Mother, who was always there to catch me when I fell and sacrificed her entire life to ensure that my brother and I would excel in all of life's pursuits.

My friend and colleague, Jeff Haden, a brilliant writer who assisted me in researching and writing this book. www.blackbirdinc.com.

My friend and mentor, Joel Bauer, who provided the method and the motivation to write this book. www.infotainer.com.

My friend and mentor, Mike Citron, who provided invaluable information on foreclosure and credit repair. www.disputesuite.com.

April Charney, Esq., a tireless attorney with Jacksonville Area Legal Aid, Inc., who finally opened my eyes to the reality of mortgage-backed securities and the widespread fraud in the mortgage industry.

My friend and gifted artist, Kathy Jacquart, who actually painted the front cover of this book. www.KJacquart.com.

My friend and talented designer, Rosie Grupp, who designed the interior and exterior of this book. BookStudio@comcast.net

My friend and brilliant copywriter, Eric Gelb, who crafted and created the message for this book. www.PublishingGold.com.

The entire staff of Price Law Firm who worked harder than ever to allow me the freedom and time to write this book. www.cpricelawfirm.com.

Introduction

I've never seen things this bad.

Over the last twenty years my law practice has focused on helping clients who face debt and credit problems. I've personally represented thousands of clients in Chapter 7 and Chapter 13 bankruptcy cases. Bankruptcy, while often the worst-case scenario, can also turn out to be a lifeline for people who face overwhelming debt and financial hardship.

In hundreds of other cases I've helped clients use bankruptcy alternatives like debt consolidation, loan modification, loan forbearance, short sales, and other legal procedures and strategies.

(By the way: If you aren't familiar with or don't understand some of the strategies I just mentioned, don't worry – by the end of this book you will.)

I also help clients avoid foreclosure... and, sadly, business is booming.

Until recently, most of my clients were people who had been struggling financially for years. Most were facing financial hardship due to circumstances outside their control: They lost jobs, had business fail, were dealing with long-term illness or injury, or were hit with unexpected expenses. Many clients had, to be blunt, bitten off more than they could chew. They lived beyond their means, took on debt they couldn't handle, or made poor financial decisions.

So I helped them, in a variety of ways, depending on their needs and their goals.

Today it's different. Today, my average client could boast (if they were in the habit of boasting) that less than a year ago they:

- Had never missed a payment
- Had a credit score of 750 to 800
- Used credit wisely and managed their finances well
- Had equity in their homes

Yet now those same people are in foreclosure and watching everything go down the tubes. And they aren't alone: Millions of Florida homeowners are either in the same boat... or are waiting in line to board that boat. The financial crisis has devastated the Florida real estate market, the Florida banking and lending system... and Florida homeowners. Sadly, I don't think relief is in sight – at least not in the near future.

My clients aren't alone. You aren't alone. Stuff has happened – and it's happened to a lot of people.

But there is hope. I know – I've worked on both sides of the foreclosure fence.

After I earned my law degree from the University of Florida College of Law, I worked for a law firm that represented creditors, handling foreclosures and collections. My job was to represent major banks in foreclosure proceedings, loan modifications, and loan workouts. I also represented major creditors and bankruptcy trustees in bankruptcy court.

In short, I came after people like you.

It was my job, but I hated it. Admittedly I was good at it, but representing banks and creditors was not where my heart was. After many sleepless nights I stopped working for creditors and formed my own practice, exclusively helping consumers – people like you. I also wrote two books about surviving – and prospering – after bankruptcy. They were minor sensations, and I have appeared as a credit and debt expert on national radio and television programs.

My message always boils down to hope. And there is hope – for my clients, and for you.

How do I know? In addition to having worked both sides of the credit fence, years ago I also stood where you now stand. I lost a job. I watched a business fail. I filed bankruptcy. I have been through foreclosure. I'm not just a bankruptcy or foreclosure attorney. I get it. I've been there. I know what you're going through... because I went through it myself.

In short, I've seen the process from all conceivable angles. Not only have I seen it – I've lived it. As a lawyer who has represented creditors, who has helped consumers, and who has survived and prospered after bankruptcy and foreclosure... I understand what you are going through.

I've never seen it this bad – but I also know how to help you.

Let's get started!

— Charlie Price

Chapter One

Create a Game Plan to Stop the Foreclosure

At some point, you start to realize that you have a problem – you know that there isn't enough money to go around. Something has happened – you lost your job, your spouse lost a job, you have extensive medical debts, etc. Whatever the cause, you now have to choose between buying food and paying the electric bill on one hand, or paying the mortgage on the other. This is usually a fairly easy choice.

But, what comes next? When you start to struggle with paying your mortgage on time, what's the next step? How do you proceed?

Unfortunately, most people usually do nothing. They bury their heads in the sand and hope that everything will just get better. They don't communicate with the lender, don't respond when they get a foreclosure complaint, and are totally shocked when a sheriff shows up at the door with a 24-hour eviction notice.

I don't want that for you. I want you to take charge of the situation and develop a game plan that will help you save your home if you wish, avoid liability if you don't, and avoid surprises during the process.

The best way to do that is to develop a game plan from the beginning. I think that there are essentially four steps to this process.

First, decide whether you want to keep the house or not. Initially, this is usually a difficult decision. Most of my clients want to keep their homes. They've often invested a lot of money into the home and have fond memories of family and friends sharing their home with them.

But, in reality, the decision usually comes down to finances versus emotions. For many of my clients, their income has changed permanently and dramatically. For example, it's not reasonable to expect to stay in a home with a $500,000 mortgage if you're income consists solely of Social Security Disability payments of $1000.00 per month – and that's never going to change. For these clients, the decision is relatively easy. I'm just trying to do damage control and limit their exposure to lawsuits and judgments.

For other clients, the decision is not so easy. Many of my clients have lost their jobs and are living on unemployment benefits. They cannot afford to pay their mortgage on this income. However, it's possible that they may find new employment in time to save their home from the foreclosure process. In these cases, I'll try to buy as much time as possible to give them an opportunity to start bringing in new income.

For other clients, it makes financial sense to walk from the home, even if they can afford to start making payments again in the future. Many of my clients, and Floridians in general, are "upside down" on their homes. This means that they owe more on their homes than they're currently worth. In many cases, this can be hundreds of thousands of dollars.

For these clients, it may take fifteen years, or longer, to break even again on the value of their home. Many of my clients ultimately determine that the best financial option is to surrender their home and start over. This option makes a lot of sense for many clients, and I enthusiastically encourage this path – especially if they can't really afford the ongoing mortgage payments.

So, the first step in this process is to determine whether you want to keep your home or not. In Chapter 2, I'll help you think through your financial situation to determine your best option. For many of my clients, this is truly the first time that they've actually sat down and analyzed their finances – and they're often surprised by the results.

Sometimes, many of my clients start down the path of saving their home, and realize after many months that they just aren't willing to make the financial sacrifices necessary to save their current home. You may come to this realization down the road as well. That's OK. I'll help you to determine the best options at every step. Just keep your mind open to all of the possibilities.

Once you've made your initial decision about keeping the home or letting it go, it's time to move on to step two – communicating with your lender. As I said before, many of my clients bury their heads in the sand and don't ever communicate with their lenders. This is a mistake. Most lenders have programs in place to help you avoid foreclosure. These programs include refinancing, forbearance, modification, short sales and deeds-in-lieu.

Although communicating with your lender is often a frustrating experience, you need to do it – at least initially. See what the lender is willing to do for you. At the very least, this may keep the lender from moving quickly to take your home.

At some point, it may make more sense for an attorney to communicate with your lender on your behalf. But, at least initially, I think it's worthwhile to talk to the lender and open the lines of communication. We'll talk more about this in Chapter 3.

Step three in this process is to learn the timeline – how long do you have before you lose your home to the foreclosure process? Many of my clients mistakenly assume that they must move out of their house after the first missed mortgage payment or when they receive a foreclosure complaint. Other clients assume that they have all the time in the world – and are unpleasantly surprised when the sheriff asks them to leave their home.

So, it's vitally important that you know the real timeline for a Florida foreclosure. Knowing how much time you have will allow you to plan your moves in the best way possible – not too fast and not too slow. We'll talk about this in Chapter 4.

Then, starting with Chapter 5, we'll talk about all of the different ways to save your home. In Chapter 5, we'll talk about your action strategy – the actual steps that you will take to fight the foreclosure process. In Chapter 6, we'll talk about loan workouts and modification agreements. In Chapter 7, we'll look at using Chapter 13 bankruptcy to save your home and address different debt problems. Finally, in Chapter 8, I'll tell you about one of my favorite strategies that combines the best techniques into one powerful home-saving weapon. I'll discuss each of these home-saving strategies and show you how they work together. By the time you've finished this section, you'll be ready to fight the foreclosure on your terms and according to your financial situation.

In Chapter 9, I'll tell you about all of the different ways to walk away from your home and minimize your liability. There are many ways to do this. However, each technique has pros and cons. I'll walk you through each technique and help you to identify the best one for you. Then, in Chapter 10, I'll tell you how to use a Chapter 7 bankruptcy case to clean up any liabilities that may come from your decision to surrender your home.

Finally, starting in Chapter 11, I'll explain how to repair your credit and dramatically increase your credit score, even if you end this process with a foreclosure, bankruptcy, or both. There are many ways to repair your credit, and I'm going to show you how to do this, step-by-step.

Do You Need a Lawyer?

Many Florida consumers wonder whether they need a lawyer to help them with the foreclosure process. As a lawyer, I know the value that I can bring to the process and to my clients. However, many clients may find that they have the time and ability to fight the foreclosure on their own. So, the simple answer is that you do not need an attorney to fight the foreclosure.

However, with that said, many consumers are simply not prepared to handle all of the steps needed to properly fight and negotiate with the mortgage companies and their attorneys. In this book, I will give you a broad overview of the different techniques available for fighting the foreclosure process. But, I can't give you everything within the space constraints of this book.

I've always believed in the division of labor – everybody does what they're best at and everybody prospers. Because I wasn't blessed with mechanical abilities, I don't repair my own car. I could probably figure it out. But, it's simply not worth the time, money or effort it would take me to repair my car. Instead, I hire someone else who likes to repair cars and is actually good at it.

I like to think of the law this way. You can probably figure out how to handle the foreclosure process on your own. But, you'll probably get a better result if you retain a lawyer who specializes in this area of the law. You don't need to hire me. But, do hire an attorney who knows how to fight the foreclosure process from start to finish.

Additional Help

You can discover more detailed information about the foreclosure process at www.SaveYourFloridaHomeNow.com. At this site, you can download sample court documents and learn about the latest developments in foreclosure and modification. In addition, you can receive advanced information about foreclosure defense and learn to properly prepare a modification packet for your lender.

Chapter Two

What Are My Financial Options – Should I Keep My Home Or Let It Go?

I know what you're thinking. If you're facing foreclosure, the last thing you want to do is review your finances – you've probably done that hundreds of times.

But, the first real step in the foreclosure process is to determine whether you should keep your home or let it go. And, you really can't make that decision unless you know whether you can afford to keep it.

So, indulge me. It will be worth it. To truly understand your options, you absolutely must take an objective look at your assets, your expenses, and your possibilities. If you absolutely cannot afford to make your mortgage payments – no matter what you do – then working to keep your house probably doesn't make sense. Sure, you can use strategies to delay the foreclosure process and stay in the house longer, but in most cases you will eventually lose the house.

On the other hand, even if you can't afford your current payment, you may be able to work out a loan modification or a forbearance plan that allows you to stay in the home – but to determine whether to pursue those options you have to know what you can and cannot afford in terms of mortgage payments (and other expenses.) Plus, at some point the lender may ask you to provide proof of your ability to meet the terms and conditions of a modification or forbearance plan – so why not take care of that ahead of time?

Think of it this way: Would you shop for a car you can't afford? The same basic premise applies to foreclosure defense: You shouldn't waste time and effort pursuing options that aren't feasible – determine what *is* feasible and work hard on those options.

We'll start with determining your net worth.

Calculate Your Net Worth

Your net worth, in simple terms, is the difference in what you own and what you owe. (Assets *minus* liabilities *equals* net worth.)

Determine Assets

We'll start with your assets. Assets are cash or items that can be turned into cash. Bank accounts, stock investments, etc. are assets.

Your home is an asset, as long as it has equity, meaning it is worth more – in terms of real market value – than what you owe. If you could sell your house for $200,000, and you only owe $150,000, your equity is $50,000. That equity is an asset. If your home is now worth less than you paid for it – which is the case for millions of Florida homeowners – your home is not an asset, it's a liability. If you owe $200,000 and your home is worth $180,000, you are upside-down and in effect your net worth is decreased by $20,000.

If your car is paid off and you could sell it for $8,000 it's an asset. If you just bought a car, and you put little or no money down, even though it's "worth" $25,000 it's not an asset because if you sold it today the proceeds wouldn't go into your pocket – they would instead go to paying off your loan. (If it sounds complicated don't worry – this process will help you figure it all out.)

Use the following **Assets Worksheet** to list all your assets. Remember, the actual value is what you can sell the item for, not what the item is theoretically "worth." A gold necklace that cost $500 isn't worth $500 unless someone will actually pay you that much for it.

Here is a list of some common assets you might have:

- Savings accounts, checking accounts, investment accounts
- 401(k) accounts, retirement accounts, life insurance policies (cash value, not the policy value)
- Home (Be honest here. Home values have dropped – a lot!)
- Automobiles, motorcycles, boats, RVs
- Jewelry
- Furniture
- Collectibles
- Antiques
- Artwork
- Cash
- Etc.

List your assets on this sheet:

Assets Worksheet

Cash on hand	______________
Checking account	______________
Savings account	______________
Money Market Funds	______________
Home(s)	______________
Life insurance (cash value)	______________
Stocks	______________
Mutual funds	______________
IRA	______________
401(k)	______________
Retirement plan (current value)	______________
Automobile(s)	______________
Jewelry	______________
Antiques and collectibles	______________
Furniture	______________
Other	______________
Total Assets	**$** ______________

List everything, but again, don't be tempted to overestimate the values. It's easy to place emotional value on an item that has little or no actual value. Your grandmother's bracelet may, to you, be priceless but is only worth $20 to someone else.

Think of it this way: If you die and all your possessions are sold, what would they be worth?

Also search for hidden or forgotten assets. You may have a savings account you've forgotten about, stock certificates collecting dust in a file drawer, savings bonds in a folder, or even old coins tucked in a cabinet.

Over the years it's easy to accumulate and then forget valuable items – hunt them down.

Determine Liabilities

Now that you've listed your assets it's time to list your liabilities.

Liabilities are what you owe. Any debt is a liability: Credit cards, personal loans, mortgages, auto loans, and even money you owe to friends or family.

Determining your liabilities is easier than determining your assets. In most cases you get a bill or a statement, unless a friend loaned you some money. (Regardless, that's still a liability.) Typical liabilities include:

- Mortgages
- Credit cards
- Automobile loans
- Medical bills
- Child support & alimony
- Household debts
- Personal loans
- Etc.

Use the following worksheet to list your liabilities.

Again, list everything. Take the time to think it through. This is probably a painful and depressing exercise, but don't be tempted to hide from reality. You must know your current situation so you can make good decisions and take the right steps to improve it – and possibly save your home.

Now fill out your sheet:

Personal Liabilities Worksheet

Mortgage	__________________
Credit cards	__________________
	__________________
	__________________
Automobile loans	__________________
	__________________
Medical bills	__________________
Personal loans	__________________
Student loans	__________________
Store loans	__________________
	__________________
Alimony & child support	__________________
Other	__________________
	__________________
Total Liabilities	$ __________________

Now that you've determined what you have and what you owe, simply subtract your liabilities from your assets to determine your net worth.

Total Assets	____________
minus Total Liabilities	____________
Equals Net Worth	____________

For example, if you have $400,000 in assets and $380,000 in liabilities, your net worth is $20,000.

When you determine your net worth, don't be tempted to take shortcuts:

- Review all records and documents.
- Find actual account statements.
- Look up fair market values for your physical assets.
- In short, don't guess – know!

You may find that your net worth is negative because your assets are worth less than your liabilities. Because most Floridians have lost as much as 50% of the value of their homes in the last several years, virtually all of my clients have a negative net worth. This, by itself, isn't a fatal problem.

However, I think it's important to think about this when you're deciding whether to keep your home. How long will it take for the value of your home to equal the mortgage balance? Depending on where you are and when you bought or refinanced your home, it may take fifteen or more years before your start to see positive equity in your home. I'm just planting a seed here.

Determine Actual Expenses and Spending

No matter how much money we have, we all spend needlessly or without thought. To get control of your finances and determine your foreclosure defense options, you must figure out what you spend.

A quick disclaimer: Determining actual expenses is at the top of most people's list of least favorite things to do... but is also why many people live beyond their means and make poor financial decisions. In your case the goal is to determine what you can and cannot do, realistically, in terms of saving your home.

How do you get started? First, gather up all your bills. Your bills will show your actual expenses for loans, utility payments, etc. (Your credit card statements will also show you how much you spend on certain items.) Pull out as many old credit card statements as you can – they'll help you identify money you've spent that you may not remember.

Then list all the ways you spend money – especially cash – that don't show up on a monthly bill.

Here's a worksheet to help you determine your monthly expenses. The list included isn't exhaustive – you're likely to have expenses not listed here. Write them in. Just make sure you list everything.

Note: No matter how hard you try, you may not remember all your weekly or monthly expenses. Take a week and track every penny you spend. Every time you write a check, use your credit card, or pay cash, write it down. You'll be surprised by how many ways you spend money that have become so automatic you don't even think about them... much less remember.

Expenses Worksheet

Mortgage	______________
Home equity loan	______________
Car payment	______________
Car payment	______________
Credit card payment	______________
Credit card payment	______________
Credit card payment	______________
Car insurance	______________
Gas and car repairs	______________
Home insurance	______________
Other loans	______________
Life insurance	______________
Child care and tuition	______________
Groceries	______________
Utility bills	______________
Phone bills	______________
Internet	______________
Cable bill	______________
Clothing	______________
Meals (eating out)	______________
Entertainment	______________
Other	______________
Other	______________
Total Expenses	**$** ______________

It can be mentally exhausting to put together your list of expenses, especially if your financial life has grown increasingly depressing. Fight through it, and identify everything you spend money on.

Then go back to your **Expenses Worksheet** and double-check to make sure you didn't miss anything. Have someone you trust look it over. Find *everything* you spend money on: You absolutely need to know where you are today.

You'll notice your expenses fall into two broad categories: Fixed expenses and variable expenses. Fixed expenses are things you spend money on that you can't easily control or change. For instance, your mortgage payment is a fixed expense – you can't quickly reduce or eliminate that spending. Insurance is also a fixed expense; while you could shop for a cheaper rate, relatively speaking you can't decide today that you'll pay less for car insurance.

But you can decide to start bringing your lunch to work today, which will immediately reduce your spending. Groceries, entertainment, gas, clothing... all these are variable expenses, because you can easily make different decisions that can reduce your spending.

Take a second and look at your **Expenses Worksheet**. Which items are variable expenses and which are truly fixed expenses? For example, you may have entered $65 for your cable bill.

You probably see that as a fixed expense, since it's a bill you pay every month, but in reality it's a variable expense: You could drop cable service altogether, or more realistically you could stop paying for premium channels you really don't watch. That's why cable is a variable expense – you can immediately decide to spend less. Almost every expense category on your sheet can, with a little creativity and a willingness to change your outlook on spending, be reduced – which puts more money in your pocket.

Before we move on, let's do a quick sense-check of your current financial position. Subtract all your current monthly expenses, fixed and variable, from your monthly net income.

(Net income) ____________

minus (Expenses) ____________

equals ____________ (your monthly surplus/shortfall)

What does this mean?

- If you spend less than you earn, that's great! (But it also means you should have no trouble keeping up with your mortgage payments... which means you haven't identified all your expenses.)
- If you spend more than you earn, you're in trouble and will have to take steps to deal with the problem.

If you're like most people, you fall into one of two categories:

- Common monthly expense are reasonable or within your income, but the extras get you in trouble
- Ongoing monthly expenses – much less the extras – are too much for your income level

Of course one other situation may apply: If you have an adjustable-rate mortgage and your payments have increased, what was a reasonable or within your income payment is no longer affordable.

Determine What You Can Cut

Now you know how you're spending your money. I'm sure you've taken steps to cut expenses, but let's take a quick look at some of the possibilities you might have missed. The goal is to free up funds to either help you make your current house payments or at the least to determine what kind of payment you can afford, assuming loan modification or forbearance is an option. Again, the overall goal is to assess where you stand so you can decide which strategies to employ... or whether it makes better sense to simply let your house go.

So: Go back to your **Expenses Worksheet**.

Take a look at each item on the worksheet. Pull out the bills or statements that document your spending in that category.

Then ask yourself the following questions for each item in that category:

1. **Do I need to spend this money at all?** For example, you may pay a monthly fee for cell phone damage or replacement insurance. (Typically that runs about $5 per month.) Does it make sense to have insurance if it will only cost $50 to replace the cell phone and the deductible is $25? Cutting off the insurance will pay for itself in three months. $5 per month may not sound like much... but it adds up to $60 per year that you in effect are currently giving away.

2. **If I do need to spend it, can I reduce the amount?** To use the cell phone example, say you pay $10 per month to send 200 text messages, plus an additional $10 because you always go over your limit. Can you convert to an unlimited plan for $12 per month? (Or better yet, can you decide the ability to text isn't really that important, and eliminate the charge

altogether?) Take a look at every bill and consider calling to ask for a rate reduction. If you're not sure, just make the call and ask. What can it hurt? All they can say is no.

3. **If I can't reduce the amount, is there another alternative?** Let's use cell phones again. Say your cell phone plan costs $40 and you get unlimited minutes, including long distance. You also have phone service in your house that costs $40 a month. Do you need both? Can you eliminate your home phone service and simply use your cell phone for all calls? (More and more people do.)

You'll be surprised by what you find if you're open to making changes. Here are few sources of savings you can find using this approach:

4. **Cable, internet, and phone services:** Consider a package deal from your local cable or phone provider. You can get digital phone service, which is provided by a broadband Internet connection, high-speed Internet, and digital channels for much less than you will pay separately. And seriously – how many of your premium cable channels do you really watch?

5. **Credit card rate reductions:** Call your credit card company and ask for a rate reduction. Simply say you want an interest rate reduction or you'll take your business elsewhere. If the first person you reach can't or won't help, ask to talk to a supervisor. If you have a $5,000 balance, even a 3% rate reduction in rate saves you $150 a year; even if it takes you an hour to get what you want, in effect you made $150 an hour for your efforts.

6. **Auto insurance:** Evaluate your policy every year. If you haven't had an accident or a ticket, ask for a reduction. If you don't ask, you won't receive.

7. **Auto loans:** Some finance companies now refinance auto loans. If you have a high interest rate and you can qualify for a lower rate because your credit rating has improved, you may be able to reduce your monthly payments by refinancing. But be careful; if you also extend the term of your loan, you may end up paying more in total. Check out the total cost, not just the difference in interest rate.

8. **Meals:** Is eating lunch out really a reward for your hard work, or just a habit you've fallen into. Bring your lunch (better yet, bring leftovers), and if you need to "get away," go outside, go to the cafeteria, or simply take a walk. Even if you only spend $5 a day eating lunch out (and if that's all you spend, please tell me where I can get such a good deal), that's still over $1,200 a year. If your net hourly income is the same as the $14.50 we calculated earlier for Jane, it takes you two weeks of work to pay for your lunches. Still worth it?

9. **Subscriptions:** Do you get a daily newspaper? (Better yet, do you still read it?) You can check out most papers online for free. Many magazines offer the same service.

These are just a few of the possibilities. My goal is to get your ideas and creativity flowing. If you're like most people, you've already thought of other ideas. Well done!

But before we move on, one more thing: Watch carefully for the details.

Audit all your bills – every month, not just today – and look at all the fine print.

If you're like most people, you only focus on the bottom line, but the devil is in the details. Your hard earned money is in those details.

Especially check your credit card bills:

- Did you sign up for a credit watch program that charges you a fee every month?
- Are you still paying for a phone line you had disconnected months ago?
- Are you paying a yearly subscription to an online service you no longer use?

Inspect every credit card bill not only for errors but also for expenses you've forgotten. If a little sleuthing doesn't turn up some unintended spending, you're in a very small minority.

Reduce the Expenses You Identified

Identifying an opportunity is nice, but acting on that opportunity is what matters most. Let's make the process easy. In a moment you'll see a worksheet to help you work through almost all your expenses and find ways to reduce spending. Simply fill out the worksheet and then every day use the time you've scheduled to work on the next item on the list.

Here's an example. The following are monthly expenses. We'll use part of the Worksheet to help you understand what to do:

Reduce Spending Worksheet

Expense	Current Amount	Action Taken	New Amount	Follow-up Required?
Cell Phone	$65			
Car Insurance	$50			
Lunch (work)	$160			

So far we've simply listed the current amount our theoretical homeowner – we'll call him George – spends on a few items.

Now we'll do a little work:

Expense	Current Amount	Action Taken	New Amount
Cell Phone	$65	Changed plan	$45
Car Insurance	$50	Dropped towing	$45
Home Phone	$40	Drop service	$0
Lunch (work)	$160	Bring from home	$80

What happened? George called the cell phone provider and dropped replacement insurance and switched to unlimited texting between other people using the same carrier. (Everyone in his family uses the same carrier, so that works.)

He also dropped towing insurance for his car since in eight years he's never needed it. He also learned that his teenage son could qualify for a lower rate if he makes the honor roll, so he'll keep that in mind at report card time.

And he's started to take his lunch to work since he was throwing away leftovers, anyway. But he does assume he may have to buy a little more food at the grocery store, so he estimated he can cut that expense at least in half.

So: In about twenty minutes, he saved $20 on his cell phone bill, $5 on his car insurance bill (with more to come), $40 on his home phone, and $80 on lunch. So in effect he "made" $145 dollars – each and every month – for about 30 minutes worth of work.

Here's what you'll do. First fill in the first two columns of the following Expense Worksheet. Then, each day, work on reducing the expense in one, two, five... however many items you can. Write down your savings – that will make you feel good about what you do. And if you start to lose motivation, remember that if you can save $20 per month after putting in an hour's time on the phone, for example, that's like making $240 an hour... because you'll save $240 per year for that one hour's work.

Reduce Spending Worksheet

Expense	Current Amount	Action Taken	New Amount
Mortgage			
Car payment			
Car payment			
Credit card			
Credit card			
Credit card			
Car insurance			
Gas			
Parking/tolls			
Home insurance			
Other loans			
Other loans			
Life insurance			
Child care			
Groceries			
Utilities			
Utilities			
Utilities			
Phone			
Internet			
Cable			
Clothing			
Meals (out)			
Entertainment			
Entertainment			
Entertainment			
Entertainment			
Entertainment			

Total Saved ____________________

One last note about this Worksheet: If you're not sure how to reduce an expense, it's easy. Ask.

Why? For example, most companies don't want to lose your business. Say you want to reduce the interest rate on your credit card. Call and ask for a rate reduction. Simply say you are looking at other options, feel your rate is too high, and you'll take your business elsewhere. If the first person you reach can't or won't help, ask to talk to a supervisor.

If you have a $5,000 balance, a 3% rate reduction in rate saves you $150 a year; even if it takes you an hour to get what you want, in effect you will have made $150 an hour for your efforts.

You can also ask for help. Call your electric company and ask if they have ways you can save money on your bill. Many will send you free information; some will even send an auditor to your home (often for free) to help you find ways to reduce your electric bill.

Many businesses will help if you ask; if they won't, and you have a choice, find another company who will.

Build a Budget

I know: The dreaded "B" word.

I'm sorry, but you need one – see a budget as your best friend.

Once you've worked through every item on the **Reduce Spending Worksheet**, your "New Amount" totals automatically create your monthly budget. Once you've eliminated what you don't need to spend and reduced what you spend on the items you need, you know exactly what you will spend each month.

The beauty of this approach is you significantly reduced your spending while creating a budget you thoroughly understand. You know exactly where you were... and exactly where you are today.

And now you know your options in terms of foreclosure defense. If your expenses still are significantly higher than your income, unless you can increase your income – or take drastic measures like selling assets in order to free up cash or eliminate monthly payments – then it's unlikely that you can save your house. If the money you spend is only slightly higher than what you earn, then you may be able to work out a loan modification or a forbearance plan. If you've found ways to have a surplus of cash each month, then you can focus on delaying the foreclosure process while you take steps to get back on track in terms of payments.

And if you're behind on payments to other creditors, you may decide bankruptcy is your best bet.

In any case, now you will have a much better sense of how realistic some of the foreclosure defense options are. But, before we look at those options, let's talk about the next step in the process – communicating with your lender. Many of my clients make the mistake of ignoring the mortgage lender when they get into trouble. In the next chapter, we'll talk about why this is the wrong thing to do, and talk about the best ways to work with your lender to solve your mortgage problems.

Chapter Three

Communicate With Your Lender

First things first: Many people mistakenly think banks and mortgage lenders want to foreclose. Lenders don't want to foreclose: They are in the business of lending money, not auctioning, owning, or selling real estate.

In fact, federal regulations prohibit banks from being in the "business" of real estate at all.

Instead, a lender wants a predictable stream of revenue that comes from homeowners making their payments. (In some ways lenders aren't particularly concerned about whether you pay on time, because late fees more than cover the cost of late payments. The late fees you pay turn out to be a nice little profit center for the lender.)

Lenders want to make loans and make money on those loans; they don't want to deal with the hassle and headaches involved in foreclosing, taking over a property, and trying to sell it. But sometimes they do foreclose.

Very often, lenders are forced to foreclose because they don't get any communication from the consumer. Because the lender doesn't know what's going on with their customer's financial situation, the lender just assumes that the customer doesn't have any intention of paying the mortgage debt, and does the only thing that it can do – start the foreclosure process.

You can stop this knee-jerk reaction from the lender by staying in constant communication with the lender regarding your financial problems. I've had many clients that were able to keep the lender from starting the foreclosure process for six months to a year, just by talking to them about their situation.

Now, I'm not saying that communicating with the lender will stop them in their tracks. But, it can't hurt. At the very least, you may be able to discover the different options that your lender has for helping you address the problem. These options may include forbearance, modification, short-sale or deed-in-lieu.

But, unless you contact your lender, you'll never know what they may be willing to do for you. So, communicate!

There's no secret or magic formula for this process. I do encourage you to keep a log of your communications with the lender. This log should include the date and time of your communication. It should also include the telephone number you dialed, the person you spoke with, and the content of the conversation.

Lenders, especially large lenders, have an unfortunate habit of misplacing the records of any communications they have with consumers. So, help them to help you and keep track of the conversations.

Who to Talk To

Many people wonder who they should talk to when they contact the lender. Part of that depends on where you are in the foreclosure process. If you've taken my advice and contacted the lender before the foreclosure process has begun, you can simply call your lender. You will be automatically directed to the correct person or department by your lender.

If the foreclosure process has already begun, you may have to initially contact the lender's attorney. You can find the contact information for the lender's attorney on the foreclosure complaint or other foreclosure documentation that you've received. Most lender attorneys will still ask you to contact the lender directly. But, you should probably start with the attorney first if you're already in the foreclosure process.

This is a short chapter. But, I wanted to emphasize how important it is to communicate with your lender. So, this step gets its own chapter. I promise you that nothing bad will come from your communication with the lender. I know that it's scary. But, it's OK. You're probably one of a thousand people that they've already heard from that day. It's not a new story to them. The lender just wants to figure out where you are in the process. Is there a solution to help you stay in the home and keep making those regular payments to them? Or, does it make more sense for everyone to find a solution where you surrender the house to the lender or a third party?

This is why I wanted you to start thinking about your financial situation before you contact your lender. It helps for you to have a general idea of what you can do, or whether you want to save the home or not. This will make your communication with the lender much more productive.

But, how long do you have to work out a solution? Many people assume that they have less time than they really do have, start to panic, and do things that they really don't need to do. All of this can be avoided if you know the real foreclosure timeline. Let's talk about that now.

Chapter Four

The Foreclosure Timeline

Florida operates under what is called judicial foreclosure: The process must go through the court system. (In some states an attorney can handle the process, making the foreclosure timeline much shorter. In Florida the procedure is relatively long – which is good for you.) As a result of judicial foreclosure, until the lender files a complaint at the courthouse and the court hears that complaint and enters a judgment against you, the lender cannot take away your house.

In effect our state legal system is set up to protect you – at least to some degree.

So let's look at the stages of foreclosure from the point of view of a homeowner facing financial difficulties. We'll pretend I am the homeowner in financial distress so you can see the typical foreclosure timeline. Keep in mind this is generally what happens; the timeline could be longer depending on the lender's backlog and the court's backlog.

In addition, many of the strategies that we'll talk about in the next chapters are designed to slow or stop this foreclosure timeline. So, what I'll review here is the basic timeline if you do nothing to stop it or slow it down.

Months One to Three: If I miss a mortgage payment I receive a letter from my lender that documents the missed payment and requests immediate payment of the past due amount. (Sometimes I'll get a phone call or two before getting a letter – it all depends on that particularly lender's operating procedures.) Typically the first letter is polite and courteous.

If I miss my next payment, the letters begin to get a little more serious in tone.

Once I've missed several payments, I get what is called an Acceleration Letter. This formal letter is typically sent by an attorney representing the mortgage lender when a borrower is considered to be in default of the mortgage agreement. The Acceleration Letter, to use common language, says, "We're accelerating your loan. The full balance is due – now. If you don't pay everything, we will foreclose." The lender must send an Acceleration Letter in order to proceed with a foreclosure action against me; it's part of the process. (Lenders must accelerate your loan because mortgage loans are installment agreements – a separate payment becomes due each month. If the lender doesn't accelerate the loan, it can only pursue the missed payments and not any future payments. Without accelerating, the lender would need to sue me every month that I miss a payment until the end of the mortgage loan term!)

Quick note: If I send a regular payment – not the full balance of the loan – after I receive the Acceleration Letter, and the lender accepts my payment, then the lender's attorney may need to send another Acceleration Letter in order to proceed with a foreclosure action.

Receiving an Acceleration Letter means I'm in trouble; the process has started in earnest.

Month Four: In most cases, after three months of non-payment the lender's attorney will file a complaint of foreclosure. While that sounds ominous, it's just the start of the process.

The sheriff – or a process server – will come to my house and hand me a copy of the complaint. If you can't reach an agreement with the lawyer you'll be served with a summons.

To enforce money judgments I have to be served personally. That's one reason foreclosure actions can take awhile – the homeowner(s) must be tracked down and handed the summons. Often the homeowners don't want to be served and will do their best to avoid it. Generally speaking if a person can't be located and all reasonable efforts have been made to find them, publication takes place. Publication is typically just a public notice printed in the classified section of my local newspaper. That lets the lender's attorney eventually proceed with the foreclosure if they can't find me to serve me. I can run... but I can't hide forever.

When they receive a summons, most people have minor nervous breakdowns. (After all, it's not every day that a deputy comes to the house and serves you with papers.) Don't be too alarmed. See a summons as an invitation to the dance, especially since the process is far from over. Some people think they need to move immediately – don't! Stay in the house. Service is just the beginning. Many of my clients are able to remain in the house for up to a year or more.

In short, when I am served, I need to stay calm. That might sound tough... but staying calm and rational is critical.

After service, when I am physically handed the summons, the lender's attorney will also file papers at the city or county courthouse. All other individuals with claims against my property (those claims are typically called "junior" obligations) like second mortgages, judgments, or other liens, are served with papers so they can try to protect their financial interests as well.

Month Five: After I receive the summons I have twenty to thirty days to "answer" the summons; the time frame depends on the lender and the lender's attorney. (The Florida Rules of Civil Procedure require that you answer the complaint within 20 days. Some lenders and their attorneys will extend this deadline to 30 days. In ether case, the summons will clearly state how much time I have to respond.) I use the word "answer" because in some cases a lawyer will file what is called a responsive pleading, like a motion to dismiss based on mistakes made in the original complaint.

If I don't answer the summons the clerk issues a default and I lose the opportunity to defend myself. (When my clients have failed to answer a complaint within the time period specified, in some cases I have been able to convince a judge to "vacate" the default – but not always.)

A response doesn't have to be a formal legal document. A response could simply be a letter I write that states, "I can't pay my mortgage right now, but I'd really like to... can I work it out?" That simple letter will be considered a response – not a particularly good one, of course, but it will keep me in the game and keep my legal options open. If I don't respond, I lose most of my legal options and rights.

Let's say I don't respond so we can see what happens. Because I did not respond, a default is entered.

Month Six: Typically, the lender will file a Motion for Summary Judgment. This Motion claims the facts are not in dispute since:

- I was supposed to make payments... but I didn't.
- I had the opportunity to respond to the summons... but I didn't.

And, as a result, the Motion says the judge should rule against me and in the lender's favor.

Put in simple terms, a Motion for Summary Judgment says: "We win – just because." That's how, in my estimation, 90 to 95% of foreclosures proceedings end: The homeowners don't respond, don't try to protect their rights or defend themselves in any way... and the lender is awarded a summary judgment. No one fights it, the process moves on... and the homeowner loses their home.

Month Seven: The hearing is held on the Motion for Summary Judgment; typically the judge enters a Judgment of Foreclosure. (And, when you think about it, why not? I didn't participate. I didn't respond. I didn't fight back in any way. What choice does the judge really have?

The Judgment of Foreclosure gives the lender the right to sell my house at auction.)

Month Eight: The lender can't sell the house right away. The lender is required to publish a notice of sale for two weeks, so normally the sale is set for thirty days after the hearing and the Judgment of Foreclosure.

Foreclosure sales can be held at any public location that is centrally located and accessible. The old stereotype of an auction held on the courthouse steps can actually be true: If the foreclosure auction notice refers to the courthouse steps as the location of the sale, it really does mean the steps of the building. But, in general, most foreclosure auctions are held in a room in the courthouse.

The auction begins and often is completed within a few minutes. A majority of auctions end with the lender that made the original loan taking legal ownership of the property.

The opening bid is usually made by the lender. Typically, this opening bid is for $100.00 and is often the winning bid. (The lender will bid up to what is often referred to as the upset price.) The upset price is the total amount due the lender, including the mortgage balance, late payment charges, other fees, and any costs of initiating and handling the foreclosure itself.

The bidding is usually opened by a representative of the lender. Lender representatives are under no obligation to identify themselves and sometimes they won't bid at all. While it may not seem logical that someone owed money secured by a property will refuse to bid on that property, it does happen.

Banks can only make a claim for the amount of the judgment. If the winning bid is for a greater amount than the judgment, the remaining funds go to junior lien holders, and then if any money is left over as the homeowner I get the remainder. Because of the severe drop in home values, surpluses are few and far between. Besides, bidders who are looking for great deals rarely pay anything close to a market price for a foreclosure property.

If the bank is the high bidder the bank now owns the property. It then becomes "bank owned" and the bank is required to sell the property. But whether a bidder buys my house or the bank ends up owning my house, within a week to ten days, the sheriff will show up with a twenty-four hour eviction notice – and I have to get out.

That's what happens if I *don't* answer the summons.

But what if I do answer the summons? The answer to that question is based on another question:

Do you want to keep the house... or let it go? While sometimes you may not know if you want to let it go until after you've tried and failed using different techniques to defend against foreclosure, often the decision is based on whether you can afford to hang on to the house. Many homeowners – even those facing foreclosure or bankruptcy – haven't taken the time to analyze their current financial situation and assess their options. That's why I had you analyze your financial situation in Step 1 of our process.

Now that you have some idea of whether you save your home or surrender it, it's finally time to get to the actual strategies for reaching your goal. I'm going to be optimistic and start with the strategies for saving your home first. Then, we'll look at the options for surrendering your home and minimizing the liabilities associated with that decision.

SECTION I

Save Your Home: Basic and Advanced Strategies

Chapter Five

Save Your Home: Basic Foreclosure Defenses

It's finally time to start looking at the actual techniques for saving your home. And I'm going to start this discussion by reviewing a variety of basic foreclosure defenses. I'm starting with foreclosure defense because it's really at the center of everything. It's possible that you'll never receive a foreclosure complaint if you deal with the problems early and quickly. However, for most people, the foreclosure process becomes a constant companion.

If you're not yet in the foreclosure process, you can skip this chapter and move on to the remaining strategies for saving your home. But, if you're already in the foreclosure process, or you know that it's coming, read on.

As you read this section, I want you to remember that you can use these foreclosure defenses regardless of whether you want to save your home or not. For most people, the goal of any foreclosure defense is to buy more time. If you want to keep your home, you may need more time to get a job or to complete a loan modification. If you plan to surrender your home, it may make sense to slow the foreclosure process down so that you have additional time to find a new home, save some money, and move.

In addition, defending the foreclosure case may provide you with leverage while negotiating with your lender. I've had many cases where the lender was initially unwilling to modify a mortgage and then reconsidered when I vigorously defended the foreclosure case. I've also had this same result when clients wanted to use a deed-in-lieu or short sale process but were initially denied by the lender. It's amazing what lenders can do when they realize that you're not going to bury your head in the sand and they can't just roll over you.

Therefore, for most of my clients, a vigorous foreclosure defense is almost always a tool in my tool bag. Sometimes it's the only tool. More often than not, however, it's just one of many tools that work together to rebuild the house.

So, let's spend some time on basic foreclosure defense. But, before we do that, let's look at the mortgage process itself – how you got the money to purchase or refinance your home. By understanding the mortgage process, and the documents associated with that process, you'll better understand the problems that arise in the foreclosure process, and how this will help you to buy more time – or leverage.

The Mortgage Process – Sign Some Documents and Get Some Money

Regardless of whether you used your current mortgage loan to purchase a new home or to refinance your existing home, the process is essentially the same. You contacted a mortgage lender or broker, explained your situation, and completed a loan application.

Once you were approved for the loan, you were scheduled for a "closing", where you signed a giant stack of legal documents. After you completed those documents, the lender gave you or some third party the proceeds from the loan and you celebrated your good fortune.

That, in a nutshell, is the process for most mortgage loan transactions. But, two of those documents you signed are vitally important to the foreclosure process and your defense of the foreclosure case – the Promissory Note and the Mortgage. (Several other documents are important as well, including the HUD-1 Settlement Statement, the Good Faith Estimate, and several other disclosure forms. However, because we're just discussing basic foreclosure defense strategies, let's focus on these two documents).

The Promissory Note and the Mortgage are the two documents that give the lender authority to file a lawsuit against you when you stop making payments, and the right to take your home at the end of that lawsuit. And, these two documents often provide the bulk of foreclosure defense strategies. So, it's important for you to understand a bit about them. Let's look at these two documents now.

Promissory Note

The Promissory Note is a document that contains your promise to repay the money the lender gave you to purchase or refinance your home. I've included a sample Promissory Note for your review. Your Promissory Note probably looks similar to this sample. The Promissory Note typically describes the amount you borrowed, the interest rate, and the terms for how you'll repay the loan.

It's important to know these things, because you can often spot problems with a foreclosure complaint by comparing the amount borrowed, the interest rate, and the terms of the loan against the foreclosure documents. For example, you may be able to discover that the lender has violated the Truth in Lending Act by not accurately listing the finance charges for your loan. (We'll talk about this briefly in a moment.)

NOTE

______________, _____	_____________________________________	_________
[Date]	[City]	[State]

____
[Property Address]

1. BORROWER'S PROMISE TO PAY

In return for a loan that I have received, I promise to pay U.S. $_______________________ (this amount is called "Principal"), plus interest, to the order of the Lender.

The Lender is____________________________________. I will make all payments under this Note in the form of cash, check or money order.

I understand that the Lender may transfer this Note. The Lender or anyone who takes this Note by transfer and who is entitled to receive payments under this Note is called the "Note Holder."

2. INTEREST

Interest will be charged on unpaid principal until the full amount of Principal has been paid. I will pay interest at a yearly rate of ________________%.

The interest rate required by this Section 2 is the rate I will pay both before and after any default described in Section 6(B) of this Note.

3. PAYMENTS

(A) Time and Place of Payments

I will pay principal and interest by making a payment every month.

I will make my monthly payment on the _______ day of each month beginning on _______________, ___________. I will make these payments every month until I have paid all of the principal and interest and any other charges described below that I may owe under this Note. Each monthly payment will be applied as of its scheduled due date and will be applied to interest before Principal. If, on ________________________, 20_____, I still owe amounts under this Note, I will pay those amounts in full on that date, which is called the "Maturity Date."

I will make my monthly payments at ____ or at a different place if required by the Note Holder.

(B) Amount of Monthly Payments

My monthly payment will be in the amount of U.S. $_____________________________.

4. BORROWER'S RIGHT TO PREPAY

I have the right to make payments of Principal at any time before they are due. A payment of Principal only is known as a "Prepayment." When I make a Prepayment, I will tell the Note Holder in writing that I am doing so. I may not designate a payment as a Prepayment if I have not made all the monthly payments due under the Note.

I may make a full Prepayment or partial Prepayments without paying a Prepayment charge. The Note Holder will use my Prepayments to reduce the amount of Principal that I owe under this Note. However, the Note Holder may apply my Prepayment to the accrued and unpaid interest on the Prepayment amount, before applying my Prepayment to reduce the Principal amount of the Note. If I make a partial Prepayment, there will be no changes in the due date or in the amount of my monthly payment unless the Note Holder agrees in writing to those changes.

5. LOAN CHARGES

If a law, which applies to this loan and which sets maximum loan charges, is finally interpreted so that the interest or other loan charges collected or to be collected in connection with this loan exceed the permitted limits, then: (a) any such loan charge shall be reduced by the amount necessary to reduce the charge to the permitted limit; and (b) any sums already collected from me which exceeded permitted limits will be refunded to me. The Note Holder may choose to make this refund by reducing the Principal I owe under this Note or by making a direct payment to me. If a refund reduces Principal, the reduction will be treated as a partial Prepayment.

6. BORROWER'S FAILURE TO PAY AS REQUIRED

(A) Late Charge for Overdue Payments

If the Note Holder has not received the full amount of any monthly payment by the end of ____________ calendar days after the date it is due, I will pay a late charge to the Note Holder. The amount of the charge will be _______________% of my overdue payment of principal and interest. I will pay this late charge promptly but only once on each late payment.

(B) Default

If I do not pay the full amount of each monthly payment on the date it is due, I will be in default.

(C) Notice of Default

If I am in default, the Note Holder may send me a written notice telling me that if I do not pay the overdue amount by a certain date, the Note Holder may require me to pay immediately the full amount of Principal which has not been paid and all the interest that I owe on that amount. That date must be at least 30 days after the date on which the notice is mailed to me or delivered by other means.

(D) No Waiver By Note Holder

Even if, at a time when I am in default, the Note Holder does not require me to pay immediately in full as described above, the Note Holder will still have the right to do so if I am in default at a later time.

(E) Payment of Note Holder's Costs and Expenses

If the Note Holder has required me to pay immediately in full as described above, the Note Holder will have the right to be paid back by me for all of its costs and expenses in enforcing this Note to the extent not prohibited by applicable law. Those expenses include, for example, reasonable attorneys' fees.

7. GIVING OF NOTICES

Unless applicable law requires a different method, any notice that must be given to me under this Note will be given by delivering it or by mailing it by first class mail to me at the Property Address above or at a different address if I give the Note Holder a notice of my different address.

Any notice that must be given to the Note Holder under this Note will be given by delivering it or by mailing it by first class mail to the Note Holder at the address stated in Section 3(A) above or at a different address if I am given a notice of that different address.

8. OBLIGATIONS OF PERSONS UNDER THIS NOTE

If more than one person signs this Note, each person is fully and personally obligated to keep all of the promises made in this Note, including the promise to pay the full amount owed. Any person who is a guarantor, surety or endorser of this Note is also obligated to do these things. Any person who takes over these obligations, including the obligations of a guarantor, surety or endorser of this Note, is also obligated to keep all of the promises made in this Note. The Note Holder may enforce its rights under this Note against each person individually or against all of us together. This means that any one of us may be required to pay all of the amounts owed under this Note.

9. WAIVERS

I and any other person who has obligations under this Note waive the rights of Presentment and Notice of Dishonor. "Presentment" means the right to require the Note Holder to demand payment of amounts due. "Notice of Dishonor" means the right to require the Note Holder to give notice to other persons that amounts due have not been paid.

10. UNIFORM SECURED NOTE

This Note is a uniform instrument with limited variations in some jurisdictions. In addition to the protections given to the Note Holder under this Note, a Mortgage, Deed of Trust, or Security Deed (the "Security Instrument"), dated the same date as this Note, protects the Note Holder from possible losses which might result if I do not keep the promises which I make in this Note. That Security Instrument describes how and under what conditions I may be required to make immediate payment in full of all amounts I owe under this Note. Some of those conditions are described as follows:

If all or any part of the Property or any Interest in the Property is sold or transferred (or if Borrower is not a natural person and a beneficial interest in Borrower is sold or transferred) without Lender's prior written consent, Lender may require immediate payment in full of all sums secured by this Security Instrument. However, this option shall not be exercised by Lender if such exercise is prohibited by Applicable Law. If Lender exercises this option, Lender shall give Borrower notice of acceleration. The notice shall provide a period of not less than 30 days from the date the notice is given in accordance with Section 15 within which Borrower must pay all sums secured by this Security Instrument. If Borrower fails to pay these sums prior to the expiration of this period, Lender may invoke any remedies permitted by this Security Instrument without further notice or demand on Borrower.

WITNESS THE HAND(S) AND SEAL(S) OF THE UNDERSIGNED.

____________________________________ (Seal)
- Borrower

____________________________________ (Seal)
- Borrower

____________________________________ (Seal)
- Borrower

[Sign Original Only]

Or, you may be able to discover that the lender is overcharging you for the amounts due on the loan. You may be able to use this information to defend the foreclosure case.

The Promissory Note also describes the two parties involved in the loan - the borrower and the lender. Generally, you're the borrower and the financial institution that gave you the money for your home is the lender. This is often vitally important to the foreclosure case. Why? Because in the vast majority of cases, the lender who originally loaned you the money is not the one that files the foreclosure complaint against you. (Very often, the lender that files the foreclosure complaint can't initially prove that it is the correct party to sue you. This is called "standing" and we'll discuss this in great detail in a moment.)

A Promissory Note is a Negotiable Instrument (Generally)

In many cases, the lender that loans you the money very quickly transfers the loan to another lender. I believe that this process, and the greed associated with this process, is one of the reasons that the housing industry collapsed. For now, I just want you to understand how a lender transfers a Promissory Note to another lender.

A Promissory Note is a form of negotiable instrument. (Sometimes a promissory note may NOT be a negotiable instrument. This can happen if there are additional terms and requirements of the promissory note that go beyond the "normal" terms and conditions. But, for now, let's keep this discussion simple, and assume that a promissory note is a negotiable instrument.)

A negotiable instrument is essentially a contract between two or more parties. One party, called the "maker", promises to pay a specified amount of money to the "payee".

A negotiable instrument is different from a normal contract, however, because the value of the instrument is linked to actual possession of the instrument (the promissory note). The Maker (you) promises to pay whoever is actually the "bearer" or "holder" of the promissory note.

If the original lender still has the promissory note, then you must pay the original lender according to the terms of the promissory note. However, as is more often the case, the original lender has transferred the promissory note to another lender or investor. Therefore, you must pay whoever is in actual possession of the promissory note Sounds simple doesn't it?

In theory, it's very simple. In practice, it very often becomes a problem. The reason that this becomes a problem is because lenders sometimes don't follow the correct procedures when transferring the promissory notes to other lenders or investors.

To transfer a promissory note, the original payee must sign, or "endorse" the promissory note to someone else. The best way to think about this is to think about one of your personal checks. (Checks are a form of negotiable instrument, just like promissory notes. It's easier to understand how promissory notes work if you think about them in terms of something you already understand, like your personal checks.)

Let's say that you owe Uncle Bob $500 for a loan that he gave you last month. To repay that loan, you write a personal check to Uncle Bob for $500 and hand it to him. He could take that check to your bank and the bank would give him $500. By having that check made payable to him, Uncle Bob gets $500. Simple enough.

But, let's say that Uncle Bob owes $500 to Aunt Sue. Instead of taking the check to your bank, getting the cash, and paying Aunt Sue, Uncle Bob wants to just give Aunt Sue the check that you gave him.

What will happen if Uncle Bob just hands Aunt Sue the check and she tries to cash it at your bank? That's right. Nothing. Your bank will not give her the $500 from your account because the check is made payable to Uncle Bob, not Aunt Sue.

However, if Uncle Bob signs, or endorses, the check in favor of Aunt Sue, your bank would be happy to give Aunt Sue the money. This is the key to transferring a negotiable instrument, be it a personal check or a promissory note. The original payee must sign, or endorse, the check or promissory note in favor of the person that will receive the payment from you.

So, for example, your original lender, Lender A, decides that it wants to transfer your promissory note to Lender B. To do this, Lender A must endorse the promissory note in favor of Lender B, just like Uncle Bob did with Aunt Sue. If properly endorsed to Lender B, you now owe lender B according to the terms of the promissory note, rather than Lender A. If it's not properly endorsed, then lender B cannot collect payment from you.

Unlike personal checks, however, many promissory notes are endorsed "in blank". This means that whoever is actually in possession on the promissory note has the right to receive payment according to the terms of the promissory note. However, a promissory note must be endorsed by one of these methods, either to a specific party or in blank, to allow a subsequent party to enforce it.

Lenders endorse promissory notes by physically signing the promissory note, typically at the end of the note. More often than not, the endorsement is a stamp with the pertinent information filled in by hand and signed by an authorized representative.

Sometimes, there are so many endorsements on a promissory note that there is no more room to add another endorsement. In this case, a lender must physically attach another paper to the promissory note and put the endorsement on the attached paper. This attachment is called an "allonge". The allonge is treated as part of the promissory note, but it must be physically attached to the promissory note to be effective.

Now you know the basic process for transferring a promissory note. Why did I spend so much time on this seemingly boring topic? You'll see the reason for this in a moment when we start talking about the actual foreclosure defense strategies. Many, if not most, foreclosure cases can be defended by attacking the process that lenders used in transferring the promissory notes. In the go-go years of the mortgage market, it seems that many lenders chose to dispense with the legal requirements for transferring promissory notes. Their haste may help you to save your home. More on that in a moment. For now, let's talk about the next major document, the mortgage.

Mortgage

A mortgage is a document that "secures" the promissory note. By signing the mortgage, you agreed to give your home as "collateral" for the loan that your lender gave you to purchase or refinance your home. If you don't repay the promissory note according to its terms, the lender can take your home from you in repayment. Without a mortgage, the bank doesn't have the right to foreclose.

The mortgage contains all of the terms that provide the security for the lender and is typically many pages in length. Most mortgages are standardized forms that conform to the Fannie Mae/Freddie Mac Uniform Mortgage. I've included a sample mortgage for your review. Your mortgage probably looks similar to this sample mortgage.

Ultimately, there are only one or two paragraphs in the mortgage that really matter to us in our attempt to save your home. We'll talk about the important paragraphs in a moment.

To be effective, the mortgage must be recorded in the county where your home is located. Once the mortgage is recorded, the lender has a "lien" against your home, and you cannot sell or transfer the property without approval from the lender. This lien will remain in effect until you pay the full amount due under the promissory note and the lender has filed a "Satisfaction of Mortgage" in the public records.

Essentially, the promissory note and mortgage work together, and cannot exist independently. If you fail to pay the promissory note as agreed, the mortgage is the document that allows the lender to take your home. Without the mortgage, the lender could only obtain a money judgment against you personally, not take your home.

Without the promissory note, the mortgage would secure nothing. The only purpose for the mortgage is to provide the mechanism for taking the collateral (your home) if you fail to pay the promissory note as agreed.

As with the promissory note, a lender must properly transfer a mortgage to allow a subsequent lender or investor to foreclose on your home. However, the process for transferring a mortgage is different from the process that we reviewed for transferring promissory notes.

Generally, the proper way for a lender to transfer a mortgage to another lender is to “assign” the mortgage. Usually, Lender A creates and signs an “Assignment of Mortgage” in favor of Lender B. Unless the mortgage is properly assigned, the subsequent lender can’t foreclose on your house.

And guess what? During the go-go days of the mortgage boom, lenders often took shortcuts when they transferred mortgages. Very often, they neglected to create and sign Assignments of Mortgage when they transferred a loan to another lender. This causes problems when the lenders want to foreclose on a promissory note. If Lender B doesn’t legally have the right to enforce the mortgage because Lender A didn’t properly assign the mortgage, then Lender B doesn’t have the right to foreclosure on your home.

After Recording Return To:

____
____
____
____

________________[Space Above This Line For Recording Data]________________

MORTGAGE

DEFINITIONS

Words used in multiple sections of this document are defined below and other words are defined in Sections 3, 11, 13, 18, 20 and 21. Certain rules regarding the usage of words used in this document are also provided in Section 16.

(A) "Security Instrument" means this document, which is dated ________________, __________, together with all Riders to this document.
(B) "Borrower" is ____. Borrower is the mortgagor under this Security Instrument.
(C) "Lender" is ____.
Lender is a ________________ organized and existing under the laws of ________________.
Lender's address is ____.
Lender is the mortgagee under this Security Instrument.
(D) "Note" means the promissory note signed by Borrower and dated ________, __________. The Note states that Borrower owes Lender ____
________ Dollars (U.S. $________________________) plus interest. Borrower has promised to pay this debt in regular Periodic Payments and to pay the debt in full not later than ________________.
(E) "Property" means the property that is described below under the heading "Transfer of Rights in the Property."
(F) "Loan" means the debt evidenced by the Note, plus interest, any prepayment charges and late charges due under the Note, and all sums due under this Security Instrument, plus interest.
(G) "Riders" means all Riders to this Security Instrument that are executed by Borrower. The following Riders are to be executed by Borrower [check box as applicable]:

☐ Adjustable Rate Rider ☐ Condominium Rider ☐ Second Home Rider

☐ Balloon Rider ☐ Planned Unit Development Rider

☐ Other(s) [specify] __________ ☐ 1-4 Family Rider ☐ Biweekly Payment Rider

(H) "Applicable Law" means all controlling applicable federal, state and local statutes, regulations, ordinances and administrative rules and orders (that have the effect of law) as well as all applicable final, non-appealable judicial opinions.
(I) "Community Association Dues, Fees, and Assessments" means all dues, fees, assessments and other charges that are imposed on Borrower or the Property by a condominium association, homeowners association or similar organization.
(J) "Electronic Funds Transfer" means any transfer of funds, other than a transaction originated by check, draft, or similar paper instrument, which is initiated through an electronic terminal, telephonic instrument, computer, or magnetic tape so as to order, instruct, or authorize a financial institution to debit or credit an account. Such term includes, but is not limited to, point-of-sale transfers, automated teller machine transactions, transfers initiated by telephone, wire transfers, and automated clearinghouse transfers.
(K) "Escrow Items" means those items that are described in Section 3.
(L) "Miscellaneous Proceeds" means any compensation, settlement, award of damages, or proceeds paid by any third party (other than insurance proceeds paid under the coverages described in Section 5) for: (i) damage to, or destruction of, the Property; (ii) condemnation or other taking of all or any part of the Property; (iii) conveyance in lieu of condemnation; or (iv) misrepresentations of, or omissions as to, the value and/or condition of the Property.

(M) "Mortgage Insurance" means insurance protecting Lender against the nonpayment of, or default on, the Loan.
(N) "Periodic Payment" means the regularly scheduled amount due for (i) principal and interest under the Note, plus (ii) any amounts under Section 3 of this Security Instrument.
(O) "RESPA" means the Real Estate Settlement Procedures Act (12 U.S.C. §2601 et seq.) and its implementing regulation, Regulation X (24 C.F.R. Part 3500), as they might be amended from time to time, or any additional or successor legislation or regulation that governs the same subject matter. As used in this Security Instrument, "RESPA" refers to all requirements and restrictions that are imposed in regard to a "federally related mortgage loan" even if the Loan does not qualify as a "federally related mortgage loan" under RESPA.
(P) "Successor in Interest of Borrower" means any party that has taken title to the Property, whether or not that party has assumed Borrower's obligations under the Note and/or this Security Instrument.

TRANSFER OF RIGHTS IN THE PROPERTY

This Security Instrument secures to Lender: (i) the repayment of the Loan, and all renewals, extensions and modifications of the Note; and (ii) the performance of Borrower's covenants and agreements under this Security Instrument and the Note. For this purpose, Borrower does hereby mortgage, grant and convey to Lender, the following described property located in the ______________________________ of ____________
____________________:
[Type of Recording Jurisdiction] [Name of Recording Jurisdiction]

which currently has the address of ____
[Street]
____________________________, Florida ______________ ("Property Address"):
[City] [Zip Code]

TOGETHER WITH all the improvements now or hereafter erected on the property, and all easements, appurtenances, and fixtures now or hereafter a part of the property. All replacements and additions shall also be covered by this Security Instrument. All of the foregoing is referred to in this Security Instrument as the "Property."

BORROWER COVENANTS that Borrower is lawfully seised of the estate hereby conveyed and has the right to mortgage, grant and convey the Property and that the Property is unencumbered, except for encumbrances of record. Borrower warrants and will defend generally the title to the Property against all claims and demands, subject to any encumbrances of record.

THIS SECURITY INSTRUMENT combines uniform covenants for national use and non-uniform covenants with limited variations by jurisdiction to constitute a uniform security instrument covering real property.

UNIFORM COVENANTS. Borrower and Lender covenant and agree as follows:

1. Payment of Principal, Interest, Escrow Items, Prepayment Charges, and Late Charges. Borrower shall pay when due the principal of, and interest on, the debt evidenced by the Note and any prepayment charges and late charges due under the Note. Borrower shall also pay funds for Escrow Items pursuant to Section 3. Payments due under the Note and this Security Instrument shall be made in U.S. currency. However, if any check or other instrument received by Lender as payment under the Note or this Security Instrument is returned to Lender unpaid, Lender may require that any or all subsequent payments due under the Note and this Security Instrument be made in one or more of the following forms, as selected by Lender: (a) cash; (b) money order; (c) certified check, bank check, treasurer's check or cashier's check, provided any such check is drawn upon an institution whose deposits are insured by a federal agency, instrumentality, or entity; or (d) Electronic Funds Transfer.

Payments are deemed received by Lender when received at the location designated in the Note or at such other location as may be designated by Lender in accordance with the notice provisions in Section 15. Lender may return any payment or partial payment if the payment or partial payments are insufficient to bring the Loan current. Lender may accept any payment or partial payment insufficient to bring the Loan current, without waiver of any rights hereunder or prejudice to its rights to refuse such payment or partial payments in the future, but Lender is not obligated to apply such payments at the time such payments are accepted. If each Periodic

Payment is applied as of its scheduled due date, then Lender need not pay interest on unapplied funds. Lender may hold such unapplied funds until Borrower makes payment to bring the Loan current. If Borrower does not do so within a reasonable period of time, Lender shall either apply such funds or return them to Borrower. If not applied earlier, such funds will be applied to the outstanding principal balance under the Note immediately prior to foreclosure. No offset or claim which Borrower might have now or in the future against Lender shall relieve Borrower from making payments due under the Note and this Security Instrument or performing the covenants and agreements secured by this Security Instrument.

2. Application of Payments or Proceeds. Except as otherwise described in this Section 2, all payments accepted and applied by Lender shall be applied in the following order of priority: (a) interest due under the Note; (b) principal due under the Note; (c) amounts due under Section 3. Such payments shall be applied to each Periodic Payment in the order in which it became due. Any remaining amounts shall be applied first to late charges, second to any other amounts due under this Security Instrument, and then to reduce the principal balance of the Note.

If Lender receives a payment from Borrower for a delinquent Periodic Payment which includes a sufficient amount to pay any late charge due, the payment may be applied to the delinquent payment and the late charge. If more than one Periodic Payment is outstanding, Lender may apply any payment received from Borrower to the repayment of the Periodic Payments if, and to the extent that, each payment can be paid in full. To the extent that any excess exists after the payment is applied to the full payment of one or more Periodic Payments, such excess may be applied to any late charges due. Voluntary prepayments shall be applied first to any prepayment charges and then as described in the Note.

Any application of payments, insurance proceeds, or Miscellaneous Proceeds to principal due under the Note shall not extend or postpone the due date, or change the amount, of the Periodic Payments.

3. Funds for Escrow Items. Borrower shall pay to Lender on the day Periodic Payments are due under the Note, until the Note is paid in full, a sum (the "Funds") to provide for payment of amounts due for: (a) taxes and assessments and other items which can attain priority over this Security Instrument as a lien or encumbrance on the Property; (b) leasehold payments or ground rents on the Property, if any; (c) premiums for any and all insurance required by Lender under Section 5; and (d) Mortgage Insurance premiums, if any, or any sums payable by Borrower to Lender in lieu of the payment of Mortgage Insurance premiums in accordance with the provisions of Section 10. These items are called "Escrow Items." At origination or at any time during the term of the Loan, Lender may require that Community Association Dues, Fees, and Assessments, if any, be escrowed by Borrower, and such dues, fees and assessments shall be an Escrow Item. Borrower shall promptly furnish to Lender all notices of amounts to be paid under this Section. Borrower shall pay Lender the Funds for Escrow Items unless Lender waives Borrower's obligation to pay the Funds for any or all Escrow Items. Lender may waive Borrower's obligation to pay to Lender Funds for any or all Escrow Items at any time. Any such waiver may only be in writing. In the event of such waiver, Borrower shall pay directly, when and where payable, the amounts due for any Escrow Items for which payment of Funds has been waived by Lender and, if Lender requires, shall furnish to Lender receipts evidencing such payment within such time period as Lender may require. Borrower's obligation to make such payments and to provide receipts shall for all purposes be deemed to be a covenant and agreement contained in this Security Instrument, as the phrase "covenant and agreement" is used in Section 9. If Borrower is obligated to pay Escrow Items directly, pursuant to a waiver, and Borrower fails to pay the amount due for an Escrow Item, Lender may exercise its rights under Section 9 and pay such amount and Borrower shall then be obligated under Section 9 to repay to Lender any such amount. Lender may revoke the waiver as to any or all Escrow Items at any time by a notice given in accordance with Section 15 and, upon such revocation, Borrower shall pay to Lender all Funds, and in such amounts, that are then required under this Section 3.

Lender may, at any time, collect and hold Funds in an amount (a) sufficient to permit Lender to apply the Funds at the time specified under RESPA, and (b) not to exceed the maximum amount a lender can require under RESPA. Lender shall estimate the amount of Funds due on the basis of current data and reasonable estimates of expenditures of future Escrow Items or otherwise in accordance with Applicable Law.

The Funds shall be held in an institution whose deposits are insured by a federal agency, instrumentality, or entity (including Lender, if Lender is an institution whose deposits are so insured) or in any Federal Home Loan Bank. Lender shall apply the Funds to pay the Escrow Items no later than the time specified under RESPA. Lender shall not charge Borrower for holding and applying the Funds, annually analyzing the escrow account, or verifying the Escrow Items, unless Lender pays Borrower interest on the Funds and Applicable Law permits Lender to make such a charge. Unless an agreement is made in writing or Applicable Law requires interest to be paid on the Funds, Lender shall not be required to pay Borrower any interest or earnings on the Funds. Borrower and Lender can agree in writing, however, that interest shall be paid on the Funds. Lender shall give so Borrower, without charge, an annual accounting of the Funds as required by RESPA.

If there is a surplus of Funds held in escrow, as defined under RESPA, Lender shall account to Borrower for the excess funds in accordance with RESPA. If there is a shortage of Funds held in escrow, as defined under RESPA, Lender shall notify Borrower as required by RESPA, and Borrower shall pay to Lender the amount necessary to make up the shortage in accordance with RESPA, but in no more than 12 monthly payments. If there is a deficiency of Funds held in escrow, as defined under RESPA, Lender shall notify Borrower as required by RESPA, and Borrower shall pay to Lender the amount necessary to make up the deficiency in accordance with RESPA, but in no more than 12 monthly payments.

Upon payment in full of all sums secured by this Security Instrument, Lender shall promptly refund to Borrower any Funds held by Lender.

4. Charges; Liens. Borrower shall pay all taxes, assessments, charges, fines, and impositions attributable to the Property which can attain priority over this Security Instrument, leasehold payments or ground rents on the Property, if any, and Community Association Dues, Fees, and Assessments, if any. To the extent that these items are Escrow Items, Borrower shall pay them in the manner provided in Section 3.

Borrower shall promptly discharge any lien which has priority over this Security Instrument unless Borrower: (a) agrees in writing to the payment of the obligation secured by the lien in a manner acceptable to Lender, but only so long as Borrower is performing such agreement; (b) contests the lien in good faith by, or defends against enforcement of the lien in, legal proceedings which in Lender's opinion operate to prevent the enforcement of the lien while those proceedings are pending, but only until such proceedings are concluded; or (c) secures from the holder of the lien an agreement satisfactory to Lender subordinating the lien to this Security Instrument. If Lender determines that any part of the Property is subject to a lien which can attain priority over this Security Instrument, Lender may give Borrower a notice identifying the lien. Within 10 days of the date on which that notice is given, Borrower shall satisfy the lien or take one or more of the actions set forth above in this Section 4.

Lender may require Borrower to pay a one-time charge for a real estate tax verification and/or reporting service used by Lender in connection with this Loan.

5. Property Insurance. Borrower shall keep the improvements now existing or hereafter erected on the Property insured against loss by fire, hazards included within the term "extended coverage," and any other hazards including, but not limited to, earthquakes and floods, for which Lender requires insurance. This insurance shall be maintained in the amounts (including deductible levels) and for the periods that Lender requires. What Lender requires pursuant to the preceding sentences can change during the term of the Loan. The insurance carrier providing the insurance shall be chosen by Borrower subject to Lender's right to disapprove Borrower's choice, which right shall not be exercised unreasonably. Lender may require Borrower to pay, in connection with this Loan, either: (a) a one-time charge for flood zone determination, certification and tracking services; or (b) a one-time charge for flood zone determination and certification services and subsequent charges each time remappings or similar changes occur which reasonably might affect such determination or certification. Borrower shall also be responsible for the payment of any fees imposed by the Federal Emergency Management Agency in connection with the review of any flood zone determination resulting from an objection by Borrower.

If Borrower fails to maintain any of the coverages described above, Lender may obtain insurance coverage, at Lender's option and Borrower's expense. Lender is under no obligation to purchase any particular type or amount of coverage. Therefore, such coverage shall cover Lender, but might or might not protect Borrower, Borrower's equity in the Property, or the contents of the Property, against any risk, hazard or liability and might provide greater or lesser coverage than was previously in effect. Borrower acknowledges that the cost of the insurance coverage so obtained might significantly exceed the cost of insurance that Borrower could have obtained. Any amounts disbursed by Lender under this Section 5 shall become additional debt of Borrower secured by this Security Instrument. These amounts shall bear interest at the Note rate from the date of disbursement and shall be payable, with such interest, upon notice from Lender to Borrower requesting payment.

All insurance policies required by Lender and renewals of such policies shall be subject to Lender's right to disapprove such policies, shall include a standard mortgage clause, and shall name Lender as mortgagee and/or as an additional loss payee. Lender shall have the right to hold the policies and renewal certificates. If Lender requires, Borrower shall promptly give to Lender all receipts of paid premiums and renewal notices. If Borrower obtains any form of insurance coverage, not otherwise required by Lender, for damage to, or destruction of, the Property, such policy shall include a standard mortgage clause and shall name Lender as mortgagee and/or as an additional loss payee.

In the event of loss, Borrower shall give prompt notice to the insurance carrier and Lender. Lender may make proof of loss if not made promptly by Borrower. Unless Lender and Borrower otherwise agree in writing, any insurance proceeds, whether or not the underlying insurance was required by Lender, shall be applied to restoration or repair of the Property, if the restoration or repair is economically feasible and Lender's security is not lessened. During such repair and restoration period, Lender shall have the right to hold such insurance proceeds until Lender has had an opportunity to inspect such Property to ensure the work has been completed to Lender's satisfaction, provided that such inspection shall be undertaken promptly. Lender may disburse proceeds for the repairs and restoration in a single payment or in a series of progress payments as the work is completed. Unless an agreement is made in writing or Applicable Law requires interest to be paid on such insurance proceeds, Lender shall not be required to pay Borrower any interest or earnings on such proceeds. Fees for public adjusters, or other third parties, retained by Borrower shall not be paid out of the insurance proceeds and shall be the sole obligation of Borrower. If the restoration or repair is not economically feasible or Lender's security would be lessened, the insurance proceeds shall be applied to the sums secured by this Security Instrument, whether or not then due, with the excess, if any, paid to Borrower. Such insurance proceeds shall be applied in the order provided for in Section 2.

If Borrower abandons the Property, Lender may file, negotiate and settle any available insurance claim and related matters. If Borrower does not respond within 30 days to a notice from Lender that the insurance carrier has offered to settle a claim, then Lender may negotiate and settle the claim. The 30-day period will begin when the notice is given. In either event, or if Lender acquires the Property under Section 22 or otherwise, Borrower hereby assigns to Lender (a) Borrower's rights to any insurance proceeds in an amount not to exceed the amounts unpaid under the Note or this Security Instrument, and (b) any other of Borrower's rights (other than the right to any refund of unearned premiums paid by Borrower) under all insurance policies covering the Property, insofar as such rights are applicable to the coverage of the Property. Lender may use the insurance proceeds either to repair or restore the Property or to pay amounts unpaid under the Note or this Security Instrument, whether or not then due.

6. Occupancy. Borrower shall occupy, establish, and use the Property as Borrower's principal residence within 60 days after the execution of this Security Instrument and shall continue to occupy the Property as Borrower's principal residence for at least one year after the date of occupancy, unless Lender otherwise agrees in writing, which consent shall not be unreasonably withheld, or unless extenuating circumstances exist which are beyond Borrower's control.

7. Preservation, Maintenance and Protection of the Property; Inspections. Borrower shall not destroy, damage or impair the Property, allow the Property to deteriorate or commit waste on the Property. Whether or not Borrower is residing in the Property, Borrower shall maintain the Property in order to prevent the Property from deteriorating or decreasing in value due to its condition. Unless it is determined pursuant to Section 5 that repair or restoration is not economically feasible, Borrower shall promptly repair the Property if damaged to avoid further deterioration or damage. If insurance or condemnation proceeds are paid in connection with damage to, or the taking of, the Property, Borrower shall be responsible for repairing or restoring the Property only if Lender has released proceeds for such purposes. Lender may disburse proceeds for the repairs and restoration in a single payment or in a series of progress payments as the work is completed. If the insurance or condemnation proceeds are not sufficient to repair or restore the Property, Borrower is not relieved of Borrower's obligation for the completion of such repair or restoration.

Lender or its agent may make reasonable entries upon and inspections of the Property. If it has reasonable cause, Lender may inspect the interior of the improvements on the Property. Lender shall give Borrower notice at the time of or prior to such an interior inspection specifying such reasonable cause.

8. Borrower's Loan Application. Borrower shall be in default if, during the Loan application process, Borrower or any persons or entities acting at the direction of Borrower or with Borrower's knowledge or consent gave materially false, misleading, or inaccurate information or statements to Lender (or failed to provide Lender with material information) in connection with the Loan. Material representations include, but are not limited to, representations concerning Borrower's occupancy of the Property as Borrower's principal residence.

9. Protection of Lender's Interest in the Property and Rights Under this Security Instrument. If (a) Borrower fails to perform the covenants and agreements contained in this Security Instrument, (b) there is a legal proceeding that might significantly affect Lender's interest in the Property and/or rights under this Security Instrument (such as a proceeding in bankruptcy, probate, for condemnation or forfeiture, for enforcement of a lien which may attain priority over this Security Instrument or to enforce laws or regulations), or (c) Borrower has abandoned the Property, then Lender may do and pay for whatever is reasonable or appropriate to protect Lender's interest in the Property and rights under this Security Instrument, including protecting and/or assessing the value of the Property, and securing and/or repairing the Property. Lender's actions can include, but are not limited to: (a) paying any sums secured by a lien which has priority over this Security Instrument; (b) appearing in court; and (c) paying reasonable attorneys' fees to protect its interest in the Property and/or rights under this Security Instrument, including its secured position in a bankruptcy proceeding. Securing the Property includes, but is not limited to, entering the Property to make repairs, change locks, replace or board up doors and windows, drain water from pipes, eliminate building or other code violations or dangerous conditions, and have utilities turned on or off. Although Lender may take action under this Section 9, Lender does not have to do so and is not under any duty or obligation to do so. It is agreed that Lender incurs no liability for not taking any or all actions authorized under this Section 9.

Any amounts disbursed by Lender under this Section 9 shall become additional debt of Borrower secured by this Security Instrument. These amounts shall bear interest at the Note rate from the date of disbursement and shall be payable, with such interest, upon notice from Lender to Borrower requesting payment.

If this Security Instrument is on a leasehold, Borrower shall comply with all the provisions of the lease. If Borrower acquires fee title to the Property, the leasehold and the fee title shall not merge unless Lender agrees to the merger in writing.

10. Mortgage Insurance. If Lender required Mortgage Insurance as a condition of making the Loan, Borrower shall pay the premiums required to maintain the Mortgage Insurance in effect. If, for any reason, the Mortgage Insurance coverage required by Lender ceases to be available from the mortgage insurer that previously provided such insurance and Borrower was required to make separately designated payments toward the premiums for Mortgage Insurance, Borrower shall pay the premiums required to obtain coverage substantially equivalent to the Mortgage Insurance previously in effect, at a cost substantially equivalent to the cost to Borrower of the Mortgage Insurance previously in effect, from an alternate mortgage insurer selected by Lender. If substantially equivalent Mortgage Insurance coverage is not available, Borrower shall continue to pay to Lender the amount of the separately designated payments that were due when the insurance coverage ceased to be in effect. Lender will accept, use and retain these payments as a non-refundable loss reserve in lieu of Mortgage Insurance. Such loss reserve shall be non-refundable, notwithstanding the fact that the Loan is ultimately paid in full, and Lender shall not be required to pay Borrower any interest or earnings on such loss reserve. Lender can no longer require loss reserve payments if Mortgage Insurance coverage (in the amount and for the period that Lender requires) provided by an insurer selected by Lender again becomes available, is obtained, and Lender requires separately designated payments toward the premiums for Mortgage Insurance. If Lender required Mortgage Insurance as a condition of making the Loan and Borrower was required to make separately designated payments toward the premiums for Mortgage Insurance, Borrower shall pay the premiums required to maintain Mortgage Insurance in effect, or to provide a non-refundable loss reserve, until Lender's requirement for Mortgage Insurance ends in accordance with any written agreement between Borrower and Lender providing for such termination or until termination is required by Applicable Law. Nothing in this Section 10 affects Borrower's obligation to pay interest at the rate provided in the Note.

Mortgage Insurance reimburses Lender (or any entity that purchases the Note) for certain losses it may incur if Borrower does not repay the Loan as agreed. Borrower is not a party to the Mortgage Insurance.

Mortgage insurers evaluate their total risk on all such insurance in force from time to time, and may enter into agreements with other parties that share or modify their risk, or reduce losses. These agreements are on terms and conditions that are satisfactory to the mortgage insurer and the other party (or parties) to these agreements. These agreements may require the mortgage insurer to make payments using any source of funds that the mortgage insurer may have available (which may include funds obtained from Mortgage Insurance premiums).

As a result of these agreements, Lender, any purchaser of the Note, another insurer, any reinsurer, any other entity, or any affiliate of any of the foregoing, may receive (directly or indirectly) amounts that derive from (or might be characterized as) a portion of Borrower's payments for Mortgage Insurance, in exchange for sharing or modifying the mortgage insurer's risk, or reducing losses. If such agreement provides that an affiliate of Lender takes a share of the insurer's risk in exchange for a share of the premiums paid to the insurer, the arrangement is often termed "captive reinsurance." Further:

(a) Any such agreements will not affect the amounts that Borrower has agreed to pay for Mortgage Insurance, or any other terms of the Loan. Such agreements will not increase the amount Borrower will owe for Mortgage Insurance, and they will not entitle Borrower to any refund.

(b) Any such agreements will not affect the rights Borrower has - if any - with respect to the Mortgage Insurance under the Homeowners Protection Act of 1998 or any other law. These rights may include the right to receive certain disclosures, to request and obtain cancellation of the Mortgage Insurance, to have the Mortgage Insurance terminated automatically, and/or to receive a refund of any Mortgage Insurance premiums that were unearned at the time of such cancellation or termination.

11. Assignment of Miscellaneous Proceeds; Forfeiture. All Miscellaneous Proceeds are hereby assigned to and shall be paid to Lender.

If the Property is damaged, such Miscellaneous Proceeds shall be applied to restoration or repair of the Property, if the restoration or repair is economically feasible and Lender's security is not lessened. During such repair and restoration period, Lender shall have the right to hold such Miscellaneous Proceeds until Lender has had an opportunity to inspect such Property to ensure the work has been completed to Lender's satisfaction, provided that such inspection shall be undertaken promptly. Lender may pay for the repairs and restoration in a single disbursement or in a series of progress payments as the work is completed. Unless an agreement is made in writing or Applicable Law requires interest to be paid on such Miscellaneous Proceeds, Lender shall not be required to pay Borrower any interest or earnings on such Miscellaneous Proceeds. If the restoration or repair is not economically feasible or Lender's security would be lessened, the Miscellaneous Proceeds shall be applied to the sums secured by this Security Instrument, whether or not then due, with the excess, if any, paid to Borrower. Such Miscellaneous Proceeds shall be applied in the order provided for in Section 2.

In the event of a total taking, destruction, or loss in value of the Property, the Miscellaneous Proceeds shall be applied to the sums secured by this Security Instrument, whether or not then due, with the excess, if any, paid to Borrower.

In the event of a partial taking, destruction, or loss in value of the Property in which the fair market value of the Property immediately before the partial taking, destruction, or loss in value is equal to or greater than the amount of the sums secured by this Security Instrument immediately before the partial taking, destruction, or loss in value, unless Borrower and Lender otherwise agree in writing, the sums secured by this Security Instrument shall be reduced by the amount of the Miscellaneous Proceeds multiplied by the following fraction: (a) the total amount of the sums secured immediately before the partial taking, destruction, or loss in value divided by (b) the fair market value of the Property immediately before the partial taking, destruction, or loss in value. Any balance shall be paid to Borrower.

In the event of a partial taking, destruction, or loss in value of the Property in which the fair market value of the Property immediately before the partial taking, destruction, or loss in value is less than the amount of the sums secured immediately before the partial taking, destruction, or loss in value, unless Borrower and Lender otherwise agree in writing, the Miscellaneous Proceeds shall be applied to the sums secured by this Security Instrument whether or not the sums are then due.

If the Property is abandoned by Borrower, or if, after notice by Lender to Borrower that the Opposing Party (as defined in the next sentence) offers to make an award to settle a claim for damages, Borrower fails to respond to Lender within 30 days after the date the notice is given, Lender is authorized to collect and apply the Miscellaneous Proceeds either to restoration or repair of the Property or to the sums secured by this Security Instrument, whether or not then due. "Opposing Party" means the third party that owes Borrower Miscellaneous Proceeds or the party against whom Borrower has a right of action in regard to Miscellaneous Proceeds.

Borrower shall be in default if any action or proceeding, whether civil or criminal, is begun that, in Lender's judgment, could result in forfeiture of the Property or other material impairment of Lender's interest in the Property or rights under this Security Instrument. Borrower can cure such a default and, if acceleration has occurred, reinstate as provided in Section 19, by causing the action or proceeding to be dismissed with a ruling that, in Lender's judgment, precludes forfeiture of the Property or other material impairment of Lender's interest in the Property or rights under this Security Instrument. The proceeds of any award or claim for damages that are attributable to the impairment of Lender's interest in the Property are hereby assigned and shall be paid to Lender.

All Miscellaneous Proceeds that are not applied to restoration or repair of the Property shall be applied in the order provided for in Section 2.

12. Borrower Not Released; Forbearance By Lender Not a Waiver. Extension of the time for payment or modification of amortization of the sums secured by this Security Instrument granted by Lender to Borrower or any Successor in Interest of Borrower shall not operate to release the liability of Borrower or any Successors in Interest of Borrower. Lender shall not be required to commence proceedings against any Successor in Interest of Borrower or to refuse to extend time for payment or otherwise modify amortization of the sums secured by this Security Instrument by reason of any demand made by the original Borrower or any Successors in Interest of Borrower. Any forbearance by Lender in exercising any right or remedy including, without limitation, Lender's acceptance of payments from third persons, entities or Successors in Interest of Borrower or in amounts less than the amount then due, shall not be a waiver of or preclude the exercise of any right or remedy.

13. Joint and Several Liability; Co-signers; Successors and Assigns Bound. Borrower covenants and agrees that Borrower's obligations and liability shall be joint and several. However, any Borrower who co-signs this Security Instrument but does not execute the Note (a "co-signer"): (a) is co-signing this Security Instrument only to mortgage, grant and convey the co-signer's interest in the Property under the terms of this Security Instrument; (b) is not personally obligated to pay the sums secured by this Security Instrument; and (c) agrees that Lender and any other Borrower can agree to extend, modify, forbear or make any accommodations with regard to the terms of this Security Instrument or the Note without the co-signer's consent.

Subject to the provisions of Section 18, any Successor in Interest of Borrower who assumes Borrower's obligations under this Security Instrument in writing, and is approved by Lender, shall obtain all of Borrower's rights and benefits under this Security Instrument. Borrower shall not be released from Borrower's obligations and liability under this Security Instrument unless Lender agrees to such release in writing. The covenants and agreements of this Security Instrument shall bind (except as provided in Section 20) and benefit the successors and assigns of Lender.

14. Loan Charges. Lender may charge Borrower fees for services performed in connection with Borrower's default, for the purpose of protecting Lender's interest in the Property and rights under this Security Instrument, including, but not limited to, attorneys' fees, property inspection and valuation fees. In regard to any other fees, the absence of express authority in this Security Instrument to charge a specific fee to Borrower shall not be construed as a prohibition on the charging of such fee. Lender may not charge fees that are expressly prohibited by this Security Instrument or by Applicable Law.

If the Loan is subject to a law which sets maximum loan charges, and that law is finally interpreted so that the interest or other loan charges collected or to be collected in connection with the Loan exceed the permitted limits, then: (a) any such loan charge shall be reduced by the amount necessary to reduce the charge to the permitted limit; and (b) any sums already collected from Borrower which exceeded permitted limits will be refunded to Borrower. Lender may choose to make this refund by reducing the principal owed under the Note or by making a direct payment to Borrower. If a refund reduces principal, the reduction will be treated as a partial prepayment without any prepayment charge (whether or not a prepayment charge is provided for under the Note). Borrower's acceptance of any such refund made by direct payment to Borrower will constitute a waiver of any right of action Borrower might have arising out of such overcharge.

15. Notices. All notices given by Borrower or Lender in connection with this Security Instrument must be in writing. Any notice to Borrower in connection with this Security Instrument shall be deemed to have been given to Borrower when mailed by first class mail or when actually delivered to Borrower's notice address if sent by other means. Notice to any one Borrower shall constitute notice to all Borrowers unless Applicable Law expressly requires otherwise. The notice address shall be the Property Address unless Borrower has designated a substitute notice address by notice to Lender. Borrower shall promptly notify Lender of Borrower's change of address. If Lender specifies a procedure for reporting Borrower's change of address, then Borrower shall only report a change of address through that specified procedure. There may be only one designated notice address under this Security Instrument at any one time. Any notice to Lender shall be given by delivering it or by mailing it by first class mail to Lender's address stated herein unless Lender has designated another address by notice to Borrower. Any notice in connection with this Security Instrument shall not be deemed to have been given to Lender until actually received by Lender. If any notice required by this Security Instrument is also required under Applicable Law, the Applicable Law requirement will satisfy the corresponding requirement under this Security Instrument.

16. Governing Law; Severability; Rules of Construction. This Security Instrument shall be governed by federal law and the law of the jurisdiction in which the Property is located. All rights and obligations contained in this Security Instrument are subject to any requirements and limitations of Applicable Law. Applicable Law might explicitly or implicitly allow the parties to agree by contract or it might be silent, but such silence shall not be construed as a prohibition against agreement by contract. In the event that any provision or clause of this Security Instrument or the Note conflicts with Applicable Law, such conflict shall not affect other provisions of this Security Instrument or the Note which can be given effect without the conflicting provision.

As used in this Security Instrument: (a) words of the masculine gender shall mean and include corresponding neuter words or words of the feminine gender; (b) words in the singular shall mean and include the plural and vice versa; and (c) the word "may" gives sole discretion without any obligation to take any action.

17. Borrower's Copy. Borrower shall be given one copy of the Note and of this Security Instrument.

18. Transfer of the Property or a Beneficial Interest in Borrower. As used in this Section 18, "Interest in the Property" means any legal or beneficial interest in the Property, including, but not limited to, those beneficial interests transferred in a bond for deed, contract for deed, installment sales contract or escrow agreement, the intent of which is the transfer of title by Borrower at a future date to a purchaser.

If all or any part of the Property or any Interest in the Property is sold or transferred (or if Borrower is not a natural person and a beneficial interest in Borrower is sold or transferred) without Lender's prior written consent, Lender may require immediate payment in full of all sums secured by this Security Instrument. However, this option shall not be exercised by Lender if such exercise is prohibited Applicable Law.

If Lender exercises this option, Lender shall give Borrower notice of acceleration. The notice shall provide a period of not less than 30 days from the date the notice is given in accordance with Section 15 within which Borrower must pay all sums secured by this Security Instrument. If Borrower fails to pay these sums prior to the expiration of this period, Lender may invoke any remedies permitted by this Security Instrument without further notice or demand on Borrower.

19. Borrower's Right to Reinstate After Acceleration. If Borrower meets certain conditions, Borrower shall have the right to have enforcement of this Security Instrument discontinued at any time prior to the earliest of: (a) five days before sale of the Property pursuant to any power of sale contained in this Security Instrument; (b) such other period as Applicable Law might specify for the termination of Borrower's right to reinstate; or (c) entry of a judgment enforcing this Security Instrument. Those conditions are that Borrower: (a) pays Lender all sums which then would be due under this Security Instrument and the Note as if no acceleration had occurred; (b) cures any default of any other covenants or agreements; (c) pays all expenses incurred in enforcing this Security Instrument, including, but not limited to, reasonable attorneys' fees, property inspection and valuation fees, and other fees incurred for the purpose of protecting Lender's interest in the Property and rights under this Security Instrument; and (d) takes such action as Lender may reasonably require to assure that Lender's interest in the Property and rights under this Security Instrument, and Borrower's obligation to pay the sums secured by this Security Instrument, shall continue unchanged. Lender may require that Borrower pay such reinstatement sums and expenses in one or more of the following forms, as selected by Lender: (a) cash; (b) money order; (c) certified check, bank check, treasurer's check or cashier's check, provided any such check is drawn upon an institution whose deposits are insured by a federal agency, instrumentality or entity; or (d) Electronic Funds Transfer. Upon reinstatement by Borrower, this Security Instrument and obligations secured hereby shall remain fully effective as if no acceleration had occurred. However, this right to reinstate shall not apply in the case of acceleration under Section 18.

20. Sale of Note; Change of Loan Servicer; Notice of Grievance. The Note or a partial interest in the Note (together with this Security Instrument) can be sold one or more times without prior notice to Borrower. A sale might result in a change in the entity (known as the "Loan Servicer") that collects Periodic Payments due under the Note and this Security Instrument and performs other mortgage loan servicing obligations under the Note, this Security Instrument, and Applicable Law. There also might be one or more changes of the Loan Servicer unrelated to a sale of the Note. If there is a change of the Loan Servicer, Borrower will be given written notice of the change which will state the name and address of the new Loan Servicer, the address to which payments should be made and any other information RESPA requires in connection with a notice of transfer of servicing. If the Note is sold and thereafter the Loan is serviced by a Loan Servicer other than the purchaser of the Note, the mortgage loan servicing obligations to Borrower will remain with the Loan Servicer or be transferred to a successor Loan Servicer and are not assumed by the Note purchaser unless otherwise provided by the Note purchaser.

Neither Borrower nor Lender may commence, join, or be joined to any judicial action (as either an individual litigant or the member of a class) that arises from the other party's actions pursuant to this Security Instrument or that alleges that the other party has breached any provision of, or any duty owed by reason of, this Security Instrument, until such Borrower or Lender has notified the other party (with such notice given in compliance with the requirements of Section 15) of such alleged breach and afforded the other party hereto a reasonable period after the giving of such notice to take corrective action. If Applicable Law provides a time period which must elapse before certain action can be taken, that time period will be deemed to be reasonable for purposes of this paragraph. The notice of acceleration and opportunity to cure given to Borrower pursuant to Section 22 and the notice of acceleration given to Borrower pursuant to Section 18 shall be deemed to satisfy the notice and opportunity to take corrective action provisions of this Section 20.

21. Hazardous Substances. As used in this Section 21: (a) "Hazardous Substances" are those substances defined as toxic or hazardous substances, pollutants, or wastes by Environmental Law and the following substances: gasoline, kerosene, other flammable or toxic petroleum products, toxic pesticides and herbicides, volatile solvents, materials containing asbestos or formaldehyde, and radioactive materials; (b) "Environmental Law" means federal laws and laws of the jurisdiction where the Property is located that relate to health, safety or environmental protection; (c) "Environmental Cleanup" includes any response action, remedial action, or removal action, as defined in Environmental Law; and (d) an "Environmental Condition" means a condition that can cause, contribute to, or otherwise trigger an Environmental Cleanup.

Borrower shall not cause or permit the presence, use, disposal, storage, or release of any Hazardous Substances, or threaten to release any Hazardous Substances, on or in the Property. Borrower shall not do, nor allow anyone else to do, anything affecting the Property (a) that is in violation of any Environmental Law, (b) which creates an Environmental Condition, or (c) which, due to the presence, use, or release of a Hazardous Substance, creates a condition that adversely affects the value of the Property. The preceding two sentences shall not apply to the presence, use, or storage on the Property of small quantities of Hazardous Substances that are generally recognized to be appropriate to normal residential uses and to maintenance of the Property (including, but not limited to, hazardous substances in consumer products).

Borrower shall promptly give Lender written notice of (a) any investigation, claim, demand, lawsuit or other action by any governmental or regulatory agency or private party involving the Property and any Hazardous Substance or Environmental Law of which Borrower has actual knowledge, (b) any Environmental Condition, including but not limited to, any spilling, leaking, discharge, release or threat of release of any Hazardous Substance, and (c) any condition caused by the presence, use or release of a Hazardous Substance which adversely affects the value of the Property. If Borrower learns, or is notified by any governmental or regulatory authority, or any private party, that any removal or other remediation of any Hazardous Substance affecting the Property is necessary, Borrower shall promptly take all necessary remedial actions in accordance with Environmental Law. Nothing herein shall create any obligation on Lender for an Environmental Cleanup.

NON-UNIFORM COVENANTS. Borrower and Lender further covenant and agree as follows:

22. Acceleration; Remedies. Lender shall give notice to Borrower prior to acceleration following Borrower's breach of any covenant or agreement in this Security Instrument (but not prior to acceleration under Section 18 unless Applicable Law provides otherwise). The notice shall specify: (a) the default; (b) the action required to cure the default; (c) a date, not less than 30 days from the date the notice is given to Borrower, by which the default must be cured; and (d) that failure to cure the default on or before the date specified in the notice may result in acceleration of the sums secured by this Security Instrument, foreclosure by judicial proceeding and sale of the Property. The notice shall further inform Borrower of the right to reinstate after acceleration and the right to assert in the foreclosure proceeding the non-existence of a default or any other defense of Borrower to acceleration and foreclosure. If the default is not cured on or before the date specified in the notice, Lender at its option may require immediate payment in full of all sums secured by this Security Instrument without further demand and may foreclose this Security Instrument by judicial proceeding. Lender shall be entitled to collect all expenses incurred in pursuing the remedies provided in this Section 22, including, but not limited to, reasonable attorneys' fees and costs of title evidence.

23. Release. Upon payment of all sums secured by this Security Instrument, Lender shall release this Security Instrument. Borrower shall pay any recordation costs. Lender may charge Borrower a fee for releasing this Security Instrument, but only if the fee is paid to a third party for services rendered and the charging of the fee is permitted under Applicable Law.

24. Attorneys' Fees. As used in this Security Instrument and the Note, attorneys' fees shall include those awarded by an appellate court and any attorneys' fees incurred in a bankruptcy proceeding.

25. Jury Trial Waiver. The Borrower hereby waives any right to a trial by jury in any action, proceeding, claim, or counterclaim, whether in contract or tort, at law or in equity, arising out of or in any way related to this Security Instrument or the Note.

BY SIGNING BELOW, Borrower accepts and agrees to the terms and covenants contained in this Security Instrument and in any Rider executed by Borrower and recorded with it.

Signed, sealed and delivered in the presence of:

____________________ ____________________

__ (Seal)
- Borrower

____________________ ____________________

__ (Seal)
- Borrower

____________[Space Below This Line For Acknowledgment]____________

The Go-Go Mortgage Years - Boom and Bust

Since I keep talking about the "go-go mortgage years" maybe it's time for me to tell you what I mean by that, and how it may help you to save your home. During the last several years, ending in 2007, housing prices rose dramatically. These ever-increasing home prices were fueled in part by a flood of mortgage money.

During this time, it seemed that virtually anyone could get approved for a mortgage loan. One of the principal reasons for this easy mortgage money was a cash infusion from Wall Street. Traditionally, major banks and mortgage lenders would lend money for mortgages based on deposits held within those institutions.

However, the creative minds on Wall Street decided it would be profitable to turn mortgages into securities that could be traded on Wall Street – just like regular stocks and bonds. Although the "securitization" of mortgages wasn't a new idea, its use grew dramatically between the mid-1990's and 2007, when the mortgage and housing industry collapsed.

Traditionally, a bank would loan the money for a mortgage, keep the loan in its own "portfolio" and collect the payments from the borrower. This was an investment for the bank, and worked perfectly as long as the interest the bank received from the mortgage loan was higher than the interest the bank paid out to people with deposits in the bank.

Of course, the bank also assumed the risk if the borrower failed to pay the loan. This made mortgage lenders very careful about the requirements for loan approval. It also limited the number of people who could receive loans because there was only so much money to go around.

With the increased use of securitization, however, all the rules changed. Now, the goal was to get a borrower, make the loan, and sell the mortgage and loan to an investor. The bank made money from selling the loan to an investor, and the cash received from the sale allowed the bank to make more loans.

As a result, the incentives changed from making a few solid loans, to making as many loans as possible. The more loans the bank could generate and sell, the more money it made.

With money coming in from American and overseas investors, banks had a seemingly endless supply of mortgage money available. This created intense competition within the mortgage industry for borrowers. This is turn created thousands and thousands of "creative" loan products that would appeal to just about any borrower and would allow just about any borrower to qualify for a mortgage - no down payment loans, interest only loans, no income verification loans, etc. The list went on and on.

(I was involved in the mortgage industry during this time, and helped hundreds of consumers in Chapter 13 bankruptcy refinance their mortgages to escape from the bankruptcy. I was constantly surprised at the loans that lenders would approve for my clients. The loans really helped my clients, but very often seemed reckless. The banks didn't care – they just wanted to fund loans.)

Title companies that handled mortgage closings were running beyond capacity. They would even send closers to borrowers' homes to get the loans closed. It was all about volume and speed – get the loan closed, get it sold, and start the process all over again.

This speed and recklessness to get loans closed has created problems for the banks that are now seeking to foreclose on loans that have defaulted. But, this speed and recklessness has also created defenses for people that want to save their homes.

I told you earlier about the proper procedures for transferring a promissory note and mortgage. Traditionally, lenders held the promissory note in their portfolio as an investment, so it wasn't really necessary to transfer these documents. And, even when a lender did transfer a loan, it was usually only one time, so they generally got the transfer process right.

However, with the securitization process, the loan was transferred several times to several different entities. I'm not going to describe the entire process because it would make your head swim. But, I want you to understand that your loan was probably transferred several times. With each transfer, the promissory note should have been endorsed or physically transferred, and the mortgage should have been assigned.

But, guess what? That rarely happened. Instead, lenders often lost or destroyed promissory notes at the beginning of the process. Therefore, they didn't properly transfer them. And, they rarely assigned the mortgages. Not a great way to do business. But, it worked – until now.

For now, I just want you to think about all of this. Next, I'm going to tell you about the foreclosure process in detail, and show you how you can use the lenders' haste to save your home.

Payment Default to Filing the Complaint

We talked about the foreclosure timeline in Chapter 2. Now, let's look at that timeline in more detail and talk about the basic foreclosure defenses that you can use to save your home during each phase of the foreclosure process.

The foreclosure process starts when you miss your first payment. As we discussed in Chapter 2, your lender will start to communicate with you within 30 days after you first miss your payment. Usually these communications are mild and polite and include offers of help.

By the 90th day of non-payment, the lender will probably transfer your file to their foreclosure attorney. As we discussed, the foreclosure attorney should then send you a Notice of Acceleration. Assuming that the lender is required to give you notice of the Default and Acceleration under the terms of the Mortgage (typically paragraph 22 of the mortgage), the lender's attorney will file a foreclosure complaint in the county where your house is located.

In addition to the foreclosure complaint, the lender's attorney will file a "Notice of Lis Pendens". Essentially, this is a notice to anyone in the future that the lender is filing a complaint that may affect the property. Any action to transfer or encumber the property done after the Lis Pendens is filed is ineffective against the lender who filed the Lis Pendens. Essentially, the Lis Pendens is a warning to the rest of the world that says "proceed at your own risk for this property".

At this time, the Clerk of Court will issue a "summons" that requires that you answer the foreclosure complaint within 20 days after it is served on you. Then, the lender will hire a private process server or the Sheriff's office to "serve" the complaint on you.

Respond to the Complaint

Under the Florida Rules of Civil Procedure, you must file a response to the foreclosure complaint within twenty days after it is served on you. (Some lenders will allow thirty days for you to respond. The specific time period will be described in the summons.)

During that time you are allowed to file an answer, or a responsive pleading.

Always file a response.

Before we talk about responding to the complaint and legal defenses, let's get something out of the way. Almost every day a client comes to us who failed to file a response. We ask why they didn't, naturally. They say, "Well, I didn't make the payments. I owe the money."

Yes, I know you owe the money. But, that doesn't necessarily mean the lender has the right to throw you out of your home. You deserve better, and there are many defenses to foreclosure.

The summons is like an invitation to a dance, and if you don't send in your RSVP... you don't get to participate in the dance. You don't get to raise defenses. You don't get to receive notice. In all likelihood a default judgment will be entered against you – and you'll lose your house.

My biggest fear for my clients is that a sheriff shows up at their house with a twenty-four hour eviction notice... and they're shocked. If you don't file a responsive pleading, you don't have to be served with notices as the process moves along... and the sheriff could show up at your house to let you know you need to leave – because you no longer own the home. If you don't file a response you won't know a Motion for Summary Judgment is filed, a hearing is scheduled, a default judgment is awarded, a sale is scheduled, the auction takes place, an eviction notice is coming... while some attorneys will deliver notices even if you don't file a response, many won't.

Imagine that you get a twenty-four hour eviction notice you had no idea was coming. Can you move in twenty-four hours? Where will you move? If the purchaser wishes to, they can bring a crew to your house after the twenty-four hour period elapses and move all your things to the curb. (If you drive by a house and see a lot of stuff in the front yard, now you know why.)

Quick note: If that does happen to you – God forbid – immediately call the lender and ask for a grace period. Beg if you have to. Ask for several days to find a place and move your things. Many will show at least some amount of compassion.

If you don't file a response, you're helpless.

Always file a response.

OK. I think I've made my point about this – FILE A RESPONSE!

But, what response should you file? Well, that depends on what you see when you first receive the complaint. You have essentially two choices – a Motion to Dismiss or an Answer. (There are others, but let's keep it simple here.)

Motion to Dismiss

Whenever possible, I try to file a Motion to Dismiss. Under Rule 1.140(b) of the Florida Rules of Civil Procedure, you can raise several defenses to a foreclosure complaint in a Motion to Dismiss. A Motion to Dismiss is a pleading that says, essentially, that the complaint has problems that require the court to dismiss it. If the judge rules in your favor, the case is dismissed and you don't even need to answer the complaint.

In reality, most foreclosure cases are not dismissed based on a Motion to Dismiss. Normally, the Plaintiff (the lender) will correct the complaint based on issues raised in the Motion to Dismiss. However, the Plaintiff needs to file a proper complaint, and you have the right to object when the Plaintiff fails to do this.

Of course, this process generally takes from one to several months to resolve itself. Then, you must generally file your answer to the complaint. In the meantime, you have the lender's attention, you know if they have a problem with their documents, and you've bought more time. So, think about using the Motion to Dismiss as your initial foreclosure defense strategy.

What Does a Motion to Dismiss Look Like?

Take a look at the sample Motion to Dismiss. There are many ways to draft a Motion to Dismiss. But, this sample Motion is fairly common.

There's nothing magic about the Motion to Dismiss. In the Motion, just state why you think the Complaint should be dismissed – explain to the judge what's wrong with it. And, since we're on that topic, let's look at the different problems with a Complaint that may allow you to file a Motion to Dismiss.

IN THE CIRCUIT OF THE 18TH JUDICIAL CIRCUIT, IN AND FOR SEMINOLE COUNTY, FLORIDA

ABC BANK, FSB, Case # 2010-CA-XXXX-14-G

Plaintiff,

vs.

JOE CONSUMER; et al.,

Defendants.

_____________________________/

DEFENDANT'S MOTION TO DISMISS FOR FAILURE TO STATE A CAUSE OF ACTION

COMES NOW the Defendant, JOE CONSUMER, by and through his undersigned attorney, and pursuant to Rule 1.140(b)(6) of the Florida Rules of Civil Procedure, moves this honorable Court to dismiss the Plaintiff's Complaint for failure to state a cause of action, and in support thereof states as follows:

1. In Count II of the Complaint, the Plaintiff seeks to reestablish a promissory note under Section 673.3091, Florida Statutes.
2. Section 673.3091(1)(a) states in relevant part that:
   A person not in possession of an instrument is entitled to enforce the instrument if … The person seeking to enforce the instrument was entitled to enforce the instrument when loss of possession occurred, or has directly or indirectly acquired ownership of the instrument from a person who was entitled to enforce the instrument when loss of possession occurred.
3. In its Complaint, the Plaintiff fails both requirements of Section 673.3091(1)(a).
4. First, the Plaintiff failed to attach to the Complaint even a copy of the Promissory Note that it seeks to reestablish. Therefore, it completely fails to establish that it was "entitled to enforce the note when loss of possession occurred."
5. Further, based on the Mortgage that the Plaintiff did attach to the Complaint, it is unlikely that the Plaintiff could establish that it is the proper party to enforce the note, even if it did have possession of the note.
6. In addition, the Plaintiff failed to attach to the Complaint any document to demonstrate that the note was transferred to the Plaintiff to prove the second element of Section 673.3091(1)(a) – that it has directly or indirectly acquired ownership of the instrument from a person who was entitled to enforce the instrument when loss of possession occurred.
7. Therefore, having failed to satisfy these conditions precedent as required by Section 673.3091(1)(a), the Plaintiff fails to state a cause of action.
8. Additionally, the Plaintiff also fails to satisfy the requirements of Section 673.3091(2), which states in relevant part that "A person seeking enforcement of an instrument under subsection (1) must prove the terms of the instrument and the person's right to enforce the instrument."
9. The Plaintiff failed to attach to the Complaint even a copy of the Promissory Note that it seeks to reestablish under Section 673.3091. Therefore, the Plaintiff is unable to prove the terms of instrument, and has failed to state a cause of action under Section 673.3091.

WHEREFORE, the Defendant respectfully requests that this Court:

1. Dismiss the Plaintiff's Complaint; and,
2. Grant such further and additional relief as this Court deems just and equitable.

I HEREBY CERTIFY that a true copy of the foregoing has been furnished by fax/U.S. Mail this ___ day of _____, 2010 to Plaintiff's Attorney, 123 Anywhere Road, Anywhere, FL 32701.

____

CHARLES W. PRICE, ESQ.
390 Maitland Ave., Suite 1000
Altamonte Springs, FL 32701
(407) 834-0090
Fla. Bar No. 0870862
Counsel for Defendant

Particular Defenses

Although Rule 1.140(b) contains several potential reasons to dismiss a complaint, I want to focus on the three primary reasons that you're likely to encounter in a typical foreclosure complaint. But, as we talk about these reasons to dismiss a complaint, and foreclosure defenses in general, I want you to understand that my goal is not to teach you to be a lawyer. My goal is to help you understand how a few of the main legal defenses work so you can make an informed choice about how to proceed. So, with that in mind, let's look at some of the basics.

Insufficiency of Service of Process – Rule 1.140(b)(5)

If you remember, I told you that a lender must serve the complaint on you using a private process server or Sheriff. But, there are rules and statutes that dictate the proper process for serving a Complaint.

Rule 48.031, of the Florida Statutes sets forth the general rules for serving a complaint against an individual. Under Rule 48.031, the process server or Sheriff must personally hand a copy of the complaint to any person who resides in the defendant's "usual place of abode" and is 15 years of age or older. The process server must also inform that person of the contents of the complaint.

In addition, a process server or Sheriff can serve you at work, but are required to serve you in a "private area designated by your employer."

I've had many cases where the process server tossed the complaint at the front door without verifying an identity of anyone in the house, or served the complaint on a child less than 15 years of age. I've also had cases where the complaint was served on neighbors or family that didn't reside in the defendant's house.

If the process server fails to follow the procedures for service as outlined in Section 48.031, the service of that complaint is subject to a Motion to Dismiss for "insufficiency of process" under Rule 1.140(b)(5).

In addition, Rule 1.070(e) of the Florida Rules of Civil Procedure requires that process servers write the date and hour of service on the original complaint and all copies. If the process server fails to do this, and this does happen, this also subjects the complaint to a Motion to Dismiss for "insufficiency of process" under Rule 1.140(b)(5).

I've had people tell me (usually plaintiff's attorneys), that filing a Motion to Dismiss for Insufficiency of Process is just "playing games". After all, the plaintiff just needs to fix the problems with the service of the complaint, and this usually isn't a fatal flaw to the foreclosure case.

However, the rules are there for a reason. Very often, people have no idea that they're being sued. If the complaint is thrown at a doorstep, or handed to a child or visitor, it's likely that the defendant may never see the complaint. The rules are there to provide "due process" for people who are being sued to give them their "day in court". I believe that it's a travesty for people to miss the opportunity to defend themselves from litigation because the plaintiff failed to comply with the rules for service. Defending improper service isn't a game – it's a defense of your rights. So, if this happens to you – fight it with a Motion to Dismiss.

Failure to State a Cause of Action – Rule 1.140(b)(6)

Most Motions to Dismiss foreclosure complaints are based on Rule 1.140(b)(6) – failure to state a cause of action. In a complaint, a plaintiff must allege enough facts to support a legal theory against you. For most foreclosure cases, this means that the lender must allege enough facts to prove that it has the right, under the terms of the mortgage, to take your home from you because you failed to pay your loan pursuant to the terms of the promissory note.

If the lender fails to allege enough facts in the complaint, or attach proper documentation to prove that it has the right to sue you for foreclosure, then you have a right to file a Motion to Dismiss the complaint. In that case, the lender has failed to "state" its right to sue you.

This is where all of our previous discussions about the promissory note and mortgage transfer process will become important. As you recall, I told you that a promissory note must be endorsed to allow a proper transfer from one lender to another. And, I told you that a mortgage must be assigned to allow proper transfer from one lender to another.

But, guess what happens in the real world? Right - the lenders don't properly transfer the promissory notes and mortgages. This allows you to file a Motion to Dismiss the foreclosure complaint. However, unlike the insufficiency of process defense that we just reviewed, this defense can sometimes be a game-ender for the mortgage lender.

If the lender can't provide proper proof that it is the true owner of the promissory note and mortgage, that lender doesn't have the right to sue you. If the transfers never properly occurred, the only lender that may have the right to file a foreclosure complaint against you is the original lender. And, in most cases, the original lender went out of business during the collapse of the mortgage industry starting in 2007. So, filing a Motion to Dismiss for failure to state a cause of action could be the first step in permanently defeating the foreclosure process against you.

Essentially, what we're talking about here is a legal concept called "standing". Standing means a plaintiff – in this case the lender – has the right to sue the defendant – in this case you. Standing means the lender has the right to sue you.

You may be thinking, "Wait a minute... I owe them the money, so why wouldn't they have the right to sue me?" And you would be right, at least in theory – but also often wrong in practice.

Here's an example. Say you receive a complaint from a lender. At the top left you'll see the plaintiff and the defendant. (For example, ACME Industries, Plaintiff, vs. John Doe, Defendant means ACME Industries is the plaintiff, or the party bringing the suit, and John Doe is the defendant, or the person being sued.)

So far so good. But then things usually take a turn. At the top left you see the Plaintiff listed; we'll pretend the Plaintiff is ACME Mortgage. In the middle of the page the Plaintiff's argument is listed; typically those arguments or positions (or facts) are called Counts. Somewhere in the first few lines you see a line like:

On June 1, 2008 at Orange County, Florida, ***John Doe*** *(that's you) executed and delivered to* ***123 Mortgage*** *a promissory note in the principal amount of $250,000.*

Oops. Who is the Plaintiff? ACME Mortgage, or 123 Mortgage? In short, who has *standing*?

One party is suing, but another party provided the money and accepted a promissory note.

Then you check out the mortgage document; it also specifies 123 Mortgage as the lender, not ACME Mortgage. Then, you check to see if the plaintiff has included an "Assignment of Mortgage" in the Complaint. But, the Plaintiff failed to attach any assignment.

Then, you check out the promissory note; it also specifies 123 Mortgage as the lender, not ACME Mortgage. After our discussion about the proper way to transfer a negotiable instrument, you look to see if there's an endorsement on the attached promissory note. But, you don't see anything.

This all seems odd, since the next line in the complaint states:

Plaintiff is the owner of said note and mortgage.

Really? How did that happen? Who knows who has the right to sue? Who has standing?

In reality, I appear to have as much right as ACME Mortgage to bring the foreclosure lawsuit against you. Just because you owe money to some lender, doesn't mean that you owe money to the lender that filed the foreclosure complaint against you. Remember that!

Before you get too excited about this, I want you to understand that in the vast majority of cases, the lender that is suing you somehow finds or produces the original promissory note and assignment – typically after receiving a Motion to Dismiss. There have been many documented cases where endorsements and assignments were forged or otherwise "created" after the foreclosure process began. I don't know how prevalent this practice is, but it does happen. The difficulty is in proving that the documents have been forged or inappropriately created. This often doesn't happen without some great detective work and detailed and extensive "discovery" of information and documents. But, even if the lender ultimately produces the documents, you should file a Motion to Dismiss if they don't have a copy of the original documents attached to the with proper endorsements of the promissory note and proper assignment for the mortgage.

Specific Problems

Now that we've talked about the failure to state a cause of action in general, let's look at some of the specific issues you can raise in your Motion to Dismiss. First let's talk about problems with the Promissory Note.

Problems With the Promissory Note

Improper Endorsement

There are two basic problems regarding promissory notes that you'll see in a foreclosure complaint. The first problem that often arises is that the Plaintiff actually has the promissory note, but it's not properly endorsed. We talked about that during our discussion on transferring promissory notes.

When you receive the foreclosure complaint, you should immediately review the attached promissory note to see who the "Lender" is on the face of the promissory note. If it's not the same lender that's suing you, look at the end of the promissory note to see if there's an endorsement.

If there's no endorsement, file a Motion to Dismiss based on lack of standing. As in the example above, if ACME Mortgage is suing you, but the lender in the promissory note is 123 Mortgage, ACME Mortgage doesn't appear to have standing. In this case, the Plaintiff has failed to state a cause of action against you.

To remedy this, the Plaintiff needs to file an original note with a proper endorsement to defeat your Motion to Dismiss. As I mentioned earlier, the lenders always seem to come up with the promissory note. But, it may take months for them to do this.

Lost Note

The second problem that arises is that the plaintiff doesn't actually have the original promissory note. In more than 50% of the foreclosure complaints that I see, the plaintiff alleges that it has lost the original promissory note and so can't attach it to the complaint.

To remedy this situation, the plaintiff must include a separate count in the complaint for "Reestablishment of a Lost Note" pursuant to section 673.3091 of the Florida Statutes. Under this statute, a plaintiff may "reestablish" and enforce a lost, destroyed or stolen promissory note if it can prove that:

(a) The person seeking to enforce the instrument was entitled to enforce the instrument when loss of possession occurred, or has directly or indirectly acquired ownership of the instrument from a person who was entitled to enforce the instrument when loss of possession occurred;

(b) The loss of possession was not the result of a transfer by the person or a lawful seizure; and

(c) The person cannot reasonably obtain possession of the instrument because the instrument was destroyed, its whereabouts cannot be determined, or it is in the wrongful possession of an unknown person or a person that cannot be found or is not amenable to service of process.

Back when I used to represent creditors, I was always shocked that lenders lost the original promissory notes and mortgages for the loans that they held in their portfolios. I can't tell you how many times I searched through the vaults at my clients' corporate headquarters in search of these original documents. Who knows what happened to them? Certainly not the lenders.

Because this happens so frequently, it was necessary for legislators to craft a statute like section 673.3091. Otherwise, lenders could never move forward in their cases.

So, when I first started seeing the rash of foreclosure complaints in 2007, I wasn't overly concerned about the count for reestablishment of a lost note. But, then I started to realize that something was different.

When I represented creditors in their foreclosure cases, my client – the plaintiff – was most often the original lender. Remember, lenders traditionally would hold the mortgage loans themselves and not transfer the loans to other investors. So, it was relatively easy for lenders to show that they owned the note when it was lost and were at that time entitled to enforce it.

But, as you recall, the mortgage industry changed substantially in the 1990's and beyond. The most common practice now is for lenders to transfer the loans to other investors, sometimes through several transactions and investors. So, the question becomes – when did the note get lost or destroyed? At what stage in the transfers did this occur?

If the plaintiff can't prove that it was the owner WHEN IT WAS LOST or was entitled to enforce the note WHEN IT WAS LOST, or received ownership from someone that could enforce the note WHEN IT WAS LOST, then the plaintiff can't "reestablish" the note under section 673.3091. If the lender can't reestablish the note, it can't enforce the note. If the lender can't enforce the note – you win!

In reality, you will probably have to conduct "discovery" to determine the chain of transfers and ownership. (We'll talk about discovery in a moment). But, at least initially, I always view a reestablishment count as a signal of problems with the foreclosure case. And, almost always, I will file a Motion to Dismiss for this reason.

But, again, be prepared for the plaintiff to magically produce the promissory note after you file the Motion to Dismiss. It happens more often than not. But, don't let this deter you. File the Motion to Dismiss and wait for a hearing on your motion.

Problems with the Mortgage

The second major problem that I see with foreclosure complaints is improper or missing mortgage assignments. We've already talked about this before. The only proper way for one lender to transfer a mortgage to another lender or investor is to assign the mortgage. Unless the mortgage is properly assigned to the plaintiff, the plaintiff doesn't have the right, or standing, to file the foreclosure complaint against you.

When you receive the foreclosure complaint, you should immediately review the attached mortgage to see who the "Lender" is on the face of the mortgage. If it's not the same lender that's suing you, look to see if the plaintiff has included an Assignment in the complaint.

If there's no Assignment, file a Motion to Dismiss based on lack of standing. As in the example above, if ACME Mortgage is suing you, but the lender in the mortgage is 123 Mortgage, ACME Mortgage doesn't appear to have standing. In this case, the Plaintiff has failed to state a cause of action against you.

To remedy this, the Plaintiff needs to file an Assignment of Mortgage to defeat your Motion to Dismiss. Very often, the assignment is dated after you file the Motion to Dismiss. There is case law that frowns on after-filing assignments, and there is case law that allows it in certain cases. For now, however, the important thing to remember is to file the Motion to Dismiss and make the lender produce the Assignment. You can always determine whether the Assignment is valid during the discovery phase of the litigation.

Problems with the Acceleration Notice

Another common problem that you can address with a Motion to Dismiss is the plaintiff's failure to attach an Acceleration Notice to the complaint. We discussed the Acceleration letter earlier and talked about why acceleration is necessary. As you recall, a lender must accelerate your loan because, without acceleration, the lender would have to sue you for every month that you miss a payment. It would take the lender years and years to resolve the problem.

So, acceleration is a necessary part of the process. However, most mortgages require that the lender give you notice of its intent to accelerate and give you time to "cure" the mortgage arrearage before this happens – typically 30 days.

You may recall that most mortgages are standardized, based on the Fannie Mae/Freddie Mac Uniform Mortgage. Because of this, you should always look at Paragraph 22 of your Mortgage to see if the acceleration paragraph is included in your Mortgage. (If it's not in Paragraph 22, see if there's an acceleration paragraph somewhere else in the mortgage. If not, you probably can't use this defense.)

If you don't have your Mortgage in front of you, review the sample Mortgage from earlier in this chapter. This is, in relevant part, what you'll find:

> 22. Acceleration; Remedies. Lender shall give notice to buyer prior to acceleration following Borrower's breach of any covenant or agreement in the Security Instrument. The notice shall specify: (a) the default; (b) the action required to cure the default; (c) a date, not less than 30 days from the date from the date the notice is given to Borrower, by which the default must be cured; and (d) that the failure to cure the default on or before the date specified in the notice may result in acceleration of the sums secured by this Security Instrument, foreclosure by judicial proceeding and sale of the Property. The notice shall further inform Borrower of the right to reinstate after acceleration and the right to assert in the foreclosure proceeding the non-existence of a default or any other defenses of Borrower to acceleration and foreclosure. If the default is not cured on or before the date specified in the notice, Lender at its option may require immediate payment in full of all sums secured by this Security Agreement without further demand and may foreclose this Security Instrument by judicial proceeding.

Therefore, pursuant to Paragraph 22, the lender must give you written notice of its intent to accelerate the loan and foreclose, and give you at least 30 days to catch up the payments before it can file a foreclosure complaint against you. And guess what? They very often don't do this.

And, plaintiffs almost never attach a copy of the Acceleration Notice to the Complaint.

The plaintiff's failure to give you proper notice of its intent to accelerate the loan, or its failure to attach a copy of a proper notice, is grounds for a Motion to Dismiss. If the lender fails to give you proper notice, as required by the mortgage, it means that the lender has failed a "condition precedent." This is legal jargon for "you didn't do something that you were required to do before you could file the lawsuit". As you can see from Paragraph 22, sending a written Acceleration Notice and giving you 30 days is a requirement BEFORE the lender can file the foreclosure complaint.

Therefore, when you receive the foreclosure complaint, you should immediately review the attached mortgage to see if it contains an acceleration notice requirement. (Look at Paragraph 22 first.) If the mortgage does require an acceleration notice, review the complaint to see if the plaintiff attached a copy of the acceleration notice to the complaint. If it is not attached, file the Motion to Dismiss.

If an acceleration notice is attached, review the date of the notice to see if the plaintiff waited the full amount of time allowed to you before it filed the complaint. If you did not receive the full time period allowed, file the Motion to Dismiss.

Failure to Join Indispensable Parties – Rule 1.140(b)(7)

Another possible reason to include in a Motion to Dismiss is the failure of the plaintiff to include "indispensable parties". An indispensable party is a person or entity that MUST be included in the lawsuit before the judge can issue a judgment.

Depending on the mood I'm in when I'm drafting a Motion to Dismiss, I may include a claim that the plaintiff has failed to include an indispensable party in the lawsuit and that it must be dismissed because of that omission. Who do you think I claim is the indispensable party?

That's right, the original lender that's listed in the promissory note and mortgage. If there's no endorsement of the promissory note, and no assignment of the mortgage, then it appears that the proper party to bring the foreclosure complaint is missing. This is essentially a standing argument. It's just another way of pleading the Motion to Dismiss.

When and How to File a Motion to Dismiss

As you recall, the Florida Rules of Civil Procedure allow you 20 days to file a response to a complaint (and some plaintiffs will allow you 30 days.) You should file the Motion to Dismiss on the LAST day of your allowed time period. I know that you're ready to do battle and get the foreclosure resolved. But, think about your goals and the big picture.

There's generally no reason to move the foreclosure case more quickly than necessary. I usually want the case to move as slowly as possible. This should be your goal as well. So, file everything on the last possible day.

And that brings us to the next point – how do you file the Motion to Dismiss and what happens next. I've included a sample Motion to Dismiss in this chapter. You can use this as a guide. Follow the "case style" that's listed at the top of the Complaint if you draft your own Motion to Dismiss. (I really don't encourage you to file your own Motion to Dismiss. You certainly can do it, I just think you'll be better served if you hire an attorney to do this for you – even if it's not me!)

Once you've drafted your Motion to Dismiss, file it with the Clerk of Court that's listed in the Complaint. You can do this by taking it to the courthouse and handing it to the clerk. Or, you can mail the Motion. Depending on your county, you may also be able to fax the Motion to the clerk. Make sure you check with the clerk to get their specific rules for filing.

You also need to mail a copy of your Motion to Dismiss to the plaintiff's attorney. They are entitled to receive anything you produce and file with the court, just as you are entitled to receive their pleadings.

The next step in the process is to schedule a hearing with the judge on your Motion to Dismiss. As with the actual filing, I'm rarely in a rush to schedule the hearing on my Motion to Dismiss. Again, there's no particular reason to move the process too fast!

Final Thoughts on Motions to Dismiss

Again, I'm not trying to make you a lawyer or tell you every possible reason for filing a Motion to Dismiss. I just want you to be aware of the issues and the possibilities. I've included a Sample Motion to Dismiss in this chapter. This Motion is not intended to provide you with legal advice and I encourage you to contact an attorney. (I'd be thrilled for you to contact my office. But, if not me, please at least talk to an attorney that handles foreclosure defense as a primary practice area.)

If you'd like additional information and more samples, go to www.SaveYourFloridaHomeNow.com. I will constantly update the web site as the case law changes and new information becomes available.

File an Answer to the Complaint

The other primary type of responsive pleading is something you're probably more familiar with – the Answer. If you don't file a Motion to Dismiss when you're first served with the Complaint, you must file an Answer within the time allowed in the Summons – 20 or 30 days.

You also will file an Answer if you originally file a Motion to Dismiss, and the Court denies your Motion. Typically, a judge will allow you a certain amount of time to file the Answer – normally 10 to 20 days.

IN THE CIRCUIT OF THE 9TH JUDICIAL CIRCUIT,
IN AND FOR ORANGE COUNTY, FLORIDA

ABC BANK, N.A. Case # 2010-CA-3031

Plaintiff,

vs.

JOE CONSUMER, et al,

Defendant(s).

______________________________/

DEFENDANT'S ANSWER TO COMPLAINT WITH AFFIRMATIVE DEFENSES

COMES NOW the Defendant, JOE CONSUMER, by and through the undersigned attorney, and for an answer to the Complaint filed in the above cause, states as follows:

GENERAL ALLEGATIONS

1. Denied.
2. Admitted.
3. Without knowledge and therefore denied.
4. Admit execution of the Note on or about April 20, 2005.
5. Without knowledge and therefore denied.
6. Denied.
7. Denied.
8. Without knowledge and therefore denied.
9. The Defendant denies the amount of the debt as alleged. The Defendant disputes the amount and characterization of this debt, affirmatively claims that many unauthorized, illegal and predatory charges and fees have been added to the claimed balance due under the subject mortgage and note and by reason thereof, and pursuant to the Federal Fair Debt Collection Practices Act, the Defendants hereby demand written and itemized verification of said debt from the Plaintiff including transaction history and accounting of the charges, fees and payments.
10. Without knowledge and therefore denied.
11. Without knowledge and therefore denied.
12. Without knowledge and therefore denied.
13. Without knowledge and therefore denied.
14. Without knowledge and therefore denied.

COUNT I
MORTGAGE FORECLOSURE

15. Without knowledge and therefore denied.
16. Admitted for jurisdictional purposes only.
17. Denied.
18. Without knowledge and therefore denied.

AFFIRMATIVE DEFENSES
FAILURE OF CONTRACTUAL CONDITION PRECEDENT

19. The Plaintiff failed to provide the Defendants with a Notice of Default and Intent to Accelerate as required by and/or that complies with Paragraph 22 of the subject mortgage. As

a result, the Defendant has been denied a good faith opportunity, pursuant to the mortgage and the servicing obligations of the Plaintiff, to avoid acceleration and this foreclosure. Plaintiff has failed to comply with statutory and contractual conditions precedent.

ILLEGAL CHARGES ADDED TO BALANCE

20. The Plaintiff has charged and/or collected payments from Defendants for attorney fees, legal fees, foreclosure costs, late charges, property inspection fees, title search expenses, filing fees, broker price opinions, appraisal fees, and other charges and advances, and predatory lending fees and charges that are not authorized by or in conformity with the terms of the subject note and mortgage which specifies the waiver of late payments and other collection charges as part of the forbearance and loan modification default loan servicing. Plaintiff wrongfully added and continues to unilaterally add these illegal charges to the balance Plaintiff claims is due and owing under the subject note and mortgage.

FAILURE OF GOOD FAITH AND FAIR DEALING: UNFAIR AND UNACCEPTABLE LOAN SERVICING

21. The Plaintiff intentionally failed to act in good faith or to deal fairly with the subject Defendant by failing to follow the applicable standards of residential single family mortgage servicing as described in these Affirmative Defenses thereby denying Defendant's access to the residential mortgage servicing protocols applicable to the subject note and mortgage.

UNCLEAN HANDS

22. The Plaintiff comes to court with unclean hands and is prohibited by reason thereof from obtaining the equitable relief of foreclosure from this Court. The Plaintiff's unclean hands result from the Plaintiff's improvident and predatory intentional failure to comply with material terms of the mortgage and note; the failure to comply with the default loan servicing requirements that apply to this loan, all as described herein above. As a matter of equity, this Court should refuse to foreclose this mortgage because acceleration of the note would be inequitable, unjust and the circumstances of this case render acceleration unconscionable. This Court should refuse the acceleration and deny foreclosure because Plaintiff has waved the right to acceleration or is estopped from doing so because of misleading conduct and unfulfilled contractual and equitable conditions precedent.

WHEREFORE, Defendant requests the Court dismiss the Plaintiff's complaint with prejudice and award this Defendant judgment against the Plaintiff for his damages, for an award of attorney's fees and for all other relief as the Court deems proper.

I HEREBY CERTIFY that a true copy of the foregoing has been furnished by fax/U.S. Mail this ____ day of _____, 2010 to Plaintiff's Attorney, 123 Anywhere Street, Anywhere, FL 32701.

____

CHARLES W. PRICE, ESQ.
390 Maitland Ave., Suite 1000
Altamonte Springs, FL 32701
(407) 834-0090
Fla. Bar No. 0870862
Counsel for Defendant

What Does an Answer Look Like?

Take a look at the sample Answer. The Answer essentially responds to each numbered paragraph in the Complaint. There are many ways to do this. However, the sample Answer is the most common form.

What to Include in the Answer

Generally, an Answer includes four basic sections – numbered responses to each numbered paragraph in the Complaint, Affirmative Defenses, a request for Mediation and a request for jury trial. (It can also include a Counter-Claim section. In this section, you can actually sue the Plaintiff for bad things that the Plaintiff has done to you. Many of the Affirmative Defenses we're going to talk about can be brought as a counter-claim. However, your ability to bring a counter-claim and its requirements are beyond the scope of this book.) Let's talk about each of these sections.

Section 1 - The Body of the Answer – Numbered Responses to the Numbered Paragraphs of the Complaint

In the first section of an Answer, you must respond to each numbered paragraph on the Complaint. When doing this, you generally have three basic responses to most of the numbered paragraphs in a Complaint. First, you can "admit" the allegation contained within the paragraph that you agree are true. Or, you can "deny" the allegations if you don't agree with them. Finally, it you don't know whether the allegation is true or not, you can say that you are "without knowledge and therefore deny" the allegation. (Sometimes, a paragraph in a Complaint contains several factual allegations. In these cases, it may be necessary to admit or deny different parts of the paragraph.)

Section 2 - Affirmative Defenses

In the second section, you should list any "Affirmative Defenses" that you have to the Complaint. Affirmative Defenses are your defenses to the complaint. They basically say, "Yes, I may have done some of the things you allege in the Complaint, but look at the bad things that you did". Let's look at some of the defenses that you may want to include as Affirmative Defenses in your Answer.

Specific Affirmative Defenses

The Most Common Defenses

Let's first review the most common defenses to a foreclosure complaint. You will probably include these defenses in your answer. Then, we'll discuss some more specialized defenses in the next section.

Lack of Standing

We discussed this issue earlier when we talked about Motions to Dismiss. As you recall, when you raise the defense of Lack of Standing, you're saying that the Plaintiff isn't the proper party to sue you. For most foreclosure cases, lack of standing is based on the Plaintiff's failure to present proper documents regarding their right to foreclose – typically problems with the promissory note and mortgage.

You should include lack of standing as an Affirmative Defense, even if you raised this defense with a Motion to Dismiss and lost. Unless all of the documents attached to the Complaint are completely correct and accurate, you may discover some real problems with the transfers of the promissory note and mortgage to the plaintiff. This could be the key to your entire foreclosure case.

Failure of Contractual Condition Precedent

A "condition precedent" is something that must happen before a Plaintiff can file a foreclosure case. This Affirmative Defense includes something we've already talked about as well. As you recall, one of the reasons I discussed earlier as a grounds for your Motion to Dismiss was the Plaintiff's failure to include a Notice of Acceleration. For most mortgages, Plaintiffs are required to give the borrower 30 days notice before they accelerate the loan and foreclose. This is a "condition precedent" for filing the foreclosure complaint. Of course, Plaintiffs very often fail to provide the proper notice. This failure gives rise to the Affirmative Defense.

You can also include under this category the Plaintiff's failure to provide foreclosure counseling. Many mortgages, especially FHA and VA mortgages, require that the lender provide foreclosure counseling before filing a complaint. Many lenders fail to do this. This failure gives rise to another Affirmative Defense that you should raise in your Answer.

Unclean Hands

This is a standard Affirmative Defense that Defendants include as a defense to many different types of cases. The defense of "Unclean Hands" essentially means that the Plaintiff did bad things that should offset anything that the Defendant did – like not paying the mortgage loan. In a foreclosure case, the reasons to allege "unclean hands" could include failure to communicate with the Defendant and failure to provide required counseling and assistance.

I sometimes include information in this defense about how a Plaintiff received TARP (Troubled Asset Relief Plan) funds from the government. As part of that money, lenders are required to provide mortgage foreclosure mitigation programs to borrowers. Their failure to do this seems like bad faith, given that these federal funds (from taxpayers) saved their businesses. The idea of including this information as part of an "unclean hands" defense is that the judge will be outraged by the mortgage companies' arrogance in using taxpayer funds to "bail out" their businesses, and then not providing any assistance to average taxpayers looking to save their homes.

There are many ways to break these affirmative defenses into multiple defenses. However, these are the basic categories of the standard affirmative defenses. Now, let's look at some very powerful defenses that you may be able to assert. (However, I must warn you that these defenses get very technical and are really beyond the scope of this book. If you believe that you can assert any of these defenses, you may want to consult with an attorney before you proceed.)

Additional Affirmative Defenses

To make it easier to understand these additional affirmative defenses, I've grouped them into three larger categories; lender abuses, servicer abuses, and miscellaneous other defenses. Most of these affirmative defenses can stand on their own as an affirmative defense or counterclaim. And, many of these defenses can give rise to other defenses, so that they work together. Let's look at these additional defenses now.

Lender Abuses

The first general category of additional affirmative defenses includes a variety of issues relating to the lender's conduct in granting and closing the mortgage loan to you. There are many federal statutes and regulations designed to protect consumers from lender abuses and provide monetary damages, attorney's fees, and some other extraordinary remedies for violations. If you can prove that a lender violated one or more of these statutes and regulations, you'll have a potent defense for your foreclosure case.

Truth in Lending Act violations.

The Truth in Lending Act ("TILA")(15 U.S.C. § 1601 et seq. as implemented by 12 CFR Part 226) is a set of statutes and regulations designed to give consumers accurate information about certain loan transactions. If applicable, TILA requires that lenders provide the consumer with information about the credit terms of the loan prior to closing.

For foreclosure actions, the most relevant TILA provision is the right of "rescission". Rescission means that you can roll back the transaction and the lien against your house. There are some problems with this remedy, given that many Floridian's are "upside down" on their mortgages – they owe more on their mortgage loans than their homes are worth. However, in the proper circumstances, TILA can provide a potent defense – and weapon – against a foreclosure action.

The TILA rescission remedy only applies to non-purchase money transactions. This means that it applies to any mortgage transaction other than a purchase transaction. So, if you refinanced your home or took out a second mortgage against your home, TILA may apply to your mortgage.

The TILA rescission remedy must be exercised no later than three years after the closing on the mortgage loan, assuming that the lender failed to correctly provide certain "material" disclosures. However, for foreclosure actions, you may be able to rescind a mortgage lien if the error in disclosing a finance charge is as small as $35.00.

For example, your lender may have calculated payments or fees incorrectly in your loan transaction. In short, the lender may not have charged you the right way. (This happens fairly frequently; loan documents are often filled with mathematical and other mistakes.)

If you believe that your mortgage loan may qualify for a TILA rescission remedy, I encourage you to speak with an attorney who understands TILA litigation. This is a highly technical area of the law and requires a great deal of expertise. But, again, in the proper circumstances, a TILA defense can be a potent defense against a foreclosure action.

RESPA Violations

The Real Estate Settlement Procedures Act ("RESPA") (12 U.S.C. §§ 2601-2617) is a set of statutes designed to protect consumers from abusive practices in the residential real estate industry. Among other things, RESPA requires that consumers receive many different disclosures during every phase of the loan process. The idea is to allow consumers to see the real cost of providing a loan so that consumers may more easily compare "apples to apples" when deciding between different loans and lenders.

Many of RESPA's requirements do not provide for civil liability. This means that you can't sue the lender and recover damages. However, several other requirements do provide for damages and attorney's fees against any lender, broker or service provider that violates those provisions.

HOEPA Violations

The Home Ownership and Equity Protection Act ("HOEPA")(primarily codified at 12 U.S.C.§ 1639 as implemented by 12 CFR Part 226) is an amendment to TILA designed to prevent predatory lending against certain consumers.

Like TILA, a violation of HOEPA can trigger a rescission claim against the lender. This could be a potent weapon in your foreclosure case. However, HOEPA violations can also trigger substantial monetary damages and attorney's fees against the lender. So, if your loan qualifies under HOPEA, you should carefully review the loan charges, etc.

So, what loans qualify under HOEPA? As with mortgages that trigger TILA provisions, to qualify under HOEPA, the loan must not have been used to purchase or construct a home. Only loans used to refinance the original purchase loan, or loans made subsequent to the purchase transaction (second mortgages, etc.) qualify.

In addition, like TILA, HOEPA contains a three-year statute of limitations. This means that you can't bring an action based on HOEPA more than three years after you closed on the loan. (You may be able to raise it as a defense in the foreclosure, even beyond this three-year limitation.)

Also, HOEPA only applies to your primary home. You can't use HOEPA as a defense in a foreclosure case if the collateral for the loan is an investment property.

Assuming that you meet all of these requirements, you should carefully review the loan. There are two "triggers" that may give rise to an action based on HOEPA. The first is the "APR Trigger". Under this test, HOEPA will apply to first mortgages if the loan has an Annual Percentage Rate that is more than 8% above the rate for Treasure securities of a comparable term. For mortgages other than the first mortgage, the trigger is 10% above the rate for comparable Treasury securities.

If all of this makes your head spin, don't worry. You're normal. I have a degree in Finance and spent several years in the mortgage industry, and this still makes my head spin. This stuff is complex and boring. If you think you may have a problem loan, talk to an experienced attorney and let them worry about it.

Unfair and Deceptive Acts and Practices

You can lump a variety of lender abuses into a broad description of unfair and deceptive acts and practices. Like many other states, Florida has a law that prohibits various unfair and deceptive practices, and that very often apply to lenders in foreclosure actions. In Florida, this law is called the Florida Deceptive and Unfair Trade Practices Act (the "Act") (Sections 501.201 et. seq.). (Generally, you would bring a claim based on the Act as a counter-claim to the complaint. For now, let's just discuss the Act as a general defense.)

Under the Act, you can complain about a host of lender misdeeds. For example, you can complain about how your lender put you into a higher rate loan than your credit score would have required. Or, maybe the lender put you into a loan that you never had a reasonable chance to repay. Or, maybe your lender added unnecessary credit life insurance to the loan. Any of these abuses, and more, can fall within a claim under the Act.

You may also be able to use the Act to dispute the lender's ability to add attorney's fees and costs to the foreclosure case if the lender failed to properly evaluate your loan for modification. Think hard, or maybe not so hard, and you can probably come up with many ways that the lender abused you during the loan process. Any or all of these abuses may give rise to a claim under the Act.

Servicer Abuses

Another broad category of defenses that you may raise in a foreclosure case revolve around the servicer. As you recall from our earlier discussion, a servicer is an entity that collects the money from you and pays that money, less its fees, to the owner of the loan. Servicers are bound by several laws that prohibit bad behavior on their part. If they violate any of these laws, the servicer subjects itself to penalties and provides you with a defense in your foreclosure case. Let's look at the common issues now. (These defenses can apply against the lender as well, if the lender is servicing its own loan).

Misallocation of funds. Some of my clients are sued even though they are current on payments, simply because the lender applied their payments to the wrong account. This is more common than you might think. The defense to this problem is to keep accurate records of your payments and other transactions with the servicer.

RESPA Violations

As with lenders, servicers can violate certain RESPA provisions that apply only to servicers (or lenders servicing their own loans). In 1990, Congress amended RESPA to include provisions that require servicers to respond to borrower's inquiries, fix problems with loan accounts, identify when servicers change, and make timely payments from escrow accounts. (12 U.S.C. § 2605). These provisions are located in Section 6 of RESPA and are known as the "Servicer Act".

The Servicer Act contains one of my favorite tools for foreclosure defense – the Qualified Written Response ("QWR"). Section 2605(e) provides that consumers can obtain information about their mortgage and escrow accounts by providing a written inquiry to the servicer.

When you send a QWR, the servicer must:

A. Within 20 days after receipt of the QWR, provide acknowledgement that it received the QWR (excluding holidays, Saturdays and Sundays);

B. Within 60 days after receipt of the QWR, make any necessary changes to your account (excluding holidays, Saturdays and Sundays); and,

C. Provide you with a written response to your QWR and a name and telephone number of a service representative that can provide assistance to you.

And, best of all, the servicer CANNOT report your mortgage account as delinquent to the credit bureaus until it has responded to your QWR. If the servicer does report your mortgage loan as delinquent before responding to your QWR, it subjects the servicer to liability under the Fair Credit Reporting Act.

Your Name
Your Address
City, State & Zip

Today's Date

Mortgage Servicer Name
Address
City, State & Zip

RE: Account No.: [Account No. Here]

To Whom It May Concern:

I hereby request information about the fees, costs, and escrow accounting of my loan. This letter is a qualified written request (QWR), pursuant to the Real Estate Settlement and Procedures Act (RESPA), 12 U.S.C. § 2605(e).

The information I request as part of this QWR is as follows:

1) A complete copy of my underwriting file.
2) The current interest rate on this account.
3) The adjustment dates of each interest rate adjustment on this account, with the corresponding adjustment amount.
4) Who the current holder of the mortgage/deed of trust is, and their mailing address for process of service, along with a current telephone number.
5) Who the current holder of the note is, and their mailing address for process of service, along with a current telephone number.
6) The date that the current holder acquired this mortgage and from whom it was acquired from.
7) The date your firm began servicing the loan.
8) The previous servicer of the loan.
9) The monthly principal and interest payments, and monthly escrow payments received from the date of the loan's closing to the date of this QWR;
10) A complete payment history of how those payments were applied, including the amounts applied to principal, interest, escrow, and other charges;
11) The total amount due of any unpaid principal, interest, escrow charges, and other charges due as of the date of this letter. Please separately and identify each amount due;
12) The total amount of principal paid on the account up to the date of this letter;
13) The payment dates, purposes of payment and recipient of any and all foreclosure fees and costs that have been charged to my account;
14) A breakdown of the current escrow charges showing how it is calculated and the reasons for any increase within the last 24 months;
15) A breakdown of any shortage, deficiency or surplus in our escrow account over the past three years.
16) A breakdown of all charges accrued on the account since the date of closing, that includes but is not limited by, late charges, appraisal fees, property inspection fees, forced placed insurance charges, legal fees, and recoverable corporate advances.
17) A statement indicating which covenants of the mortgage and/or note authorize each charge.
18) Please provide a copy of all appraisals, property inspections, and risk assessments completed for this account.
19) Please provide a copy of all trust agreements pertaining to this account.
20) Please provide a copy of all servicing agreements (master, sub-servicing, contingency, specialty, and back-up) pertaining to this account.
21) Please provide a copy of all written loss-mitigation rules and work-out procedures for this account.
22) Please provide a copy of all manuals pertaining to the servicing of this account.
23) Please provide a copy of the LSAMS Transaction History Report for this account, and include a description of all fee codes.
24) If this account is registered with MERS, state its MIN number.
25) A statement indicating the amount to pay this loan off in full as [pick date about 30 days after this letter is dated].

I hereby dispute all late fees, charges, inspection fees, property appraisal fees, forced placed insurance charges, legal fees, and corporate advances charged to this account. Additionally, I believe my account is in error for the following reasons: [state reasons here]. Pursuant to 12 U.S.C. § 2605(e), you are hereby notified that placing any negative coding on my credit report before responding to this letter is a violation of RESPA and the FCRA. Your organization will be subject to civil liability if negative coding appears for this account before a response to this QWR is issued to me.

Please provide me confirmation that you have received this QWR within 20 days, as required under 12 U.S.C. § 2605(e). Thereafter, please respond to these questions within 60 days of receipt of this letter, also as required under 12 U.S.C. § 2605(e).

Regards,

Your Name

[1] [Not necessary, but you may indicate reasons here.]

Why is the QWR one of my favorite foreclosure defense tools? First, it provides you with "accurate" information regarding your loan and its' servicing. Very often, there are conflicts between the information provided to you pursuant to the QWR and other sources such as the plaintiff's attorney in the foreclosure. You may be able to use these discrepancies as the case unfolds.

In addition, the QWR prevents the servicer from reporting your mortgage loan as delinquent until it responds to the QWR. This may protect your credit rating long enough to allow you to pursue foreclosure options that may not be available to you with poor credit.

Finally, the servicer's failure to comply with your QWR can subject it to damages under Section 6, and damages pursuant to the FCRA if it reports your delinquency before responding to the QWR. So, you should always prepare and send a QWR to the servicer – you'll be glad that you did this.

FCRA Violations

Since we started talking about the Fair Credit Reporting Act, let's look at it a little closer. The Fair Credit Reporting Act ("FCRA")(15 U.S.C. § 1681 et seq.) is a set of statutes that regulate the use, collection and dissemination of consumer credit information. As we discussed in the last section, servicers can violate the FCRA by reporting your mortgage loan as delinquent to the credit bureaus before responding to your QWR.

In addition, servicers can violate the FCRA by inaccurately reporting your mortgage loan to the credit bureaus. For example, as we saw earlier, servicers sometimes misapply payments to the wrong account and allege that a consumer is delinquent. Very often, the servicer will then report this negative account history to the credit bureaus.

If a servicer inaccurately reports your mortgage loan to the credit bureaus, you may have an action, or defense, against the servicer or lender based on the FCRA. Violations of the FRCA may subject the servicer to pay for your actual damages, punitive damages and attorney's fees.

FDCPA Violations

Another potential claim that you may assert against a servicer is based on the Fair Debt Collection Practices Act ("FDCPA")(15 U.S.C. § 1692 et seq.). Congress passed the FDCPA in 1978 to eliminate abusive practices in the collection of consumer debts.

The FDCPA generally only applies to collection agencies or other entities that collect debts on behalf of the original creditor. However, servicers can fall within the provisions of the FDCPA if the loan is transferred to the servicer after the loan goes into default. (Additionally, attorneys that represent the servicer or the lender are always subject to the FDCPA).

The FDCPA generally prohibits the use of any false, deceptive, or misleading representations, the use of any unfair or unconscionable means to collect a debt, and any conduct to harass, oppress or abuse the consumer. In addition, the FDCPA contains many specific actions that are prohibited and that give rise to damages under the FDCPA.

If you believe that the servicer or the servicer's attorney has violated the FDCPA, you should review the specific provisions of the FDCPA and include these violations as a defense to your foreclosure complaint. Or, as always, contact an attorney who understands how to use the FDCPA as a defense in a foreclosure action.

Additional Defenses

There are two additional defenses that I wanted to discuss that don't really fit under the broad categories of lender or servicer abuse, but that might still be applicable to your foreclosure case – the Servicemembers Civil Relief Act and violations of the Pooling and Servicing Agreement. Let's look at these two defenses now.

The Servicemembers Civil Relief Act

The Servicemembers Civil Relief Act ("SCRA")(50 U.S.C. App. § 501 et seq.) is a set of statutes designed to protect military service personnel on active duty and their dependents. The SCRA is a revision of the Soldiers' and Sailors' Civil Relief Act of 1940 and provides important protections against foreclosure for active-duty military personnel and their dependents.

The SCRA applies to active-duty members of the Army, Navy, Air Force, Marine Corps and Coast Guard. The SCRA also applies to members of the National Guard if they are ordered to report for military service. The SCRA also applies to dependents of active-duty service personnel.

The provisions of the SCRA apply whenever a qualifying service member is on active duty or until 90 days after the end of active duty. If a consumer qualifies under the SCRA, a judge must stay a foreclosure proceeding against that consumer for at least 90 days (and probably longer) to allow the consumer an opportunity to present a defense to the foreclosure.

In addition, a judge may, under the SCRA, adjust the payment obligations due under a mortgage loan. This could include lowering the interest rate, adjusting the due date for a balloon payment, or lowering or even suspending payments due under the promissory note.

Therefore, as you can see, the SCRA can be a very powerful weapon in your foreclosure case. If you qualify under the SCRA, immediately raise the SCRA as a defense. You will see a very quick end to your foreclosure case (at least until you leave active duty).

Violations of the Pooling and Servicing Agreement

As you recall, we talked about how the mortgage industry moved in a big way to making mortgages "securitized". For most mortgage-backed securities transactions, a trust is created to hold the mortgage loans. Then, a Pooling and Servicing Agreement ("PSA") is created to specify the terms of the trust and how mortgage loans are to move into the trust.

Generally, PSA's require that a trust receive the mortgage loan into the trust within four months after the trust is opened to receive mortgages. Under the terms of the PSA, any mortgage loans received after this period are NOT part of the trust.

Therefore, if the plaintiff is a trust, you may be able to defend the foreclosure complaint by alleging that the plaintiff does not have standing to bring the action because it never brought the mortgage into the trust within the time allowed by the PSA and so it doesn't own the mortgage. Judges generally don't understand this argument, so you'll need to lay it out for them step-by-step.

How do you know if your mortgage was properly transferred to the trust? First, verify that the alleged holder of your mortgage is a trust. (You can see this easily if the plaintiff is a trust. In addition, you can discover the true identity of the alleged mortgage holder by sending a QWR or by doing discovery)

After identifying that the alleged holder of your mortgage is a trust, try to locate the PSA for this particular trust. I can usually find a PSA just by entering the name of the trust into a Google search. If this doesn't work, you should use the SEC's EDGAR system at http://www.sec.gov/edgar.shtml. If that doesn't work, you should try to obtain the PSA with a QWR or during discovery.

Next, review the terms of the PSA. Identify when the Trust was opened to receive mortgage loans and when it was closed. You may have a defense to the foreclosure complaint if the assignment of mortgage or endorsement of the promissory note is dated AFTER the last date identified for mortgages to be admitted into the trust.

As with many of these additional defenses, raising a defense to the foreclosure complaint based on the PSA is very technical and requires a high level of expertise. Please do your homework or contact an attorney who understands the way that PSA's affect foreclosure actions.

Final Thoughts on Basic Foreclosure Defenses

In this section, we've reviewed some of the most common defenses to a foreclosure complaint. There are other defenses that we haven't discussed, but I'm concerned that I may have already strayed too deep into complex legal theories. So, to save the average reader, let's stop there for now.

Again, my goal isn't to train you to be a lawyer; my goal is to show you that a skilled, experienced lawyer can find a variety of ways to raise affirmative defenses on your behalf – and to make sure your rights are protected. Even if those defenses don't result in a dismissal of the suit, or in you getting a free house, raising affirmative defenses does buy you time to explore other options.

For now, let's look at the last two parts of a standard foreclosure answer.

Section 3 – Request for Mediation

Although I'm calling this a "section", it really doesn't quite merit that description. The normal request for mediation is simply that – "I request mediation".

I gave this request for mediation its own "section" in the Answer because I wanted to emphasize to you how important mediation can be during the foreclosure process. I'm going to talk about mediation in great detail in the next section. So, for now, just make sure that you include this request in your Answer.

Section 4 – Request for Jury Trial

OK. This isn't really a "section" either. But, as with the request for mediation in Section 3, I believe that it's very important to include this request in your Answer. The standard foreclosure case typically doesn't give rise to a right to trial by jury. However, many of the affirmative defenses that you may raise to the complaint may provide you with a right to a jury trial.

Why do you care if a jury hears this? Well, if the case actually gets to a jury, you may find that average citizens are sick of the way that mortgage companies are treating them too. You may find a more sympathetic crowd in a jury, rather than with a judge. This can be a crapshoot either way. But, mortgage companies really don't like to take their chances with juries. So, ask for the jury trial!

The Next Step – Discovery

After you file and serve your Answer, you should immediately draft and serve different requests for discovery. These requests typically include "Interrogatories"," Requests for Production"," Requests for Admissions" and depositions.

I'm not going to devote a lot of time to this section, because it's really beyond the scope of this book. However, I want you to at least be familiar with the concept of discovery and understand why it's important to your foreclosure case. (You can review sample discovery requests at www.SaveYourFloridaHomeNow.com.)

There are several reasons to pursue discovery in a foreclosure case. Of course, the most obvious reason is to discover information that will help your case and hurt the Plaintiff's case. Often, the only real way to do this is with discovery.

Another important reason to engage in discovery is to prevent the Plaintiff from moving for Summary Judgment. (We'll talk about this is in the next section.)

Interrogatories

Interrogatories are questions that you ask the opposing party – in this case the Plaintiff in your foreclosure case. You want to find out as much information as you can about the Plaintiff and its case against you. Ultimately, you're trying to find out information that will help your case and hurt the Plaintiff's case.

Requests for Production

In a Request for Production, you try to get documents from the opposing party – the Plaintiff in your foreclosure case. As with the Interrogatories, your trying to find documents that will support your case and hurt the Plaintiff's case.

Requests for Admission

In a Request for Admission, you try to get the opposing party to admit or deny various elements of its case or yours. As with the other discovery requests, you're trying to get the Plaintiff to admit to certain elements of the case that will help your case and hurt its case against you.

Depositions

A deposition is a face-to-face question and answer session. In a deposition, you get to ask the Plaintiff, or the Plaintiff's representative, direct questions about your case. As with the other discovery requests, the point of a deposition is to discover facts that will help you to support your case and hurt the Plaintiff's case.

Motion for Summary Judgment

After you file your Answer, the plaintiff will file a Motion for Summary Judgment. In a Motion for Summary Judgment, the Plaintiff essentially says that there is no need to have a trial because the Plaintiff is right – you didn't pay and the lender can take your home pursuant to the terms of the promissory note and mortgage. Amazingly, this is how the vast majority of foreclosure cases are decided – without a fight.

Whenever I'm in court to defend a client's case, I'm almost always the only defense attorney in the courtroom. Generally, the judge is sitting in front of a stack of case files – each of these files representing someone's home about to be lost to the system. One by one the judge and the Plaintiff's attorney dispense with the stack of cases (Sometimes, the Plaintiff's attorney isn't even present in the courtroom. It's a common practice for plaintiff's attorneys to appear by phone).

This is what happens when you don't defend the foreclosure case – you lose without a trial and without a fight. I don't want this to happen to you – so don't let it happen to you!

So, the Motion for Summary Judgment is the Plaintiff's next move after you Answer the Complaint. But, you can prevent the Plaintiff from winning its case against you with a Summary Judgment.

A Motion for Summary Judgment really says that there's "no dispute as to material facts" and that the judge can determine the case based on the law. So, you can do two things to defeat the Motion for Summary Judgment. First, you can show that there IS a dispute as to material facts in the case. That's why it's important to do discovery. Second, you can defeat the Motion for Summary Judgment by winning the legal arguments, including the various affirmative defenses that we discussed in the last section.

Mediation

Mediation is a process for resolving conflicts between parties, usually with the help of a third-party "mediator" who helps the parties settle their differences. Traditionally, homeowners did not have a right to mediation in a foreclosure case. However, with the dramatic increase in foreclosure cases, Florida judges became agitated that consumers could never seem to speak with a decision-maker at the mortgage companies. This communication problem was contributing to a huge backlog of foreclosure cases in the court system.

To find a solution, the Florida Supreme Court formed a task force to study the problems behind the foreclosure crisis. Based in part on the task force's recommendations, in December 2009, the Florida Supreme Court ordered a statewide mediation program for foreclosure cases.

Under this new mediation program, homeowners finally get the chance to actually speak to a decision-maker at the mortgage company, generally with the assistance of a neutral mediator in the room. I've had very good results with this mediation process and I'm a strong supporter of the program.

The goal of mediation in the foreclosure process is generally to modify the terms of the loan to make the payments affordable for the homeowner. Really, mediation is an attempt at modification within the foreclosure case, and the goal is generally the same – to lower the mortgage payment. (This isn't always true. You may agree on a repayment plan that doesn't modify the terms of the mortgage. Or, you may reach an agreement on surrendering the home pursuant to a short sale or deed-in-lieu. However, these alternative outcomes are much less common than a standard loan modification.)

For this reason, you should always analyze your income and expenses to see if you will qualify for a modification. I'm going to explain the mortgage modification process in great detail in the next chapter. Before proceeding to mediation, I advise you to carefully review the information on modification programs and requirements. If you don't have the correct numbers when you go to mediation, the lender will NOT approve your loan for modification, and you're right back to fighting the foreclosure.

I like the mediation process because it often allows us to shortcut the modification process. It's not unusual for the modification process to take many months to produce a modification. This process generally requires months of frustrating contacts with the lender, including multiple instances of the lender "losing" the documentation.

With mediation, the process comes down to an hour or two of actual communication with the lender's representative. I'll take that process any day over the traditional modification process.

Of course, the primary reason for engaging in mediation is to modify the terms of your mortgage. It's unlikely that a lender is going to mediate any other issues that you may have raised in your Answer. If you really have no intention of seeking a modification of your mortgage payments, it probably doesn't make sense to participate in mediation – other than slowing down the foreclosure process.

What Do You Need to Do to Participate in the Mediation Program?

To qualify for the mediation program, the home that you're seeking to save with this mediation process must be your primary residence. The foreclosure mediation program does not apply to investment properties.

Next, you must file a responsive pleading to the Complaint and request mediation. This is why I wanted you to include a request for mediation in your Answer.

Next, you must provide financial documentation to the plaintiff/lender no less than 10 days before the scheduled mediation. This will probably include your most recent paycheck stubs, recent bank statements, and recent tax returns.

Finally, you must show up to the mediation. The mediation is held in your county, usually in the mediator's office or an executive suite that the mediator is using for the mediation. At the mediation, the parties in attendance will include the mediator, the plaintiff's attorney, you, and your attorney. The mortgage company representative typically appears by phone. That's OK. At least you get to talk to someone that can actually make a decision.

What Does the Lender Need to Do for the Mediation Program?

OK. We've talked about your requirements. What does the mortgage company need to do? First, they must coordinate the mediation with you and the mediator. Under the Florida Supreme Court's Order, they must schedule the mediation no less than 60 days after the case is filed, but no more than 120 days after it is filed.

In addition, the mortgage company must pay for the mediation. This is an important consideration for most defendants. In traditional mediation, each party splits the cost of the mediator. Depending on how long the mediation lasts, and the hourly rate of the mediator, a defendant could end up paying a lot of money for the mediation process. So, this mediation is free for foreclosure defendants.

Finally, and perhaps most important, the mortgage company must provide a representative for the mediation that has actual authority to resolve the foreclosure case. Generally, the lender's representative appears by telephone. Who cares? At least you get to talk to them.

If no agreement is reached, of course, the lender can move forward with foreclosure proceedings. This does happen occasionally. But, at the very least, the mediation process will slow down the foreclosure process.

If your goal is to stay in the house, always participate in the mediation process. Asking for mediation automatically gives you more time to work out other potential defenses or options to help you avoid foreclosure. Why give away time that could be used to help you?

Hearing on the Motion for Summary Judgment

Assuming that the mediation wasn't successful, the next step in the foreclosure process will be the hearing on the Plaintiff's Motion for Summary Judgment. It's common for Plaintiffs to file the Motion for Summary Judgment very early in the foreclosure case. (Under Rule 1.150 of the Florida Rules of Civil Procedure, a plaintiff must only wait for 20 days after the commencement of the case before it files the Motion.) However, the filing of the Motion isn't really the important thing – it's the hearing on the Motion that matters.

In the normal foreclosure case, the hearing on the Motion is generally held two to three months after the case is filed. At a minimum, the Plaintiff must wait at least 20 days after serving the Motion for Summary Judgment before the hearing on that Motion can occur.

If you have outstanding discovery requests at the time of the hearing, the Plaintiff is not entitled to Summary Judgment. As you recall, the point of a summary judgment is that there are no disputes as to material facts. If you don't yet have responses to your discovery requests, you can't really determine if there's a dispute. So, courts require that the parties complete all discovery before allowing summary judgment. (I hope this makes you want to pursue discovery!)

If you do reach the hearing on the Motion, and you prevail on any of your defenses or arguments, the judge will schedule a trial in the case. If, however, you do NOT prevail on your defenses, the judge will schedule a foreclosure sale of your home.

Traditionally, foreclosure sales were scheduled 30 days after the hearing on the Motion. This allowed the lender to publish notice of the sale as required by Florida law.

Now, however, most judges are willing to allow homeowners additional time before the foreclosure sale is scheduled. If you lose your case with the judge, at least ask for 60 or 90 days before the sale occurs. This should allow you additional time to pursue modification or other remedies to save your home. (If necessary, you can always file a Chapter 13 bankruptcy even one minute before the sale to save your home.)

In addition, if you lose your arguments with the judge, you always have the right to appeal your case to an appellate court. The appeals process is beyond the scope of this book, and beyond the abilities of most non-attorneys. Therefore, I strongly encourage you to speak with an attorney before you appeal your foreclosure case.

The Foreclosure Sale

The next step in the foreclosure process is the foreclosure sale. My hope for you is that you never reach this point in the foreclosure process unless you've determined that you can no longer afford the property or don't otherwise want to retain possession. But, I want to make sure we finish our discussion to the logical end.

Typically, foreclosure sales are scheduled for 11:00 am at the county courthouse. Anyone is allowed to bid during a foreclosure sale. However, the mortgage company is generally the successful bidder.

At the completion of the sale, the clerk will issue a Certificate of Sale to the successful bidder. Then unless someone objects to the sale, the clerk will issue a Certificate of Title to the successful bidder after 10 days. The property now officially belongs to the successful bidder.

With the Certificate of Title in hand, the successful bidder can now ask the court for a Writ of Possession. The Writ of Possession allows the new owner to evict you from your home. Generally, a sheriff posts a notice on your door that you have 24 hours to vacate the house. If you fail to vacate within the 24-hour periods, the lender can hire people to throw you and your possessions in the street.

This actually happens. If you've ever seen a pile of household belongings sitting in a yard, you've probably seen the sad aftermath of this process. Don't ever let this happen to you. The easy way to avoid this is to participate in the foreclosure process. You'll never be surprised if you know what's going on at every stage of the process.

Final Thoughts on Defending the Foreclosure Action

Before we move on, let's get this out of the way. Occasionally someone will say that raising defenses to a foreclosure action is like playing legal games. If you owe the money – and you do – but you raise legal defenses, aren't you just playing games if you require the lender to produce the Promissory Note, produce the mortgage, or verify that no Truth in Lending Act violations took place? (Or respond to the fact that violations did in fact take place, even if those violations were not intended?)

Absolutely not.

I don't play games. I help you exercise your legal rights – rights you are guaranteed as an American citizen.

More importantly, I'm working hard to buy you time. I'm not trying to "get you off on a technicality." I'm trying to buy you time: Time for your financial situation to improve, for you to sell other assets, for you to get help from family or friends...

Think about it this way. Say you lost your job and couldn't make payments. But after a few months you get a new job and start to get back on track. You can start making payments again, especially if we work out a loan modification plan with your lender. That creates a win-win situation: The lender is not forced to foreclose and receives payments. You don't lose your house and are allowed to make payments you can afford.

By buying time, I helped you and your lender reach a win-win solution. (When that happens I'm happy for the lender, but what I really care about is that the outcome is beneficial to you.) So if I need to stall – I will.

As we'll see in the next chapter, many of my clients receive mortgage modifications that help them to save their home. However, the average loan modification takes three to four months to work out. The average foreclosure, once the Acceleration Letter is sent, takes three to four months. You need time. It's my goal to get you that time.

Most lenders run foreclosures on a dual-track system: A loan modification track and a foreclosure track. They run both processes concurrently. So while you're negotiating a loan modification, the lender is still working through the foreclosure process... just in case.

And if the foreclosure process goes more quickly than the loan modification process – you lose.

Raising legal defenses buys time to work out a loan modification.

Raising legal defenses also creates leverage. Time creates leverage; the longer the lender has to wait, the more expensive the process. Raising foreclosure defenses also create leverage; if we can create doubt in the mind of the lender – about finding a Promissory Note, or finding an original mortgage document, or successfully working through the Reestablishment Statute, or Predatory Lending violations – the lender may be more likely to agree to favorable loan modification terms.

The more leverage you have, the stronger your negotiating position.

If you like, think about foreclosure as a balance scale. When the original complaint is filed, all the "weight" is on the lender's side. When you file a response, you add weight to your side. When you raise defenses to the foreclosure, you add more weight to your side. As time passes more and more weight is added to your side of the scale. Your goal is to level the scales and level the playing field – simply by exercising your legal rights.

OK. I think I've made my point about this – vigorously defend your foreclosure case! Now, let's look at the other non-foreclosure options available to you to save your home.

Chapter Six

Save Your Home: Workout Agreements and Modification

There are many ways to keep your house that don't involve foreclosure defense or bankruptcy. Generally, these alternatives involve a "loan workout" with the lender to change the repayment terms of the loan, or a modification of the actual terms of the loan

In large part, the options available to you depend on the type of loan you have and which entity holds the loan. For example, your loan may be held by Fannie Mae, Freddie Mac or Ginnie Mae. Each of these entities provides different workout options for borrowers. In addition, FHA and VA loans have their own set of workout options. Finally, loans that are held by securitized trusts have workout options that are described in the Pooling and Servicing Agreement.

So, what options are available depends on a number of situations. In this section I will describe the standard options that may be available to you. You should check with your lender to discover the workout options that are available based on your specific circumstances.

We'll start with some basic premises and an overview of the subject; then we'll dive a lot deeper into the actual process and give you a look at how workout agreements and modifications work "from the inside."

Forbearance

If you aren't familiar with the term, think of forbearance as a way to "catch up" on late payments; think of loan modification as changing the terms of the mortgage itself: Interest rate, principal amount due, or term.

Forbearance occurs when you are allowed, through an agreement with your lender, to pay a different amount than originally agreed to or to be put on a different payment schedule for a specified period of time. At the end of that time your terms go back to what you originally committed to when you took out the mortgage.

For example, say you are three months behind on your payments. The lender could agree for you to make a payment and a half until you catch up, instead of requiring the full amount be paid all at once. If your monthly payment is $1,000 and you're three months behind, you'll need to pay $3,000 to bring your mortgage current (plus fees and additional interest, of course.) If the lender agrees you could make monthly payments of approximately $1,500 for six months, bringing your mortgage current at the end of that six-month period. (You'll have made your normal payments of $1,000 per month, plus six payments of $500 per month to satisfy the $3,000 you are behind.)

If you can show detailed records of your income and expenses, some lenders may be willing to offer forbearance plans for up to eighteen months. Just keep in mind the lender will want to see solid proof that the plan is reasonable and is one you have every chance of meeting.

A lender may also be willing to offer what is called a "temporary indulgence." Under a temporary indulgence, the lender agrees to suspend payments for a specified period of time with the assumption that all payments will be brought back up to date when the term of the indulgence is over. (It's a little like a forbearance plan, but with a balloon payment at the end instead of increased monthly payments.) In most cases you will have to demonstrate that a temporary problem has caused your financial distress – and you will have to show exactly how the problem will be overcome. For example, you may be in the process of finalizing the sale of another property and are waiting for the proceeds to be distributed. Or you expect to receive a settlement from an insurance company or receive a settlement as the result of another legal proceeding.

Those are logical reasons why a lender might agree to a temporary indulgence. It's your job, not the lender's, to develop, present, and provide backup for those logical reasons. Simply saying, "I promise I will try really hard," is not a solid reason for a lender to work with you.

I can't stress enough that mortgage forbearance is in no way "mortgage forgiveness." Under a forbearance plan your mortgage is modified for a short period of time; none of your debt or responsibility is forgiven. The goal of forbearance is to work out a plan that allows you to bring the loan current, not to eliminate some or all of your debt.

Lenders tend to be more likely to agree to a forbearance plan when your income is temporarily reduced: Loss of job, unpaid leave, long-term illness, or family emergency. The lender will want to see that you are making every effort to reduce expenses and meet your obligations.

Also keep in mind that if you have an adjustable-rate mortgage and your payments have increased dramatically, forbearance is a short-term and not a long-term cure for payments you can't afford. If that's the case, requesting forbearance is fairly likely to be a waste of your time.

Loan Modification

A loan modification is a permanent change in one or more of the terms of a mortgage loan. After the modification is put in place the loan is reinstated and the homeowner is no longer in default... and hopefully the homeowner can afford the new payment amount. (Otherwise why would the lender agree to a modification?)

Loan modification is another hot topic, and like all hot topics is surrounded by a lot of misinformation and misunderstanding. Some loan modification advertisements remind me of the "But wait, there's more!" infomercials: Some loan modification companies claim they can cut homeowner mortgage payments in half.

Does that sound too good to be true? It usually is. In general, lenders won't agree to extreme mortgage modifications. (But, they will agree to reasonable modifications based on government guidelines and their own internal procedures.)

In reality, when we help our clients with loan modifications, our goal is to modify the loan so that payments fall in a range of 31 to 38% of the client's gross monthly income. For example, say your salary is $60,000 per year. That's $5,000 a month; 38% of $5,000 is $1,900.

If the current payments are higher than, as in this example, $1,900 a month, we negotiate with the lender to try to reduce the interest rate or the loan term so payments fall at or below $1,900; that way our client can better afford the mortgage payments and therefore avoid foreclosure. (Keep in mind that 38% may not be easy for many people to afford; after tax that means approximately half of your take-home pay will go to making mortgage payments.)

Watch Out For Non-Attorney Modification Companies

Before we look at an example of a loan modification, allow me to cover one other topic. The Florida Attorney General's Office stated the most frequent subject of complaints from Florida consumers in 2008 regarded "loan rescue" and loan modification offers from various companies and individuals. Some companies actually guaranteed they could stop foreclosure, reduce mortgage payments and/or provide other services that, bottom line, they couldn't. To make matters worse, many were advising consumers not to seek or consult with an attorney or other financial or legal professional.

As a result, many Florida consumers lost payments they made, up front, based on those promises... and received nothing in return.

So, in 2008, the Florida legislature passed The Foreclosure Rescue Fraud Prevention Act of 2008, codified at Section 501.1377 of the Florida Statues. Under the Act, among other things, loan modification companies cannot charge consumers an upfront fee for services – the goal is to protect consumers from predatory practices. Although attorneys were not specifically exempted from the Act's provisions, Florida's Attorney General issued a letter specifically exempting attorneys from the Act and its enforcement.

So: If you are considering working with a loan modification company and not a lawyer, be aware of the law and the ban on upfront charges. Some companies and individuals try to take advantage of people when they are their most vulnerable – don't let that happen to you.

An Overview of the Loan Modification Process

Now let's look at an example of loan modification. Say you currently make $50,000 a year. You have an adjustable-rate mortgage, and when you took out the loan your payment was approximately $1,800 a month; after the interest rate was adjusted the payment increased to $2,100 a month.

The combination of a higher monthly payment and some unforeseen expenses has made it difficult for you to make your payments on time, and you've missed a few payments.

Your goal is to get your monthly mortgage payments to equal approximately 31% to 38% of your monthly gross income, or approximately $1,290 to $1,580 per month. You can accomplish that in two basic ways: By convincing the lender to agree to a lower interest rate or by convincing the lender to extend the term of the loan. (There are a few other possibilities, but those are the main options.)

So you contact your lender after putting together a package of information. Different lenders have different requirements; many have loan modification applications that you can download; those applications include a list of required documents. Fortunately, you've already pulled most of this information together based on your efforts in Chapter Two.

In general, you will need:

- Proof of income (W-2s, tax returns, etc)
- An accurate financial statement: Assets, liabilities, monthly expenses
- Proof of financial hardship. Often this is called a hardship letter, because you describe the reasons behind why you can't make payments on your mortgage.

Everyone is different, and everyone has different circumstances that created their financial distress, but typically lenders consider situations like these to reflect hardship:

- Divorce and separation
- Loss of income
- Death of a spouse or family member
- Death of a co-signor or co-borrower
- Illness or injury
- Job relocation
- Military service

The hardship letter is an important part of the loan modification application; lenders don't just want to know that you are struggling – they want to know *why* you are struggling.

Then you apply for a loan modification. Some homeowners are successful on their own; others need skilled representation to help them. We have found that our knowledge of the lending system, the legal system, and our clients' rights makes it easier for us to achieve a reasonable loan modification solution. Why? Keep in mind the lender's representative reviews loan modifications every day; he or she is an expert on the subject, at least from a lending point of view. The average consumer is not an expert, either from a lending point of view or a legal point of view. With hard work, preparation, and tenacity you may be able to work out a solution you can afford – but you also may need help. Many of our clients have seen their payments drop dramatically; before you consider other, more drastic measures, make sure you explore loan modification possibilities.

Frankly, one of the biggest problems that I see with consumer-prepared modification applications is the lack of cash flow needed to pay even a modified mortgage payment. Most consumers want to show the lender how "bad off" they are and list their expenses as exceeding their income. This helps the lenders understand why the consumer fell behind on their mortgage payments. Unfortunately, it almost always brings an automatic denial for the modification.

Think about it. Would you lend money to someone who clearly demonstrated that they didn't have the ability to repay it? Of course not. So don't put the lender in that position. I always say that your income and expenses should be in the "sweet spot": not too high and not too low, but just right. Think about this is as you're preparing your own modification application.

The loan modification process can often take three to five months; how long it takes depends on your lender and on whether you pull together and provide the required information as quickly as possible. That's another instance where experience plays a huge role; experienced lawyers know how to prepare your application package, know how to present it, and know how to work within the system to make the process go as quickly as possible. Remember, while you're working on a loan modification the foreclosure clock is still ticking... and even ninety days may be too long to wait for an answer, especially if the answer turns out to be "no."

The Modification Process – From the Inside

Over the past few years loan modifications have become much more prevalent. If you think about it, the lending industry really had no choice – the explosion in foreclosures in many ways forced lenders to be more liberal about working with homeowners in financial distress... otherwise they might find themselves with even more foreclosed properties to deal with (and greater public outcry about predatory lending practices.)

The government has also stepped in. For example, the Home Affordable Modification Program (HAMP), one of the more widely-known initiatives, is designed to provide eligible homeowners with the opportunity to modify their mortgages and make payments more affordable. Over a million homeowners have already received help under the program. The goal is to help three to four million homeowners by 2012. The original HAMP was put into place in 2009; in March 2010 the administration announced enhancements to the Home Affordable Modification Program designed to provide additional resources for struggling homeowners. (We'll look at those enhancements shortly.)

Do you qualify for a modification under the Home Affordable Modification Program? As you might guess, determining whether or not you meet the requirements can be complicated. Also keep in mind that words like "may" and "might" and "do not constitute a contract offer binding" appear in the wording of the legislation. Even if you do qualify, you may need an experienced advocate on your side to convince your lender to work with you, and under terms you can financially live with.

Here are the basics. Eligibility is based on meeting the following criteria:

- The borrower is delinquent on their mortgage or faces imminent risk of default
- The property is the borrower's primary residence and is occupied by the borrower
- The mortgage was originated on or before January 1, 2009, and the unpaid principal balance is no more than $729,750. (In other words, if you took out a loan after January 1, 2009, or your loan is for an amount greater than $729,750, you do not qualify under HAMP.)
- The current monthly mortgage payment (including taxes, insurance, and any homeowner's association dues) is greater than 31% of the borrower's monthly gross income.
- The current mortgage payment is not affordable due to a financial hardship that can be documented.

Once a borrower is determined to be eligible for the program, the mortgage holder can take a series of steps to adjust the monthly mortgage payment to 31% of the borrower's total pre-tax monthly income:

1. Reduce the interest rate to as low as 2%; if that is not sufficient, then
2. Extend the loan term to 40 years; if that is still not sufficient, then

3. Defer a portion of the principal until the loan is paid off, and waive interest on the deferred amount

The above series of steps is called a waterfall; the lender applies the first step, and if that is not sufficient, the lender moves on and adds the next step.

I should warn you, however, that lenders rarely move to the third step of this waterfall process. Lenders will almost never defer or waive principal amounts due on the loan, even if that would make the modification work. Although it does happen, it's still rare. Personally, I think that more homeowners would stay in their homes if lenders reduced the principal amounts of the loans to bring them more in line with the current market value of the homes securing the loans. Unfortunately, for now at least, it's not a common practice.

To help insure lenders participate, HAMP provides financial incentives to the lender. For example, lenders receive an up-front Servicer Incentive Payment of $1,000 for every eligible loan modification. Lenders can also receive Pay for Success payments – based on whether the borrower stays in the program – of up to $1,000 per year for up to three years. And if the borrower is still current on their mortgage but is faced with imminent default, the lender may be eligible to receive from $500 to $1,500 if it agrees to a loan modification. (The goal of the "still current" incentive is to make it more attractive for lenders to work with borrowers who are current on their payments but facing financial distress that will make *staying* current unlikely.)

In short, the lenders now have a financial incentive to work with borrowers in distress – aside from potentially avoiding the cost of foreclosing on properties. The government provides those incentives; don't think lenders have suddenly become more considerate or compassionate. Mortgage lending is a business, first and foremost, and decisions are made based on business reasons.

HAMP is designed to help struggling homeowners stay in their homes by providing business reasons for lenders to offer loan modifications.

Does Your Lender Participate?

Participation in HAMP is mandatory for servicers of loans owned or guaranteed by Fannie Mae or Freddie Mac. Participation in HAMP is voluntary for lenders or servicers of non-government sponsored enterprises (in other words, non Fannie Mae or Freddie Mac) loans.

Quick aside: What is a "servicer"? We discussed servicers back in Chapter 5, but let's look at this again. A loan servicer collects payments, maintains records, pays insurance, taxes, and other escrowed fees... basically a servicer "handles" your mortgage. Often the servicer is a different entity than the original lender. Many mortgages are sold to another company. For example, when you first received your mortgage you may have gotten the loan from a local bank. Then a month or so later you may have gotten a notice explaining that the loan had been sold or reassigned to another lender. The terms of your loan didn't change; in effect the only thing that changed was whom you wrote your check to, and where you mailed that check. The new owner of your mortgage is now servicing your loan.

To make things more complicated, some companies specialize in servicing loans on behalf of lenders – in effect, those companies take care of all the paperwork for the lender. So while a bank may own your loan, another company is responsible for handling that loan... including serving as a point of contact for you. If that is the case, you will deal with the loan servicer, not with the mortgage company.

Much of the time, dealing with a loan servicer is like dealing with the lender; they follow guidelines and policies established by the lender. But, in some cases, a loan servicer may not be particularly responsive to your requests. We often have to contact Fannie Mae, Freddie Mac, or a major lender directly to put pressure on and ensure that the loan servicer is responsive to our clients' needs.

But, in most cases, servicers are responsive, especially since HAMP provides financial incentives to servicers who complete loan modifications under HAMP guidelines.

If your loan is handled by a servicer that does not own the loan itself, your servicer may need to get permission from the owner of the loan before they can change any of the terms of your loan. But in most cases the servicer operates under guidelines stating what actions the servicer is allowed to take. Those guidelines are typically called a "servicing agreement" or a "Pooling and Servicing Agreement" (PSA). In most cases the PSAs are intended to give the servicer flexibility to make modification decisions as long as the modification provides a better financial outcome for the lender or investor than not modifying the loan. HAMP has made it more likely that modification will provide a better financial outcome for the lender.

To find out if your lender or servicer participates in HAMP, check the list at www.makinghomeaffordable.gov/contact_servicer.html. (You can also go to www.SaveMyFloridaHomeNow.com for the most current list of participating lenders and servicers.

HAMP: The Basic Process

Let's say your lender (or servicer) participates in HAMP and you feel you meet the guidelines; what happens? Here's a slightly more detailed overview of the process.

Step One: The lender determines eligibility. Before moving forward, the lender determines whether you meet the minimum eligibility requirements: You occupy the property, you took out the loan on or before January 1, 2009, the principal balance is less than $729,750, your mortgage payment is greater than 31% of your gross monthly income, and you face a documentable financial hardship (which can, of course, simply be the fact you can't afford to make payments.)

Step Two: The lender evaluates your financial situation. Once your loan is determined to meet minimum eligibility requirements, the lender asks for information and documentation about your financial situation. You will be asked to provide information about current income, current assets, current expenses, and any hardships that cause you to be unable to make mortgage payments. In the early stages the lender may accept information verbally, but at some point the lender will require actual documentation (bank statements, W-2 forms, tax returns, copies of receipts, etc) to verify any statements you make.

Step Three: Determine if your monthly first lien mortgage payment is greater than 31% of your gross or pre-tax monthly income. With documentation in hand, this step is easy for the lender to determine. (You can too – simply divide your monthly gross income amount into the amount of your mortgage payment. For example, if you make $3,000 a month and your monthly mortgage payment is $1,400, then your payment makes up 46% of your pay. ($1,400 / $3,000 = .46, or 46%.)

Step Four: The lender runs a Net Present Value (NPV) test. The goal of a NPV test is to determine whether the value of the loan to the investor will be greater if the loan is modified. If the modified loan is not of greater value, the investor and servicer may still modify the loan, but modification is *not* required.

Step Five: Offer trial loan modification. If the modified loan is of greater value (based on the NPV calculation) the servicer must offer modification under HAMP, and, if you accept the offer, put you on a trial modification (typically three months) at the new payment level.

Step Six: Put an official modification agreement in place. If you successfully make all of the required trial payments during the trial period and the income and expense information you provided is determined to be accurate, your lender will provide an official modification agreement. Think of Step Five as a trial period; if you "pass" the test, then long-term modification will be extended to you. If you don't... modification may no longer be an option.

Sound fairly straightforward? In concept it is – but in practice the loan modification process can become extremely complicated and at times contentious. (Some lenders are more "modification friendly" than others; we find that some require a not-so-gentle push.)

One of the more complicated areas of the HAMP program involves the Net Present Value calculation. It's an important piece of the HAMP puzzle, since successfully qualifying is based in part on meeting the NPV test.

Let's take a closer look at how Net Present Value is calculated. (I originally planned to leave the Net Present Value concept out of this book. It's fairly complicated and boring. However, I've recently had modifications denied or altered based on the lender's analysis of the Net Present Value test, using their own proprietary – and secret – calculations. So, I want you to at least understand the concept so that you'll know what you're up against.)

Net Present Value (NPV)

First the definition: Net Present Value is the difference between the present value of cash inflows and the present value of cash outflows. (I know – your head is starting to spin.) NPV is typically used by companies that are analyzing whether to invest capital in a project; it's one way to determine the potential of profits and in general terms to decide whether the investment makes sense.

Think of it this way: NPV is a way to compare the value of money now with the value of money at some time in the future. In simple terms, a dollar in your pocket today is worth more than a dollar in the future, if only because inflation eats away at the buying power of the future dollar; the dollar you have today can be invested so it earns some kind of return. If I agree to give you a dollar ten years from now, that dollar won't be worth anything near what it is worth today.

Put yourself in the lender's shoes. If you borrowed $200,000 to buy a home, the money you borrowed has a value to the lender. To compensate the lender for losing access to that money, you pay interest on the loan.

Everyone is happy until you are unable to make payments. Then the lender has a decision to make. On one hand, the lender could decide to foreclose if you go into default; eventually the lender will get its money back when the property is sold at auction or otherwise disposed of. Then it can lend that money to another borrower.

But foreclosing does come with costs: Administrative costs, legal fees, interest lost while the process takes place, etc. And, in today's economy, it's very likely that the lender may only receive a fraction of the loan amount due from the eventual sale of the property.

So, on the other hand, the lender might be better off taking less by modifying the loan – like granting a lower interest rate, allowing a longer payment term, or even forgiving some portion of the loan – than if it foreclosed on the loan.

Both options – foreclosing or modifying the loan – come with positives and negatives. NPV calculations help the lender understand those positives and negatives from a financial point of view.

That's why, where loan modification is concerned, the NPV test is one of the formulas used to determine whether your loan is eligible for modification. Running an NPV calculation helps the lender decide if they will be better off, in financial terms, by modifying your loan or by letting you default and foreclosing on the property. As you can probably guess by now, that calculation and decision isn't simple to make. NPV takes into account factors like the current value of the property, the cost of foreclosing, how long it might take to sell the property, etc, and compares that scenario against what happens if your interest rate is reduced, the term of the loan is extended, whether any interest will be waived, etc.

All the different factors are called "inputs." The HAMP NPV calculation includes tons of inputs: Simple ones, like the balance of your loan, when you took out the loan, the amount of your payment... all the way to complicated ones like the risk of default, an estimate of project home price declines, a mark-to-market loan-to-value ratio... in short, items and calculations most people in no way understand.

The results of the calculation are called "outputs."

So let's go back to basics: Simply put, NPV helps the lender answer this question, in financial and business terms: "Should I modify the loan... or not?" The lender runs two basic scenarios:

- The NPV of the loan if a modification is *not* offered
- The NPV of the loan if a modification *is* offered

If the NPV of the modification scenario is greater, your loan qualifies for modification – your loan is considered to be NPV "positive."

If the NPV of the non-modification (meaning foreclosure) scenario is greater, your loan does not automatically qualify, but the lender could still choose to allow modification – the lender can qualify for incentives even if the NPV calculation is not in favor of modification as long as your loan meets other eligibility requirements and the modification is performed according to standard guidelines.

HAMP and NPV

A participating lender in HAMP is required to modify any loan that meets the program's eligibility criteria if the modification also tests "positive" for NPV – in other words, if the NPV is higher if the loan is modified. The underlying premise of the system is that if the NPV is positive, everyone – lenders, servicers, and borrowers – is better off if the loan is modified and the risk of foreclosure is reduced.

HAMP spells out the method under which NPV is determined, but it does allow for lender customization. Every lender is given discretion, within limits, to choose a discount rate, or the interest rate used to determine the present value of future cash flows. Larger lenders (lenders that have more than $40 billion in loans on the books) are also allowed to develop their own default rates – the assumed overall rate of loan defaults – to be used as an input for NPV calculations. In many cases lenders do not modify the calculations or inputs, but some do.

Then, here's what happens. The lender follows this basic process:

Step One: Compute the NPV of the mortgage under the assumption it is not modified

1. Determine the probability that the mortgage will default

2, Project the future cash flows of the mortgage if it defaults, along with the present value of those future cash flows

3. Project the future expected cash flows of the mortgage if it does not default, along with the present value of those future cash flows

4. Take the probability weighted average of the two present values

Step Two: Compute the NPV of the mortgage under the assumption it is not modified (using similar inputs as above)

Step Three: Compare the two NPV results to determine if modification is the better alternative

If modification is the better alternative (in the business, that means NPV is "positive"), the loan qualifies. Keep in mind a number of factors and scenarios are evaluated as a part of the calculations, including:

- The value of the home relative to the size of the mortgage
- The likelihood the loan will be foreclosed on
- Overall and (sometimes) market-specific trends in home prices
- The cost of foreclosure:
  - legal expenses
  - lost interest during the time required to complete foreclosure
  - property maintenance costs
  - expenses involved in reselling the property
- The cost of granting modification:
  - lower monthly payment from the borrower
  - likelihood a borrower will default even after the loan is modified
  - financial incentives provided by the government
  - likelihood the loan will be paid off before its term expires (in other words, an assumed "prepayment probability")

Basic NPV Model Assumptions

The HAMP NPV model includes a few basic assumptions. As you know, some of those assumptions (inputs) can be customized by some lenders. The HAMP NPV model includes a broad range of inputs. Knowing those inputs – and how they were determined – can be critical when working with lenders during the loan modification process.

Here are a few examples of assumptions that can and cannot be modified:

Discount Rate: A lender that owns a mortgage expects future cash payments from a borrower. The promise of those payments is worth less to the lender than cash in hand today, however. How much less those future payments are worth is determined based on a discount rate. The higher the discount rate, the less a future payment is worth to a lender today.

For example, a $2,000 payment made a year from now is only worth $1,900 at a 5% discount rate (5% of $2,000 is $100.) Think of the discount rate as an amount the lender must make in order to feel good about lending money in the first place. (After all, if I can make more by lending money to someone else at a higher rate, shouldn't I do that? Or shouldn't I invest in a CD paying 5% instead of one paying a 3% return? If it helps, think of a discount rate as a "rate of return I expect in order for this investment to make sense" amount.)

In the base NPV model, all lenders are given limited discretion to adjust the discount rate by up to 2.5%, since different lenders and investors place different values on future payments versus the payments received today. (In short, different lenders and investors have different expectations.)

The discount rate the lender uses may be as low as Freddie Mac's Primary Mortgage Market Survey (PMMS) weekly rate for 30-year fixed-rate conforming loans, and as high as the PMMS weekly rate plus 2.5%.

For loans not owned or guaranteed by Fannie Mae or Freddie Mac, the lender may apply a single discount rate or two discount rates, one for loans it owns and another for loans serviced for all other investors and lenders. But in no case can a lender use a higher discount rate for loans in its own portfolio than the rate used for loans it services for other investors. If a loan is owned or guaranteed by Fannie Mae or Freddie Mac, a loan servicer must apply the rate specified in Fannie Mae and Freddie Mac guidelines.

Default Rate: The base NPV model projects a default rate in two basic ways: The probability of default if the loan is not modified and the probability of default if the loan is modified.

Default rates depend on a number of variables that are specific to each loan. Basically, the default rate is assumed to vary based on the credit quality of the borrower, the borrower's debt burden, the loan-to-value (LTV) of the home at the time of modification, and whether the loan is modified before default, early in default, or in the late stages of default.

Default rates are currently set based on the broader loan performance experience.

Large lenders and servicers – the ones with portfolios exceeding $40 billion – can, if they choose, customize the NPV model to use default rates that reflect their experience with their own loans. (But they are required to validate the rates they use.)

As a result, the default rate used rates may vary widely from one large lender to another based on differences in their portfolios. (Lenders that made a lot of "bad" loans are likely to use a higher default rate, since a number of their loans have likely entered default.) The default rate used can have a sizable impact on the NPV calculation result.

Home Values: When home prices continue to fall, some homeowners are more likely to cut their losses and let the house be foreclosed on. If prices are stable or even rising, homeowners are more likely to do what they can to weather the financial storm. That's why the likelihood of future increases or decreases in home prices impacts a borrower's willingness to stay in a house; increases and decreases also affect the lender's potential financial loss in the event of foreclosure. Lenders must use the home price projection values included in the base NPV model. Lenders do not have discretion to substitute a different value projection.

REO Discount: A real estate owned (REO) property – a property that did not sell at foreclosure auction and is owned by the lender – generally tends to sell for a lower price than a similar home that is not an REO property. The difference is known as the "REO Discount." The REO discount takes into account the lower perceived value buyers tend to place on homes that have been foreclosed on. Because of differences in foreclosure rates and other housing trends, the REO Discount varies based on where the home is located and by its relative value. So, a $1,000,000 home in Florida may use a different REO Discount than a $150,000 home in Iowa. In either case, the REO Discount is set by HAMP and is not open to lender modification.

NPV: The Bottom Line

When a homeowner faces financial distress, the lender or servicer has a choice: Modify the mortgage, or leave it as is.

Although it would be nice to think that lenders make decisions based on "heart," in reality the decision comes down to an objective process. If the loan is modified the lender assumes there is a greater chance that the borrower will eventually repay the loan in full – and along the way the lender can receive incentives from HAMP. If the loan is not modified, the loan may go to foreclosure, but using the NPV calculation the lender has determined that absorbing the cost of foreclosing is offset by other financial factors.

HAMP is designed to create modifications that are more likely to test NPV positive, which should increase the number of modifications and keep more people in their homes. Lower monthly payments mean borrowers are less likely to default.

Keep in mind that lenders and servicers are required to offer modification on all NPV positive loans. If the loan is not NPV positive, the servicer is required to at least consider other options. So while you shouldn't lose all hope if NPV is negative, you should realize that you may need assistance in convincing the lender to agree to a loan modification.

HAMP Enhancements

While we're on the subject of HAMP, let's look at some changes to the program that were enacted in March 2010. The enhancements are designed to extend HAMP to more homeowners. The changes made are intended to provide temporary mortgage assistance to (some) unemployed homeowners, make it possible for a greater number of people to qualify for loan modification, and provide assistance for people to move to more affordable housing when loan modification is not possible.

Here's the nutshell version of those changes:

Unemployed borrowers who meet eligibility criteria may have mortgage payments temporarily reduced to an affordable level for at least three months and up to six months while they look for a new job. If the homeowner does not find a job before the temporary assistance period is over, or if they do find a job with one with a lower income level than their previous job, they will then be evaluated for a permanent HAMP modification.

Better lender "outreach" so more borrowers can complete a HAMP application. Lenders are expected to reach out to borrowers and better communicate options, and in return receive increased incentives.

And, "Pay for Success" initiatives have been expanded to include homeowners with FHA loans.

Relocation assistance payments will be increased for borrowers who use the foreclosure alternative program. Some borrowers continue to struggle financially and are unable to meet the terms of a modification. Payments to borrowers who use the foreclosure alternatives program will be doubled, and incentives will be increased for lenders and servicers.

And here's the detail:

Temporary Assistance for Unemployed Homeowners

Mortgage payments can be reduced to an affordable level for a minimum of three months and up to six months for some borrowers, while they look for new job.

- Payments are temporarily set at 31% of monthly income (or less) while the borrower is unemployed (basically, this is type of forbearance plan.)

- The plan is offered for a minimum of three months and up to as much as six months, depending on the individual circumstances of the borrower. In any case the plan ends when the borrower is re-employed. Any borrower who finds a new job during the assistance period and has a mortgage payment that is above 31% of their new monthly gross income must be considered for general HAMP assistance.

- Who is eligible?

  – Home is owner-occupied

  – The loan balance is below $729,750

  – The loan was originated before January 1, 2009

- The borrower must provide proof they are receiving unemployment insurance benefits.

- The borrower must request temporary assistance in the first ninety days of delinquency.

Better Lender "Outreach"

The goal of this enhancement is to improve how lenders communicate with borrowers, and to ensure more borrowers are aware of their options. One part of this enhancement is that lenders are required to make a reasonable effort to reach out to borrowers who are struggling to make mortgage payments.

- Requires lenders to solicit the participation of borrowers who meet the HAMP eligibility profile and who have missed two or more payments.

- Prohibits lenders from seeking foreclosure until the borrower has been evaluated and found to be ineligible for HAMP modification.

- Requires lenders to stop foreclosure actions after a borrower enters into a trial modification plan, as long as that plan was based on verified borrower income.

- Requires the lender to certify, in writing, that the borrower was not eligible for HAMP before an attorney or trustee can conduct a foreclosure sale or auction.

- Establishes a 30-day "borrower response period" from the date of a non-approval notice; during this time the foreclosure sale is prohibited. (Basically this period gives the borrower some breathing space to consider other options.)

- Requires lenders to consider borrowers who are in bankruptcy for HAMP modification.

Also, if bankruptcy is part of the picture, in some cases the trial period may be waived if the borrower is already performing successfully under a bankruptcy plan. In other words, if you are in a bankruptcy plan and are meeting the obligations of that plan, the trial period for a HAMP modification may be waived and you may immediately qualify for a permanent modification.

Increased Relocation Assistance Payments

The goal of this enhancement is to provide borrowers with foreclosure alternatives, and to help borrowers move to more affordable housing if necessary.

One way is to increase payoffs to junior lien holders who agree to release borrowers from debt; that makes foreclosure alternatives like short sales more likely to be an option. Another is to increase lender incentive payments (the money the lender receives from the government) from $1,000 to $1,500 in order to hopefully increase the use of foreclosure alternatives and encourage the lenders to reach out to homeowners who are unable to complete a modification plan.

Borrowers who successfully complete a foreclosure, like a short sale or a deed-in-lieu, receive a $3,000 relocation assistance payment to help them quickly move to housing they can afford.

Additional Notes on HAMP

A few other things you should know about HAMP:

1. **Your lender will not require you to pay a modification fee.** Homeowners who qualify for a modification under HAMP

are never required to pay modification fees or pay late fees. If there are other costs associated with your modification, like the payment of back taxes you owe, your lender can give you the option of adding those costs to the amount you owe on your mortgage, or to pay some or all of those expenses up front.

2. **You don't have to currently be behind on payments in order to qualify.** If you are struggling to stay current on your mortgage payments and have reason to believe you are likely to default on your mortgage soon, you may still qualify. (Reasons why you are likely to default could include an increase in mortgage payment, loss of job, reduced pay rate, or other financial situation. You will be required to document the reasons why you feel you are likely to default on your mortgage, but you may qualify for a modification even if you have not missed a payment – yet.

3. **You may still qualify even if you face foreclosure.** Participating lenders and loan servicers are not allowed to proceed with a foreclosure sale on an eligible loan until the homeowner has been evaluated for HAMP participation. And, once you enter into a trial period, the lender or servicer is not allowed to initiate a new foreclosure as long as you make your payments. If you face foreclosure, applying for HAMP may at the very least help buy you time.

4. **HAMP will not immediately reduce the amount you owe.** The goal of HAMP is to help homeowners keep their homes by lowering the monthly payment; the goal is not to reduce the overall loan balance. Lenders can offer a reduction in principal, but that is not likely. In most cases the modification will include lower interest rates and longer

payment terms. Don't expect to see a reduction in your balance. It could happen – but it's not likely.

5. **But you might still receive incentives.** Homeowners who make timely payments on modified loans receive what are called "success incentives." Every month you make a payment on time you accrue an incentive that reduces the principal balance on your loan. Each year the incentive will be applied directly to your loan balance; the incentive is $1,000 per year for five total years. (The goal of the incentive is to help you build up equity in the home.) But, if your loan is no longer considered to be in good standing success payments will not be made.

Currently the HAMP program is set to expire on HAMP expires on December 31, 2012. Trial modifications must be in place by that date.

The FDIC Loan Modification Model

Some lenders and servicers do not participate in the Home Affordable Modification Program; if that is the case, you still have options. While HAMP is relatively new, we have been helping clients with loan modifications for years. Many lenders have their own in-house modification programs that vary from the HAMP guidelines. However, they can still offer significant payment reduction for eligible homeowners.

In short, HAMP is not the only modification game in town.

The key to successfully negotiating a loan modification or workout is to understand the financial repercussions for the lender and to put together an attractive package that appeals to the lender's bottom-line financial interests. Instead of using the HAMP NPV model, the Federal Deposit Insurance Corporation (FDIC) created a publicly-available tool to evaluate NPV to assist lenders – and borrowers – determine whether, and under what terms, a modification makes sense.

It also offers some advantages compared to the HAMP NPV model:

- It requires very few inputs; most of the information required is publicly available, which means it's easy for the borrower (or the borrower's attorney) to understand how the calculations were made.

- It uses conservative assumptions, which sometimes works against the homeowner.

- It's widely recognized as a useful tool; in fact, some states recommend using the FDIC calculation as a tool during foreclosure mediation.

Let's take a closer look!

FDIC Model Basic Features

Ratio of Affordability: Like HAMP, the FDIC model assumes the homeowner's monthly payment should fall between 31 and 38% of their gross monthly pay. If the homeowner's ratio is already under 31% (and the payment includes an amount covering principal, interest, taxes, and insurance – in short, the typical mortgage payment) then the modification will not be approved.

Keep in mind that when we help our clients work out a loan modification we set a "target" ratio that we want to hit. Obviously the lower the ratio we target the better, since a lower ratio means a lower and therefore more affordable monthly payment. As a rule of thumb we shoot for 31%, but that is not always achievable. Keep in mind that as a rule of thumb lenders will shoot for a ratio of 38%; the higher the ratio, the more money they receive. For example, say you earn $4,000 per month in gross wages.

A 38% ratio means your monthly payment will be $1,520; a 31% ratio means your payment will be $1,240, a difference of $280 per month.

Payment Reduction: Under the FDIC program, monthly payments must be reduced by at least 10%. If a 10% reduction results in a payment with a ratio under 31%, loan modification is denied. Roughly speaking unless your payment is more than 38% of your monthly gross income, you won't qualify under the 10% rule.

Payment Modification: Once the affordability standard is set (the target ratio) then the modified payment is determined. The FDIC program, just like the HAMP program, uses a "waterfall" system.

- First, interest rates are reduced. The "floor" rate is 3%.
- If that change doesn't result in a payment that meets the target ratio, then the term of the loan is extended to forty years. (The longer it takes to pay off a loan, the lower the monthly payment.)
- If that change doesn't work, then some amount of principal may be eliminated in order to meet the target.

Once the new payment is in place, that payment amount stays in place for five years. At the end of five years, the interest rate increases by 1% per year until it reaches the rate effective at the time of the loan modification.

Foreclosure Effect: The FDIC tool also takes into account the potential of a property having a lower perceived value in the marketplace if it is foreclosed on. It also accounts for foreclosure costs and interest losses if the property is foreclosed on. The result is an REO value, which is compared to the current principal balance to calculate a discount to present value – basically a reduced value of the property due to the current financial situation of its owner. The greater the assumed cost of foreclosure, the more likely the lender is to modify the loan. Lenders try to make smart financial decisions; if foreclosing will cost more than modifying the loan the lender is much more likely to modify the loan. The foreclosure effect calculation is similar to the...

Value of Modification: The value of the modification (in the financial world, it's called the Loan Modification Value) is based on evaluating the present value of the payments and the anticipated loss from foreclosing on the property. The result is a set of probabilities that allows the lender to determine how risky the modification is, the likelihood it will fail, and the cost if it does fail.

Then all the values are input and the numbers get run.

As long as the value of the loan modification is greater (or represents a smaller loss to the lender) than the present value of foreclosing, the NPV test is considered to be "passed" and a loan modification is in the best interest of the lender. If the present value of foreclosing has a higher value than the value of the loan modification, the lender has no financial incentive to work out a loan modification.

Loan Modifications: Items to Watch For

Some lenders offer loan modifications based on the HAMP program; others offer modifications based on their own guidelines and procedures. Even though HAMP has made the process somewhat easier, in many cases it can be tough for an individual borrower to reach an agreement that makes short-term and long-term sense. Lenders are under no obligation to be "fair" to the borrower; the only obligation the lender feels is to maximize returns and profits.

But say you do reach terms on a loan modification. Great – but the process isn't done. You will then sign a loan modification agreement – and that agreement may include terms and provisions that are less than advantageous to you. Before you sign any agreement, watch for these potential pitfalls.

Tax Implications: If any of your debt is forgiven, that amount is considered to be taxable income. For example, say in the loan modification process you not only receive a lower interest rate and a longer term but also $10,000 of your principal balance is forgiven by the lender. (While unlikely, it does happen.) While you won't have to pay the $10,000 to the lender, either now or in the future, you may owe tax on that amount since the IRS considers forgiven debt to be income. (The same is true if a credit card company forgives or charges off a portion of your credit card balance.) That's the general rule, but exceptions do exist – you may not owe tax on the forgiven amount under certain circumstances. For example, you may not owe tax if you were insolvent before the debt was discharged or if the discharge occurred as part of a bankruptcy case. (Review this discussion in Chapter 9. I address this issue in great detail in that chapter.)

Either way, you should know what to expect so you aren't hit with a nasty surprise at tax time.

Waivers: Many loan modification agreements contain waivers. (You shouldn't be surprised; many legal documents – even simple contracts – contain waivers.) In most cases the waivers are designed to protect the lender or servicer from any past or future claims that you as a borrower might have. If, like some people, you were "pushed" into an unaffordable repayment plan by an unscrupulous loan modification company, you may lose any chance at relief – or at making a legitimate claim – based on a waiver buried somewhere in all the legal phrases and wording at the end of the loan modification document.

Only agree to waivers that fit the circumstances. If you enter into a short-term repayment plan, waiving your rights doesn't make sense. If your loan is voided, some waivers may make sense. Also make sure that any waivers apply to subsequent owners or servicers of your loan. If your loan is sold, the terms of your modification should apply to any of those subsequent owners or servicers.

Keep in mind "blanket" waivers are often not defensible. Sometimes clients come to us seeking help when they have signed all-inclusive waivers; those waivers may not be enforceable. We may be able to fight the waivers using contract law legal issues like lack of consideration, unconscionability (meaning excessive, unreasonable, or grossly unfair), and lack of mutuality. But also keep in mind that your best defense against unfair or one-sided waivers is to not sign an agreement containing unfair or one-sided waivers.

Enforcement: Agreements are not enforceable unless all the legal bases have been covered. Even if you are successful in reaching a loan modification agreement with your lender, it makes sense to have an attorney review the agreement to make sure it is not only in your best interest but that all the terms are enforceable. An agreement you can't enforce isn't an agreement at all.

Credit repair: Most homeowners seeking loan modifications have missed at least one, if not more, payments. Worse, the lender may have initiated foreclosure proceedings somewhere along the way. As a result, your credit has been damaged. Requiring the lender to take steps to help repair your credit should be a part of the loan modification agreement. (We always seek credit repair as part of the modifications we arrange on behalf of our clients.)

Additional Modification Possibilities

But wait – there's more! Let's look at a few other loan modification possibilities.

HOPE for Homeowners

The Housing and Economic Recovery Act of 2008 (HOPE) created HOPE for Homeowners, a voluntary program that authorized the Federal Home Administration (FHA) to insure loans made to refinance homeowners into 30-year or 40-year fixed-rate mortgages. (In short, the goal is to make qualifying for refinancing more likely since the FHA will insure those loans and reduce the original lender's risk, at least to a degree.)

The program ends in 2012, but while it's in place HOPE for Homeowners can reduce the interest rate and principal balance for eligible homeowners; refinancing is based on current, not older (often meaning higher) property values. Unfortunately, the program is voluntary, so lenders don't have to participate.

You may be eligible if you have not intentionally defaulted on your mortgage or other substantial debt. What does "intentional" mean? Intentionally defaulting occurs when you had funds available to make payments, without hardship, but simply chose not to. In addition:

- You must have made at least six full payments on the first mortgage on the property.
- You must have a debt to income ratio of greater than 31% (meaning all your debt payments must add up to at least 31% of your gross income) but not more than 43%.
- You cannot have been convicted of fraud in the last ten years.
- You must certify that you did not provide false information to obtain the mortgage you hope to refinance.
- The mortgage must have been originated on or before January 1, 2008, and the property must be your primary and only residence. (That means you cannot own other residential properties like vacation homes or even rental properties.)

Other conditions apply:

- The amount of the mortgage cannot exceed $550,440.
- The mortgage cannot have a loan to value (LTV) ratio of more than 96.5% of the current appraised value of the property. LTV is a simple ratio; divide the amount of the loan by the current appraised value of the home. If the home is worth $100,000 and the loan is for $96,000, the LTV is 96%. ($96,000 / $100,000 = .96, or 96%.)

What's the downside? A result of the HOPE for Homeowners program is that you will enter into an equity sharing agreement with the department of Housing and Urban Development (HUD). As a result you will share a portion of the initial equity in the property as well as a portion of any future increase in value. If you sell or refinance the property, HUD gets a cut based on this chart:

If you sell during year:	HUD receives:	You receive:
1	100% of equity	0% of equity
2	90% of equity	10% of equity
3	80% of equity	20% of equity
4	70% of equity	30% of equity
5	60% of equity	40% of equity
Additional years	50% of equity	50% of equity

Basically you share any property value gains with HUD in return for entering into the program.

Also, you will not be allowed to get a second mortgage, home equity loan, or any other type of loan using the property as security or collateral (except under very specific conditions.)

As you can see, HOPE for Homeowners isn't right for everyone, but depending on your circumstances and long-term goals, it might be right for you

Project Lifeline

If your situation is relatively dire, another program that could provide at least temporary relief is Project Lifeline. Project Lifeline is a program that grants eligible homeowners a 30-day delay in foreclosure proceedings. To qualify, you must be at least 90 days delinquent on your mortgage and not less than 30 days away from a scheduled foreclosure sale. Any type of home loan is eligible, including home equity loans and second mortgages.

The goal of Project Lifeline is to give you additional time to try to work out a loan modification before you lose your home. Of course, 30 days is often not enough – many loan modifications and workouts can take up to 60 days. If you haven't started the process, asking for 30 days is not likely to be of much help. We shoot for at least a 60-day "grace" period so we have a better chance of reaching an agreement with the lender.

If you take advantage of Project Lifeline – or if you are able to get your lender to put a hold on foreclosure proceedings for any reason – make sure you get that agreement in writing. Verbal agreements are rarely enforceable; get everything in writing.

Fannie Mae HomeSaver Advance Loan

This tool has received relatively little press or media attention. The HomeSaver Advance loan is an unsecured personal loan the homeowner can use to bring a delinquent mortgage back to current status. Basically, you receive a loan that you use to pay past-due payments on a first mortgage. The loan is unsecured, meaning you do not have to provide collateral in order to secure the loan, and the interest rate is set at 5%, for 15 years, with no payments required for the first six months.

You can use the money to pay principal, interest, taxes, insurance, and homeowner association fees, but the money cannot be used to pay late fees or other costs.

But there is a limit to what you can borrow: You can borrow no more than $15,000, or, if it turns out to be a lower amount, no more than 15% of the original unpaid principal balance.

To qualify, the mortgage must be one that was purchased or secured by Fannie Mae, and the mortgage must be at least six months old. On the plus side, you don't have to occupy the property, so unlike most programs investment properties or second homes do qualify under this program.

Keep in mind that receiving a HomeSaver loan does not change the terms of your original mortgage: The interest rate, terms, principal balance, etc all remain the same. The HomeSaver loan is designed solely to help you bring your mortgage current. For that reason it's a great option for homeowners who have faced a short-term financial crisis or burden but feel that over the long term they can successfully meet their financial obligations. If you lost your job and can't afford to make payments, the HomeSaver loan will only provide short-term relief.

What if You Have a VA Loan?

VA loans are underwritten by the Veterans Administration. In some ways a VA loan is like an FHA loan, except VA loans are intended for veterans of military service. The basic purpose of the VA home loan program is to help eligible veterans get home loans when financing is not generally available, and to help veterans purchase properties with no down payment.

New guidelines make it easier for the VA to modify mortgage loans for borrowers in distress. And loan servicers can qualify for incentives if they implement certain modification options.

The VA expects the lender to try reasonable alternatives before foreclosing on a property. The basic alternatives are repayment plans, forbearance, and loan modification. Here's a quick look at each:

Repayment Plans: Repayment plans are possible if the loan is more than 60 days delinquent. Under a repayment plan, the borrower pays the normal monthly payment plus a certain amount towards the amount of delinquency. The period of repayment is unlimited, so the additional portion can be fairly small. Repayment plans are best suited to people who had temporary financial setbacks but are now back on their feet and able to make regular payments (plus a little extra.)

Forbearance: Under forbearance, the lender agrees to suspend payments or reduce the amount of the payments for some number of months. The money that was not paid must be repaid at a later date, either as a lump sum or through some type of payment plan. Forbearance, like a repayment plan, is best suited to borrowers who have a temporary financial setback but who are able, within a fairly short period of time, to be able to get back on track and make regular payments.

Loan Modification: Lenders can also modify VA loans in ways similar to how conventional loans are modified. The lender can lower the interest rate and increase the term. In order to qualify, the loan must be at least 12 months old and in default. The borrower must also be considered a good credit risk based on a current credit report. While that sounds contradictory (since if your credit is good you probably are not struggling to make payments), the default is not considered to be part of the "credit worthy" determination. What matters most is whether you are judged to be able to make the new payments based on your income, expenses, and obligations. Loans can be modified for one to three times without VA approval, and for an unlimited number of times if the VA approves.

If a loan modification or workout is unsuccessful, you still have options. The lender may grant forbearance for a period of time that allows you to sell or transfer the property. Even though you will lose the house, you may at least be able to do so under your terms and not under the terms of a foreclosure.

I recognize the programs and options for forbearance or loan modification seem complicated and almost endless. The key is to understand the guidelines, understand the system, and use the tools at your disposal to get the best possible outcome for your situation and your goals. There are tons of strategies you can employ... but for many people, those financial strategies still aren't enough to save their homes.

If that is the situation you find yourself in... read on. I have two more, very powerful, strategies for saving your home!

Chapter 7

Save Your Home: Chapter 13 Bankruptcy

Now let's talk about bankruptcy, which can be another powerful form of foreclosure defense. Back in the "old days" – before the foreclosure crisis – bankruptcy was generally my favorite tool for saving a home from foreclosure. (Now, I prefer a combination strategy of modification and bankruptcy, which generally provides the most affordable monthly payment. I'll tell you about that in a moment.)

Yes, the "B" word. I know what you're thinking. "There is no way," you're probably saying to yourself, "that I'll ever file for bankruptcy." But, before you dismiss bankruptcy as an option, I want you to read this chapter and think about it.

Bankruptcy is a tool – sometimes a wonderful tool under the right circumstances. Sometimes bankruptcy is the absolute best move – other times it's not.

What is Bankruptcy?

Bankruptcy is a federal court process that is intended to help consumers and businesses eliminate their debts or repay those debts under the "protection" of the bankruptcy court. Bankruptcy releases the debtor from liability for certain types of debts. ("Debtor" is a term for someone who has filed a bankruptcy case.)

- In many cases, if you owe money and you declare bankruptcy, the lender can no longer expect repayment of that loan. The lender also cannot attempt to collect the debt at a later date. Letters, phone calls, and legal actions disappear. In some cases, it's as if the loan never happened. In other cases, if property was used to secure a debt, the lender may be able to recover that property in order to at least partially satisfy the debt.

When you say "bankruptcy", most people think "Chapter 7". (By the way, we refer to the different types of bankruptcies as "Chapters", because they are literally chapters in the Bankruptcy Code.) However, there are many different types of bankruptcies that serve different purposes.

Depending on their situation, most consumers file either a Chapter 7 or a Chapter 13 bankruptcy case. For our purposes in discussing your home, the choice of bankruptcy will generally come down to whether you want a long-term solution to your mortgage problem, or a short-term solution.

Generally, you file a Chapter 13 bankruptcy as a long-term solution to foreclosure, and a Chapter 7 bankruptcy as a short-term solution. In this chapter, we'll look at the Chapter 13 bankruptcy as a powerful tool for saving your home from foreclosure. In a later chapter, we'll look at the Chapter 7 bankruptcy and see how it can eliminate the liabilities that may follow you as the result of letting your home go.

Chapter 13 - The "Rehabilitation Bankruptcy"

Chapter 13 is officially called the "Adjustment of Debts of an Individual with Regular Income" bankruptcy. Under Chapter 13, you typically are allowed to keep all of your assets. However, you must repay some, or all, of your outstanding debts to your creditors. This debt repayment is accomplished pursuant to a Chapter 13 "Plan".

A Chapter 13 case typically lasts for three to five years. During this time, you generally make monthly payments to the Chapter 13 trustee who then distributes portions of these payments to each of your creditors pursuant to the Chapter 13 Plan. During these three to five years, you are "in" bankruptcy and must pay all of your disposable income to the Chapter 13 trustee to repay your creditors. You are also subject to the rules and restrictions of the bankruptcy trustee and court during this time.

Chapter 13 allows you to repay a mortgage arrearage over the life of the plan, which typically lasts three to five years. With creative drafting of the Chapter 13 plan, it's possible to keep a debtor's first-year Chapter 13 payments equal to, or less than, the payments they were making to their mortgage company and their other creditors. This allows them to catch their breath and regain their financial footing.

In a Chapter 13 case, your attorney drafts a plan that lists your debts and assets and proposes a timetable for you to repay your creditors. During this time, you pay your ongoing monthly mortgage payment, your mortgage arrearage, and some percentage of your total debts. In return, you generally get to keep all of your assets. But, the bankruptcy court and trustee maintain a constant watch on your financial affairs and they expect you to live a frugal life. That's the trade-off for the Chapter 13.

When you successfully complete your payments pursuant to the Plan, the bankruptcy court generally discharges most of your remaining debts. From that point on, you are free to begin your new financial life with a fresh start and a current mortgage.

In a nutshell, that's how a Chapter 13 bankruptcy case works. Now, let's look at the specific benefits that a Chapter 13 can offer you if you're facing a mortgage foreclosure. I believe that there are at least five specific benefits that you can receive from filing a Chapter 13 case: the automatic stay, long-term repayment of mortgage arrearages, second mortgage stripping, other debt resolution, and credit improvement.

The Automatic Stay

The main reason that people actually file bankruptcy is because their creditors are doing bad things to them, or threatening to do bad things to them. To provide immediate relief from creditor harassment (sorry, "collection activities"), Congress created the "automatic stay". The automatic stay goes into effect when the bankruptcy case is filed. The automatic stay prevents most creditors from pursuing collection activities against the debtor.

The point of the automatic stay is to provide immediate relief from creditor harassment. The automatic stay also stops creditors from calling at home and at work, prevents landlords from evicting tenants, and prevents creditors from repossessing property.

In the foreclosure process, the automatic stay will immediately stop a foreclosure case, dead in its tracks. It will even stop a foreclosure sale – one minute before the sale.

I've filed hundreds of Chapter 13 cases over the years literally minutes before the foreclosure sale was scheduled to occur. Once the bankruptcy case is filed, the foreclosure sale must stop. Even if the clerk still holds the foreclosure sale, it is void if the bankruptcy case was filed prior to the sale.

So, the automatic stay is an extremely powerful tool. You should know that the automatic stay goes into effect when you file a Chapter 7 case as well. However, the difference is how long the automatic stay will stop the foreclosure case.

In a Chapter 7 case, a mortgage lender will quickly file a motion in the bankruptcy court to "lift the automatic stay". In most cases, if you are behind on your mortgage payments, the bankruptcy judge will grant the mortgage lender's motion, and they will be able to restart the foreclosure case. This will generally buy you about two months before the foreclosure case gets moving again.

However, in a Chapter 13 case, the bankruptcy judge will not allow the mortgage lender to get relief from the automatic stay, as long as you have addressed the mortgage debt in your Chapter 13 Plan. This is why a Chapter 13 bankruptcy is a long-term strategy for addressing the mortgage problem.

Allows Flexible Repayment of Mortgage Arrearages Over Five Years

Another reason that Chapter 13 bankruptcy is a long-term strategy for addressing a mortgage problem is that it allows you to repay your mortgage arrearages over five years. Therefore, instead of needing to come up with a lump-sum repayment of $30,000, or make double mortgage payments, the Chapter 13 bankruptcy allows you to decide the best way for you to repay the mortgage arrearages.

For many of my clients, I generally structure a "step-up" plan that provides for little or no payment of mortgage arrearages in the initial year of the plan, followed by increasing payments each year as income improves. This allows clients to get back on track financially before contributing more income to their mortgage repayment.

The choice of how you repay the mortgage arrearages is really up to you and your attorney. As long as you repay the arrearages in full by the end of the plan, the mortgage lender must generally go along with the plan. This puts you in control of your future for a change.

Allows "Stripping" of Second Mortgage Loans

One of my very favorite reasons for using Chapter 13 bankruptcy is the ability to "strip" second mortgages. In a Chapter 13 bankruptcy, you can "strip" a second mortgage if the first mortgage exceeds the value of your home.

Because the prices of homes have dropped so dramatically in the last several years, many of my clients with more than one mortgage have second mortgages that are "unsecured" by their home because the first mortgage balance exceeds the property value.

Assuming that an appraisal supports the value of your home, it's relatively easy to make a second mortgage "go away" in a Chapter 13 case. The second mortgage loan becomes a general unsecured claim in the Chapter 13. Very often, unsecured creditors receive little, if anything, from the Chapter 13 case. Therefore, if you can strip your second mortgage in the Chapter 13 case, you may end up paying virtually nothing towards that second mortgage.

At the end of the Chapter 13 case, the judge will issue an order that removes the second mortgage as a lien against your home. At that point, you're first mortgage will be current, and you're other debts will be addressed as well. Let's see how that works.

Addresses Other Debts

The Chapter 13 bankruptcy is meant to be an all-encompassing solution to your debt problems, not just your mortgage. Therefore, you generally address all of your debts in the Chapter 13 case at the same time.

In addition to their mortgage problems, most of my clients are behind on credit card and personal loan payments when they come to see me. That's OK. A Chapter 13 bankruptcy case can fix a lot of things.

How these other debts get "fixed" depends on the type of debt and the type of creditor. You see, in addition to protecting you, the bankruptcy laws attempt to protect your creditors - from you, and from each other. To do this, the bankruptcy laws provide different methods for dividing your non-exempt assets and income between and among your creditors.

Without these methods, creditors would start a "feeding frenzy" for your assets and income. Some creditors would receive full repayment and others would get nothing. However, by providing specific methods for dividing your assets and income among your various creditors, Congress has attempted to provide a level playing field for all creditors.

However, the bankruptcy laws do not treat all creditors equally. Instead, the bankruptcy laws divide creditors into three major categories - priority creditors, secured creditors, and unsecured creditors.

Priority Creditors

The bankruptcy laws allow some creditors to receive payment from you before other creditors receive payment. These creditors are called priority creditors. The order of payment to creditors is important because in most bankruptcy cases, there isn't enough money to repay all creditors. Therefore, the creditors with a higher priority under the bankruptcy laws receive a greater percentage of their claim than the creditors with a lower priority.

The bankruptcy laws specify several creditors that have priority claims, and also set forth a priority order among these creditors. The most common priority creditors include: (1) the bankruptcy trustee; (2) your employees; (3) your former spouse; and, (4) governmental entities to which you owe taxes and penalties.

In a Chapter 13 case, you must fully repay priority debts. Therefore, if you're behind on your alimony or child support payments, or you owe the IRS for recent income taxes, you must find a way to pay these amounts in full by the end of the Chapter 13 Plan.

However, the good news is that the Chapter 13 allows you to flexibly repay these debts over the life of the Plan. Without the ability to repay these priority debts over time, you might find yourself in jail or having your wages garnished at an unreasonably high amount. I've filed many Chapter 13 cases over the years specifically to address these types of debts. So, if you've got a problem with priority debts, in addition to your mortgage arrearages, Chapter 13 may be your solution.

Secured Creditors

"Secured" or "unsecured" identifies whether your debt is backed up by one of your assets. Creditors refer to this as "collateral". A creditor is secured if you pledge one of your assets as collateral for the loan. If you don't repay this secured creditor, then the creditor may seize the asset that you pledged. This gives the creditor some security for the loan, other than your simple promise to repay.

The most common secured creditor is the bank or financial institution that financed your new car. You pledge the car as collateral for the loan, the bank pays the dealership for the car, and you drive away with a smile on your face. But, if you fail to make your monthly loan payments, the bank can repossess your car and sell it to repay the loan.

Another common secured creditor – and the reason you're reading this book - is your mortgage company. The mortgage company lends you money to purchase a house. As a condition for lending you this money, the mortgage company insists that you pledge the house as collateral for the loan. But, if you fail to make your monthly mortgage payments, the mortgage company can take your house and sell it to repay the loan.

Under the bankruptcy code, a secured creditor generally receives payment up to the current value of the pledged asset, or is entitled to take the pledged asset. Therefore, secured creditors generally receive a large percentage of their claim.

A Chapter 13 case can be a powerful tool for addressing secured debts. Except for the mortgage on your primary residence, it is generally possible to "cram down" a secured debt to the current market value of the collateral in a Chapter 13 case. For example, many of my clients are "upside down" on their vehicle loans. This means that the vehicle is worth less than the amount of the secured loan.

Depending on the age of the loan, it's possible to "cram down" the secured loan to the fair market value of the vehicle. In addition, it's often possible to extend the duration of the loan to equal the term of the Chapter 13 Plan, and reduce the interest rate. By taking all of these steps, I can often cut a car payment in half. The savings from modifying car loans in a Chapter 13 case can go a long way towards repaying the mortgage arrearage. (Now you're starting to see the power of the Chapter 13 case. Think about this. How much would your monthly payments drop if were able to cut your car payments in half and eliminate your second mortgage payment? Bankruptcy isn't sounding so bad now, is it?)

Unsecured Creditors

As you might have guessed, an unsecured creditor is a creditor that does not have the safety of collateral to ensure repayment of the loan. Therefore, if you fail to repay the loan, an unsecured creditor can only receive payment if they can seize nonexempt assets or if you agree to voluntarily repay the loan - which means they're generally out of luck. Without a specific asset to seize, unsecured creditors must file a lawsuit against you, get a judgment, and then try to seize one of your nonexempt assets or garnish your wages.

Unfortunately for unsecured creditors, most states exempt a variety of assets and income from creditor seizure. This makes many people "judgment proof". For most unsecured creditors, a court judgment is a worthless piece of paper.

Unsecured creditors include major bank cards like Visa and MasterCard, and department stores that issue their own credit cards. Other unsecured creditors may include your landlord, local utility, cable, and telephone companies, and medical providers. In fact, most creditors are unsecured creditors.

In a bankruptcy, unsecured creditors generally receive very little, if any, of their total claim. This is because of the priority system that the bankruptcy code establishes among and between your creditors. Secured creditors can seize their collateral from you, and repay some, or all, of the loan. Priority creditors receive first payment from the remaining assets or income. And the poor unsecured creditors receive anything that's left.

In a Chapter 13 case, unsecured creditors receive the remaining available income from your plan. This means that they generally receive a very small percentage of their total claim.

Many consumers mistakenly assume that your must repay all of your debts in a Chapter 13 case. However, for most consumers, this simply isn't true.

For example, you may owe $50,000 in credit card debts when you file the Chapter 13 case, but repay 1% or less of that amount during the Chapter 13 case. Assuming that you make all of the payments according to your Chapter 13 plan, the remaining balances on most unsecured debt is "discharged". That means that it goes away forever. (The amount that you repay to unsecured creditors during the Chapter 13 case depends on your income, expenses, household size, and assets).

Therefore, if you have unsecured debts, the Chapter 13 bankruptcy can free you from those debts and help you to get back on track with all of your other payments. As we discussed with secured creditors, any reduction in your monthly payments will go a long way towards resolving your mortgage problem and saving your home. So, you see, Chapter 13 can be a very powerful tool.

But, guess what? It can also improve your credit. Really. Let's see how that works as we look at the last major benefit of Chapter 13 bankruptcy.

Credit May Actually Improve

It may surprise you to learn that a Chapter 13 bankruptcy can actually improve your credit. Based on the current credit scoring models, bankruptcy often dramatically improves credit scores, frequently within a year or so of the date of filing.

(I'm going to spend a great deal of time addressing credit in the last section of this book. For now, let me give you a quick overview of how bankruptcy can actually improve your credit).

The most common credit scoring model is the "FICO" score developed by the Fair Isaac Corporation. Under the most common model, 30% of the score is based on the "Amounts Owed" on your debts.

A large part of that calculation is based on the ratio of your balances to your credit lines. Ideally, that ratio should be less than 30%. So, for example, if you have credit card limits of $10,000, you should owe less than $3,000 on those credit cards to get the best FICO score.

Unfortunately, many of my clients have ratios that exceed 100% because the balances on their credit cards are higher than the credit limits on those credit cards. This will absolutely kill your credit score – even without late payments. (This is one reason why someone who has never missed a payment on a debt can have a lower credit score than someone who has been late on payments.)

In the bankruptcy, debts get reclassified as "Included in Bankruptcy" on your credit report. If the creditor is properly updating the information, the credit account of someone in bankruptcy should report with a zero balance. This resets the ratios and helps to raise the credit score. (This isn't always the case. Many creditors are reluctant to update balances in a Chapter 13 case because they believe that the case may fail.)

In addition, accounts included in a Chapter 13 case should not report as "late". Under the most common FICO score, 35% of the credit score is based on "Payment History" If you're late on your credit accounts when you file the Chapter 13, that information should be removed once you file the Chapter 13 case. This will also help to increase your credit score. And, because mortgage debt is weighted more heavily than other forms of debt in the FICO model, you'll get an even bigger increase in your FICO score by brining the mortgage current pursuant to the Chapter 13 Plan.

Surprising – but true.

The Chapter 13 Process

Now that you understand a little bit about the Chapter 13 bankruptcy, let me give you a quick overview of the process so you'll understand how it works.

After talking to your attorney about whether it's appropriate to file a Chapter 13 bankruptcy, you must first complete a credit counseling course. The first course is designed to see whether you have any alternatives to filing bankruptcy. There are many ways to take this course, and many approved vendors. Typically, you can complete the course over the phone or online – usually in less than one hour.

You will be asked to provide you income, expenses, assets and liabilities and will review the different types of bankruptcy cases and other non-bankruptcy options. For the most part, your completion is a given. I have never referred a client to a credit counselor who then said that the client was ineligible to file a bankruptcy. This is because I know that the client needs to file the bankruptcy – the counselor just confirms this. So, don't be afraid of this course – it's a no-brainer.

Once you complete the first credit counseling course, the counselor will send your attorney a copy of the course completion certificate. With this certificate in hand, the attorney is free to file your case with the bankruptcy court.

In the old days, we would do this by physically handing the bankruptcy clerk a copy of the bankruptcy documents. Now, however, it's all done electronically. As a result, I can file a bankruptcy case within minutes from my office. (This is extremely important when we're talking about an emergency filing to stop a foreclosure sale!).

At the moment the case is filed, the automatic stay goes into effect. As you recall from our discussion before, the automatic stay stops any collection activity against you – creditors can't call you, write you, sue you, or continue to sue you. Everything stops the moment you file the case. I always tell my clients to answer the phone once I file the bankruptcy case and give each creditor the bankruptcy case number. This stops all calls that same day and goes a long way towards stopping the stress of creditor harassment.

Within four to five weeks after the bankruptcy case is filed, you must go to the Meeting of Creditors. Although this sounds ominous, there's usually not much to it. At this meeting, the Chapter 13 Trustee will interview you and creditors have a right to do the same.

In reality, creditors rarely show for the Meeting of Creditors. In addition, there's no judge and no courtroom. Generally, five to eight people are scheduled during the same 30-minute time block. That means for most consumers, the Meeting of Creditors lasts for three to five minutes.

A good attorney will fully prepare you for the questions you'll receive, so you'll know what to expect. Most of my clients are still scared to death before the Meeting. But, without fail, they all walk away and say "That was easy". Yeah. I told you. It will be the same for you too.

Around this time, you will probably start making your payments to the Chapter 13 Trustee pursuant to your Chapter 13 Plan. You and your attorney will have developed the plan and the payments based on the requirements of the Bankruptcy Code and your ability to pay.

If you're smart, you will set the payments to come out automatically from your paycheck pursuant to a Wage Deduction Order. In the Orlando bankruptcy court where I most often practice, there is a 90% success rate for Chapter 13 cases with a Wage Deduction Order in place, and a 50% success rate for those cases without a Wage Deduction Order. You do the math. If you want your Chapter 13 case to succeed, set up a Wage Deduction Order.

You'll also need to take a second credit-counseling course. The second course is called "Debtor Education" and is supposed to keep you out of trouble in the future. It will give you information about budgeting and money-management. Many of my clients actually enjoy this class. Like the first credit-counseling course, you can take the Debtor Education course by telephone or online and generally takes about one hour. You don't officially need to take this course until the end of your case – which may be several years later. But, do yourself a favor and do it at the beginning so that you don't forget about it. If you forget to take the course, you don't get your discharge! So, get it done.

At some point in this process, your creditors will start filing "Proofs of Claim" with the Bankruptcy Clerk. These Proofs of Claim set forth what the creditor believes is the balance and terms of your debt with that creditor. Your attorney will then review these claims and either amend the Chapter 13 Plan or object to the claim. This is all part of the process, but you're generally not involved in much of it.

Once your attorney has reviewed all of the Proofs of Claim, and objected to those that don't seem accurate, it may be necessary to file an Amended Chapter 13 Plan to account for the right account balances and terms. This is very common.

The final step in the Chapter 13 process is the Confirmation Hearing. At this hearing, the bankruptcy judge will "confirm" that everybody agrees that the Plan you have in place at that time, be it the original Chapter 13 Plan or an Amended Chapter 13 Plan, is the right plan. At that point, the judge will confirm the Plan and much of the legal maneuvering is complete. The only thing left is for you to make your plan payments each month and wait for the end of your plan.

Once you've completed all payments according to your Chapter 13 Plan, the bankruptcy judge will issue your discharge and all of your dischargeable debts are eliminated. This includes any second mortgage debts that you stripped off pursuant to the Plan. At this point, all of your debts should be current or discharged, and you're ready to start your new life – your fresh start.

Final Words on Chapter 13 Bankruptcy

The Chapter 13 bankruptcy is a very powerful tool to fight foreclosure, and address all of your other debts at the same time. In the right case, it can be the answer to all of your problems. So, please consider adding this tool to your arsenal.

If you think that bankruptcy may be an option, please consult with an attorney that understands – and has experience with – Chapter 13 cases. Because of the economic fallout from the housing crisis, many attorneys have suddenly become "bankruptcy attorneys". Very often, these attorneys have little experience with bankruptcy in general, and with Chapter 13 cases in particular. A Chapter 13 case can be very complex and many attorneys that "dabble" in bankruptcy don't offer them at all.

So, ask the attorney a lot of questions. How long have they been an attorney? How long have they practiced bankruptcy? How many bankruptcy cases have they filed? How many Chapter 13 cases have they filed? You get the idea. Be an informed consumer, hire the best attorney that you can, and save your home. That's my wish for you.

Chapter 8

Save Your Home: The Combo Strategy

I mentioned in the last chapter that I have a new favorite strategy for addressing mortgage issues. Now it's time to share this strategy with you.

This strategy may work great for you if you have a second mortgage that is "upside down" because the balance of your first mortgage loan exceeds the current market value of your home. If you're in this category, keep reading.

The combo strategy is a two-step process that combines two of my favorite mortgage foreclosure tools – modification and Chapter 13 bankruptcy. Here's how it works.

First, you negotiate a mortgage modification using all of the techniques that we discussed in Chapter 6. This should allow you get your mortgage payments to an affordable level, probably based on 31% of your gross income. This should also eliminate your mortgage arrearages, as they will likely be "rolled back" into the mortgage balance.

Then, you should file a Chapter 13 bankruptcy. As we discussed in Chapter 7, you can then "strip off" the second mortgage and eliminate that payment. In addition, as we discussed, you should be able to modify or eliminate many of your other debts.

The net result of this comb strategy is lower mortgage payments, no more second mortgage payments, and a repayment plan you can more easily live with and succeed under. Your payments are dramatically reduced, and you are much less upside-down on your mortgage, since the debt tied up in your second mortgage has disappeared.

And now you know why it's my favorite strategy.

Yes, this is a short chapter. But, the combo strategy deserves its own chapter. It's very powerful if used properly. I hope it works for you!

SECTION 2

Let It Go – Strategies for Leaving Your Home

Chapter Nine

Let It Go – Strategies for Leaving Your Home

In the last section, we spent a lot of time discussing the best ways to save your home. However, in many cases, the best solution is to simply let it go. Sometimes, letting your home go is the only answer.

If you've determined that your best option is to sell or walk away from your home, there are many things that you need to consider about the best way to do this. Almost every option for leaving your home, other than a simple sale, carries risks and liabilities. The trick is to find the option that causes the least pain.

In this section, we'll talk about several ways to let your home go and discuss the best ways to minimize the problems that come from each option.

As I mentioned earlier, foreclosure defense options hinge on one simple question:

Do I want to keep the house... or let it go?

Say you own a $500,000 house and have a mortgage of $480,000. (At least you're not upside-down, like a huge percentage of Florida homeowners.) That's the good news; the bad news is you were injured and are living on $1,500 a month disability payments – and that's all you will earn for the foreseeable future. No matter how much you may want to, you will not be able to keep the house.

You simply can't afford it... and no legal strategies will ever overcome that fact.

You'll have to let it go. But what are your options?

In this chapter, we'll review all of the options available to you once you realize that keeping the house just doesn't make sense. This can often be a difficult decision to make, and I spend a lot of time with my clients discussing the cold reality of making strict financial decisions. This usually involves a lot of tears and tissues. But, sometimes the right decision is to let the house go.

Once we've decided that this is the only option, my goal for my clients is to minimize the financial fallout from letting the house go. Almost every option carries a cost of some kind. The trick is to find the option that hurts the least. Let's spend some time looking at these options now and hopefully find the best option for you too.

Normal Sale

This first option should be obvious, but often it is not. If you have a little equity in your home, and you either decide you don't want to keep the house or know you won't be able to keep the house – just sell it. Some of my clients are in the middle of foreclosure and yet are trying to hang on to the house because of the equity.

If you have equity – sell it! Don't get greedy, and don't be penny-wise and pound-foolish. Contact a Realtor, list the home, and take what you can. If you are in the foreclosure process, in a few months much if not all of your equity will be gone... leaving you with nothing. If you decide to let the house go, just do it.

Deed-in-Lieu of Foreclosure

A deed-in-lieu of foreclosure is the process where you give your home back to the lender because you are no longer able – or sometimes willing – to make payments. The "deed" is provided "in lieu" of foreclosure, but the end result is the same: The lender sells the property in order to get part or all of the loan balance you owe.

A few legal documents are required. You may need to sign an Agreement in Lieu of Foreclosure, and a quit claim deed (which basically says you relinquish all legal claims to the property.) The Agreement specifies the terms and conditions of the deed-in-lieu, the quit claim deed conveys legal ownership of the property to the lender. (Think of one as the contract and the other as the deed.)

The end result is like saying, "Take it back. We're done. No foreclosure or other legal processes are necessary."

Why would you pursue this option? The main goal is to avoid a "deficiency" on the property. A deficiency means you owe more than it's worth. If the property goes to foreclosure auction and the purchase price is lower than the amount you owed, the lender can come after you for that deficiency. (Often they don't, but in the foreclosure process the lender does retain the right to pursue deficiency judgments. Think of foreclosure as the gift that could keep on *taking*.)

In effect the deed-in-lieu makes the process a little easier and less time-consuming for the lender; in return, they give up the right to pursue a deficiency judgment. This is the traditional reason that someone would want to do a deed-in-lieu.

However, you should know that lenders have become much more aggressive in pursuing deficiency claims. During the last year, I have seen lenders become unwilling to waive a deficiency claim for doing a deed-in-lieu., and instead are "reserving the right" to pursue a deficiency. I don't allow my clients to enter into a deed-in-lieu agreement unless the lender specifically states they will not pursue a deficiency. You shouldn't either.

As part of the Agreement, the lender marks the homeowner's mortgage as paid and provides documentation stating the debt is canceled and the lender has waived the right to seeking a deficiency judgment.

Keep in mind lenders generally prefer to pursue foreclosure rather than accept a deed-in-lieu. If you have other liens on the property, like a second mortgage, an IRS lien, or other tax liens, the lender is stuck with those liens if they accept a deed-in-lieu. A foreclosure wipes out secondary or junior liens, making the process much easier for a lender when those liens exist.

So, if you don't have other liens on the property, a deed-in-lieu might be a smart choice.

If you do have other liens, you can ask the lender about a deed-in-lieu, but the lender may be unwilling to offer that option.

Short Sale

If you've heard any real estate terms lately, I feel sure one of the terms you heard is "short sale." There is nothing complicated about a short sale: A short sale is the sale of a property for less than the amount owed on the mortgage(s). In "short," you sell for less than you owe. That's the situation many Florida homeowners find themselves in; if they want to sell their homes, they'll have to take less than what they owe. Hence a short sale.

For example, let's say a house appraises for a market value of $250,000. The homeowner has a first mortgage in the amount of $275,000 and a second mortgage in the amount of $50,000. In that case there is no equity left in the property; the house is worth $250,000 but the mortgages total $325,000. (Sadly, this is a very typical situation.)

In order to sell the house under the above condition, the lender will have to agree to let you do so. The lender "owns" the house, so they have to give you permission to make a short sale. If they do, the second mortgage holder may get a few thousand dollars, with the remainder going to the first mortgage holder. (If the house goes to foreclosure, the second mortgage holder – and any other junior lien holders – will get nothing. Typically the second mortgage holders agree to short sales because at least they get *something* – something is always better than nothing.)

Sounds great, right? Not so fast. While a short sale does avoid foreclosure and can avoid a deficiency judgment, there are disadvantages as well. Let's look at the positives and negatives of short sales.

Credit Score Impact

One of the big myths about short sales is that they don't affect your credit as much as a foreclosure. However, this is just a myth. In reality, you will lose just as many points on your credit report with a short sale as with a foreclosure. This misconception arises because a foreclosure appears in the "Public Records" section of your credit report, along with bankruptcies and judgments. A short sale (and a deed-in-lieu, by the way) will not appear as a public record on your credit report. Therefore, many people assume that a foreclosure has a larger credit score impact. However, the credit bureaus report a short sale as a "settled debt", a "charge-off", or a "short sale." All of these descriptions are negative entries on your credit report and will lower your credit score just as much as a "foreclosure" entry in the Public Records section of the credit report. So, be careful if your primary goal in completing a short sale is to save your credit.

Future Mortgage Qualification

A short sale may allow you to qualify for a new mortgage much more quickly than if you are foreclosed on. In general terms, a conventional mortgage lender may allow you to qualify for a mortgage two years after a short sale – if you are foreclosed on, a conventional mortgage lender will typically require you to wait five years before you are able to qualify. (Where the FHA is concerned, you will probably have to wait three years whether you do a short sale or are foreclosed on.) So if you are hoping to buy another house in the relatively near future, a short sale may make that possible.

Deficiency

The primary goal of a short sale should be to get all lenders (first and second mortgage holders) to agree not to pursue a deficiency judgment. If you don't get the second mortgage holder to agree and you do a short sale, the second mortgage holder will come after you. They will sue you personally; if your second mortgage was for $50,000, they will sue for that amount. If, however, you also plan to declare bankruptcy, you may not care about deficiency judgments. Otherwise, the goal is to get all mortgage holders to agree *not* to seek collection of the deficiency.

Recently lenders have been reserving the right to seek deficiencies; don't do a short sale under those conditions. (Or have your lawyer explain that you can simply declare bankruptcy if the deal is not consummated.) Be careful about what you sign: Don't sign a short sale agreement unless deficiency judgment rights are waived – or the transaction is part of an overall strategy you and your lawyer have developed.

Tax Liability

The potential tax liability of entering into a short sale is perhaps my biggest concern. This is a problem that most promoters of short sales seem to "gloss over" or not understand. You see, the IRS considers canceled or settled debt as income. Say the lenders agree to a short sale in the example above; you sell the house for $250,000, the mortgages totaled $325,000, so the total the sale was "short" is $75,000. The $75,000 difference may be considered income by the IRS, and the lenders will send you and the IRS 1099 forms reporting that income. The IRS will assume you "made" $75,000 (even though none of that money ended up in your pocket) and you'll owe income taxes on $75,000. Since no money was withheld like it is on a normal paycheck, you'll have to come up with the tax. (For a good explanation of this issue, download Publication 4681 – Canceled Debts, Foreclosures, Repossessions and Abandonments - from the IRS at www.irs.gov.)

Short sales and foreclosures can result in cancelled debt and a potential tax liability.

But there are ways to get around the tax liability. Let's look at the three primary ways that you can avoid having to pay the IRS for letting your house go.

Mortgage Forgiveness Debt Relief Act of 2007

On December 20, 2007, Congress passed the Mortgage Forgiveness Debt Relief Act of 2007 (the "Act") to minimize the tax problems associated with the housing crisis. Because so many homes were worth less than the mortgage loans, homeowners across America were getting large tax bills as a result of letting their homes go. The Act was a way to stop this.

Unfortunately, many people don't fully understand the Act's guidelines. You see, the Act doesn't apply in every case. I can't tell you how many times I've argued with realtors and real estate professionals who assume that this Act wipes out tax liability on all short sales. That is not always the case.

I want my clients to understand all of the problems that come with any foreclosure solution and potential tax liability is a real problem with short sales. Because I want you to understand the problems too, let's look at the Act's guidelines to see if it will help you to avoid tax liability:

- The house must be your principal residence. The house cannot be a second home. It can't be an investment property that you rent to others. You must live there as your principle residence. If the house is not your principle residence, the deficiency is taxable.

- The debt must have been used to acquire, construct, or substantially improve the principle residence. Sound complicated? It's not. Let's look at a simple scenario to illustrate the point. Say you have a first mortgage for $250,000 on your home; when you purchased the property it was worth $275,000, so that entire amount went to acquiring your principle residence. Then real estate values skyrocketed; at one time your home was worth $350,000, and you took out a second mortgage for $50,000. But you didn't use that money to improve the property – to add on, build a deck, or renovate your kitchen – but instead used it to go on vacation, pay off a few credit cards, and buy a motorcycle. (After all, it's your money and you can spend it as you please, right?) Now the home is worth $250,000. The second mortgage debt you took on did not improve your principle residence – and the deficiency is not excluded under the Debt Relief Act.

If you don't meet the guidelines, your 1099 income is considered income and you will face a tax liability. That might be okay, especially if the house is your only real debt and you would prefer to pay the income tax on the deficiency rather than declare bankruptcy or go through foreclosure.

If you do meet the guidelines, the Act provides relief from the tax repercussions of a short sale. Decisions about whether to do a short sale should be made on a case by case basis, taking into account your individual circumstances, needs, and long-term goals.

Bankruptcy

The second major way to avoid tax liability from a short sale or foreclosure is to file bankruptcy. The Bankruptcy Code has a provision that negates the income provision in the Tax Code. If the Bankruptcy Code didn't contain this provision, everyone that filed bankruptcy would have tax consequences because all of the debt in the bankruptcy is forgiven.

Although I haven't seen any case law to support this, I believe that you should file the bankruptcy BEFORE the short sale or foreclosure sale occurs. This is because the income is generated when the debt is forgiven. You may be able to wipe out a deficiency from a short sale after the fact, but I believe that the income event that triggers the tax liability happens at the time of the short sale or foreclosure sale. So, it you're planning on filing a bankruptcy anyway, file it before the short sale or foreclosure – just to be safe.

Insolvency

The third major way to avoid tax liability is to prove that you were "insolvent" at the time of the short sale or foreclosure. If you receive a 1099 from your mortgage lender after a short sale or foreclosure, you can file IRS Form 982 with your tax return stating that you were insolvent at the time. The IRS uses a very simple test for insolvency: If your liabilities exceed your assets, you are considered to be insolvent. In the last chapter you determined your net assets and your liabilities – you know whether insolvency is a valid claim you can make.

However, you should know that the amount of your insolvency is important. To get the full benefit of this provision, your insolvency amount must exceed the amount of debt that was forgiven. So, for example, let's say that you sold your home in a short sale transaction for $30,000 less than the amount of the mortgage debt. Therefore, the lender forgave $30,000 of your debt to make the short sale work. This $30,000 would normally be considered income to you.

However, after completing the insolvency worksheet from IRS Publication 4681, you discover that your liabilities exceed your assets by $40,000. Because the $40,000 of "insolvency" exceeds the $30,000 of debt forgiveness, you won't have any tax liability.

But, let's say that instead you discover that your liabilities only exceed your assets by $20,000. In this case, because your insolvency is only $20,000, the difference between the debt forgiveness amount of $30,000 and your $20,000 insolvency amount is income to you. In this case, that means that you must pay taxes on the $10,000 difference.

If you think that the insolvency exception may help you, I encourage you to speak with a tax professional. Although the concept of insolvency is simple, the actual calculations may not be so simple. Review Publication 4681 and get some professional advice. There's nothing worse than getting a big tax bill on top of losing your house!

Foreclosure

If you can't do a normal sale, can't do deed-in-lieu, can't do a short sale... nothing else works... foreclosure is a reality. If you plan on declaring bankruptcy anyway, let it go. At the end of the day the lender will get the property back somehow... so just let it go and focus on ways to make your life better in other areas. While there are many ways to fight and delay the process, foreclosure may be inevitable.

The foreclosure process is just a way of getting the title to the property transferred from you to someone else, usually the lender. Many of my clients are confused about the foreclosure process. For example, they often think that when I file a bankruptcy case for them, that the house will just go back as part of the bankruptcy. They're confused when they keep getting notices of the foreclosure process after I file their bankruptcy case.

You don't need to be afraid of the foreclosure process. If you've decided to let your home go, and you weren't able or willing to sell the house or enter into a deed-in-lieu or short sale, then foreclosure is the only option available. That's OK. Just let it go.

However, make sure that you're prepared. If you're facing a deficiency or tax liability from the foreclosure sale, think about filing a Chapter 7 bankruptcy case. This will eliminate any deficiency or tax liability, and take care of most other debts as well. We'll talk about this option in the next chapter.

In addition, once the foreclosure sale option is the only choice, make sure that you understand the timelines. Go back and review our discussion of the foreclosure timeline so that you have a good understanding on when you'll need to be out of the house. There's nothing worse than seeing a 24-hour eviction notice attached to your door. Don't let this happen to you! Know the timelines, make the right moves, and protect yourself. That's my wish for you!

Chapter Ten

Chapter 7 Bankruptcy

The Chapter 7 bankruptcy is really in a class by itself when we're talking about the foreclosure process. Although it can be used as a tool in your foreclosure defense, the defense is only temporary. As we discussed before, the automatic stay provided by the Bankruptcy Code will stop a foreclosure case regardless of whether you file a Chapter 7 bankruptcy case or a Chapter 13 bankruptcy case. However, with a Chapter 7, the lender will ask the bankruptcy judge for relief from the automatic stay – and the judge will grant that relief.

Therefore, a Chapter 7 bankruptcy is only a temporary solution to the foreclosure. I generally use it as a tool in the overall process. So, for example, if my client is able to modify their mortgage, I may file a Chapter 7 bankruptcy to wipe out other delinquent debts.

More often than not, however, I'll file a Chapter 7 bankruptcy for clients who are letting their homes go. As we discussed in the last chapter, most of the options for letting your home go come with some potential liability, generally a deficiency or tax bill. The Chapter 7 bankruptcy is an effective tool for "cleaning up" all of the problems associated with letting your home go and for addressing all of the other debt at the same time.

Let's take a few minutes now and look at the Chapter 7 bankruptcy and see if it may be right for you.

Chapter 7 Basics

Differences Between Chapter 7 and Chapter 13

Chapter 7 bankruptcy shares many similarities with Chapter 13 bankruptcy. For that reason I won't go into as much detail about the process, but there are things to keep in mind.

First, a Chapter 7 bankruptcy does not use a repayment plan. Instead of setting up a repayment plan, a Chapter 7 Trustee gathers up your assets, sells (liquidates) them, and uses the proceeds to pay off your creditors. This is why Chapter 7 is called a "liquidation" bankruptcy.

In reality, most consumers in Florida who file a Chapter 7 bankruptcy case lose few, if any, assets as a result of filing the bankruptcy. In my experience, approximately 95% of my clients have "no asset" cases. This means that they have no assets to lose in the bankruptcy case.

The reason that most consumers have no asset cases is because there is little or no equity in their "stuff" or it's just not worth the hassle to take and sell. As you may know, "equity" is the value of the property after liens on that property. So, as we've discussed throughout this book, if your home is worth $250,000 and you owe $200,000, you have $50,000 in equity in your home.

However, the reality for most Floridians right now is that they owe more on their assets than they're worth. So, for example, if you own a car that has a current market value of $15,000, but you owe $25,000 on that car, you don't have any equity in the car. If a Chapter 7 Trustee took your car and tried to sell it at auction, they would have to pay the lien on the car before distributing any money to creditors. Because there's nothing to gain by doing this, you keep the car – as long as you keep making payments to the car lender.

Another reason that most people have no asset bankruptcy cases is because we have "exemptions" under Florida law that protect certain assets from seizure in the bankruptcy case. One of the primary goals of bankruptcy is to give you a "fresh start". If creditors could take everything from you, it would be very difficult for you to get that fresh start. This is why we have exemptions.

Although the Bankruptcy Code provides a list of federal exemptions, Florida has "opted out" of the federal exemptions and uses its own list of exemptions. Perhaps the most valuable exemption is called the "homestead" exemption, which protects all of the equity in your house. (Of course, this isn't as valuable as it used to be.) You also get exemptions for vehicle equity and personal property, and most retirement accounts are fully exempt. These exemptions work with liens on your assets to protect most people from losing anything in the typical Chapter 7 case.

The final reason that most people don't lose any assets in the Chapter 7 case is because many assets aren't worth taking, even if they're not covered by an exemption. Chapter 7 cases are administered by "Trustees" whose job is to find any non-exempt assets, liquidate these assets, and give the proceeds from their sale to your creditors.

To encourage this process, the Bankruptcy Code allows Chapter 7 Trustees to keep as much as 25% of whatever they liquidate. So, in essence, being a Chapter 7 Trustee is a business. As a result, they always need to look at cases from a cost-benefit standpoint – what will it cost to take an asset versus what how much money will be generated by the sale of that asset.

This drives every decision they make. So, for example, household goods like couches, lamps and tables may not be covered by exemptions. However, Chapter 7 Trustees rarely take these items because the cost of taking them almost always exceeds the revenue that will be generated by the sale of these assets. This analysis applies to old boats, trailers, cars, etc. If it's not worth taking, the Trustee won't take it.

Therefore, even if you appear to have assets, you may not lose them when you file a Chapter 7 case. So, don't be afraid of a Chapter 7 bankruptcy because you're afraid of losing property – you probably won't.

The other major difference between a Chapter 7 bankruptcy and a Chapter 13 is the amount of time that you're actually "in" bankruptcy. Under a Chapter 13 case, you are in bankruptcy for three to five years. In a Chapter 7 case, you're generally only in the bankruptcy case for four to six months. Therefore, once the Chapter 7 process is complete, you're done. You can move on with your life and get a fresh start.

How Debts are Resolved in a Chapter 7 Case

You get a fresh start in a Chapter 7 case because most of your unsecured debts are "discharged". However, not all unsecured debts are dischargeable, and other debts receive special treatment. How these debts are resolved in a Chapter 7 case depend on the type of debt and the creditor.

You may remember in our discussion of Chapter 13 bankruptcy that the bankruptcy laws don't treat all creditors equally. As we discussed, the bankruptcy laws divide creditors into three major categories - priority creditors, secured creditors, and unsecured creditors.

Priority Creditors

The bankruptcy laws allow some creditors to receive payment from you before other creditors receive payment. These creditors are called priority creditors. The order of payment to creditors is important because in most bankruptcy cases, there isn't enough money to repay all creditors. Therefore, the creditors with a higher priority under the bankruptcy laws receive a greater percentage of their claim than the creditors with a lower priority.

The bankruptcy laws specify several creditors that have priority claims, and also set forth a priority order among these creditors. The most common priority creditors include: (1) the bankruptcy trustee; (2) your employees; (3) your former spouse; and, (4) governmental entities to which you owe taxes and penalties.

In a Chapter 7 case, priority creditors receive payment before other creditors, and you may not be able to escape them after the bankruptcy. For example, let's say that you owe the IRS money for your 1040 taxes from last year. Because this particular debt doesn't meet one of the exceptions to discharge it, it would be one of the first creditors in line for distribution if the Trustee did sell any of your assets. And, if you didn't have any assets to liquidate, you'd still owe the IRS for this debt after your Chapter 7 case was completed.

Secured Creditors

As we discussed before, "secured" or "unsecured" identifies whether your debt is backed up by one of your assets. Creditors refer to this as "collateral". A creditor is secured if you pledge one of your assets as collateral for the loan. If you don't repay this secured creditor, then the creditor may seize the asset that you pledged. This gives the creditor some security for the loan, other than your simple promise to repay.

The most common secured creditors include mortgage lenders and car lenders. These lenders take a security interest in your home or car, and can take your home or car if you fail to repay the loan as agreed.

Under the Bankruptcy Code, you have three ways to address a secured debt; reaffirm the debt, surrender the collateral, or redeem the collateral. Let's look at these choices now.

Reaffirm the Debt

The first option you have with secured debts in a Chapter 7 case is to reaffirm the debt. This means that you just keep making payments as if the bankruptcy never happened. You sign a "reaffirmation agreement", keep the collateral, and keep making payments. This happens frequently with automobile loans and mortgages that aren't delinquent when you file the Chapter 7 case.

Many of my clients are afraid that they'll lose their car or home if they file a Chapter 7 case. But, if you can afford the payments, want to keep the collateral, and are current, you can easily keep your stuff. No problem.

Surrender the Collateral

But what happens if you can't afford to make the payments on secured debts, or simply don't want the collateral any longer. That's not a problem either. In the Chapter 7, you can simply "surrender" the collateral to the lender and wipe out any liability from doing this.

This happens frequently with cars and homes. Many of my clients owe much more on their car loans than the car is worth, and the monthly payments are much too high. By surrendering your car in the bankruptcy, you can get out from under oppressive loans and payments and get your fresh start.

This applies to home mortgages as well. Many of my clients have multiple investment properties that are upside down and aren't producing income. The Chapter 7 bankruptcy allows these clients to surrender the investment properties in the bankruptcy and eliminate any liabilities that may come from doing this.

This is also why I explained that I file a Chapter 7 bankruptcy case for my clients that want to walk away from their primary homes. The Chapter 7 bankruptcy allows them to surrender the house, get away from the loan and payments, and eliminate any deficiency or tax liability associated with the surrender. So, this is a very powerful part of the Chapter 7 bankruptcy.

Redeem the Collateral

The final option that you may choose with secured property is to "redeem" the collateral. This means that you pay the fair market value for the property at the time you file the bankruptcy case. If you can come up with a lump sum payment for the fair market value, you can keep the property and eliminate the remaining balance of the loan.

For example, let's say that you own a car and you really want to keep it. However, you owe $30,000 for the car but it's only worth $20,000. You can redeem the car by paying the creditor $20,000 and you get to keep the car. The remaining $10,000 of the loan is eliminated by the bankruptcy.

Of course, the trick to redeeming property is that you need to have the lump sum payment to complete the redemption. If you can't come up with this lump sum payment, you'll need to reaffirm the debt or surrender the property. (There are lenders that will finance redemptions of vehicles in a Chapter 7 case. They typically charge high interest rates. But, depending on how much debt is eliminated in the redemption process, it very often makes sense to use one of these lenders to complete the redemption).

The Fourth Option

OK. I know that I told you there's only three options with secured property, but there's really one more – the fourth option. In the old days, we'd call this option the "ride through". This option means you don't do anything with the collateral.

Traditionally, we'd use this technique with auto loans. Instead of reaffirming a car loan that was upside down, the debtor could just keep making payments and not remain contractually liable for that debt.

However, when Congress passed the Bankruptcy Abuse Prevention and Consumer Protection Act in 2005, it attempted to eliminate the ride through option. As a result, the ride through option isn't used nearly as often.

But, there's one type of loan that always cries out for this option – second mortgages that are really unsecured. How can a second mortgage be unsecured? If you remember, we talked about this issue when we looked at Chapter 13 bankruptcy. In a Chapter 13, you can "strip off" a second mortgage if the first mortgage balance exceeds the value of the property. If so, the second mortgage is really unsecured against the house.

In a Chapter 7 case, you can't strip off the mortgage like you can in a Chapter 13 case. However, when you file the Chapter 7, ALL of your dischargeable debts are eliminated, unless you reaffirm them. This includes secured debts.

So, think of it this way. When you file the Chapter 7, you don't owe the mortgage debt any longer, but your house still does because the secured lender retains a lien against the house. If you don't pay the mortgage after you file the Chapter 7, the lender can foreclose on your house, but they can't ever pursue you personally for the debt.

If that's true, why would you want to encourage the mortgage lender to foreclose on your house? Because the lender won't do it. Think about it. If the second mortgage is upside down because the first mortgage balance exceeds the value of the property, there's no reason that the second mortgage lender would want to foreclose on your house. If it did, all of the proceeds from the foreclosure sale would go to the first mortgage company. So, why do it?

When a client has an unsecured second mortgage, but wants to keep their home, I encourage them to not sign a reaffirmation agreement for the second mortgage. Signing the reaffirmation agreement just puts them back on the hook personally for the mortgage debt. This could really become a problem if they ultimately give up their home down the road.

Very often, unsecured second mortgage lenders are willing to settle for pennies on the dollar after a client files a Chapter 7 case and fails to enter into a reaffirmation agreement. These lenders know that they can never pursue the client, and it will be many years, if ever, before they could receive any proceeds from a foreclosure sale.

So, if you plan to keep your home, and have an unsecured second mortgage, please be very careful when deciding whether to reaffirm that debt. I would advise against it. Then, when the bankruptcy is finished, contact the second mortgage lender and try to negotiate a settlement with them. (You need to negotiate with them because the lien will just sit there against your home. Some day, when you go to sell or refinance your home, the lien will appear and you'll need to pay the lender to complete your sale or refinance. By that point, your home will probably have increased in value and you will have to pay more to the lender to resolve the lien. So, do it now while you have some negotiating leverage!)

Unsecured Creditors

Finally, as we discussed before, an unsecured creditor is a creditor that does not have the safety of collateral to ensure repayment of the loan. Unsecured creditors include major bank cards like Visa and MasterCard, and department stores that issue their own credit cards. Other unsecured creditors may include your landlord, local utility, cable, and telephone companies, and medical providers. In fact, most creditors are unsecured creditors.

In a Chapter 7 bankruptcy case, unsecured creditors generally receive very little, if any, of their total claim. This is because of the priority system that the bankruptcy code establishes among and between your creditors. Secured creditors can seize their collateral from you, and repay some, or all, of the loan. Priority creditors receive first payment from the remaining assets or income. And the poor unsecured creditors receive anything that's left.

Therefore, at the end of your Chapter 7 case, most of your unsecured debts will be eliminated. We call these debts "discharged" debts. Discharged debts are debts that your creditors can never force you to repay. Debts become "discharged" towards the end of the bankruptcy case, when the bankruptcy trustee and judge are satisfied that you have completed your obligations under the Bankruptcy Code.

However, not all debts are dischargeable. Certain types of debts are "nondischargeable". Congress believed that certain types of debts, like student loans, some tax obligations, and child support, are important enough to prevent them from being wiped out in bankruptcy. Therefore, you may still be responsible for repaying some of your debts after the bankruptcy.

The Chapter 7 Process

Now that you understand a little bit about the Chapter 7 bankruptcy, let me give you a quick overview of the process so you'll understand how it works.

After talking to your attorney about whether it's appropriate to file a Chapter 7 bankruptcy, you must first complete a credit counseling course. The first course is designed to see whether you have any alternatives to filing bankruptcy. There are many ways to take this course, and many approved vendors. Typically, you can complete the course over the phone or online – usually in less than one hour.

You will be asked to provide you income, expenses, assets and liabilities and will review the different types of bankruptcy cases and other non-bankruptcy options. For the most part, your completion is a given. I have never referred a client to a credit counselor who then said that the client was ineligible to file a bankruptcy. This is because I know that the client needs to file the bankruptcy – the counselor just confirms this. So, don't be afraid of this course – it's a no-brainer.

Once you complete the first credit counseling course, the counselor will send your attorney a copy of the course completion certificate. With this certificate in hand, the attorney is free to file your case with the bankruptcy court.

In the old days, we would do this by physically handing the bankruptcy clerk a copy of the bankruptcy documents. Now, however, it's all done electronically. As a result, I can file a bankruptcy case within minutes from my office. (This is extremely important when we're talking about an emergency filing to stop a foreclosure sale!).

At the moment the case is filed, the automatic stay goes into effect. As you recall from our discussion before, the automatic stay stops any collection activity against you – creditors can't call you, write you, sue you, or continue to sue you. Everything stops the moment you file the case. I always tell my clients to answer the phone once I file the bankruptcy case and give each creditor the bankruptcy case number. This stops all calls that same day and goes a long way towards stopping the stress of creditor harassment.

Within four to five weeks after the bankruptcy case is filed, you must go to the Meeting of Creditors. Although this sounds ominous, there's usually not much to it. At this meeting, the Chapter 7 Trustee will interview you and creditors have a right to do the same.

In reality, creditors rarely show for the Meeting of Creditors. In addition, there's no judge and no courtroom. Generally, five to eight people are scheduled during the same 30-minute time block. That means for most consumers, the Meeting of Creditors lasts for three to five minutes.

A good attorney will fully prepare you for the questions you'll receive, so you'll know what to expect. Most of my clients are still scared to death before the Meeting. But, without fail, they all walk away and say "That was easy". Yeah. I told you. It will be the same for you too.

The final part of the process is to take your second credit-counseling course. The second course is called "Debtor Education" and is supposed to keep you out of trouble in the future. It will give you information about budgeting and money-management. Many of my clients actually enjoy this class. Like the first credit-counseling course, you can take the Debtor Education course by telephone or online and generally takes about one hour.

Once you complete your Debtor Education course, you're home free. Now, you're just waiting for different time frames to run and for the bankruptcy clerk to process your discharge. In my area, it generally takes four to six months to complete the entire bankruptcy process, from start to finish. In reality, you're only involved in the first month. After that, you're just waiting for the discharge to come in the mail. It's a pretty simple process, isn't it?

But, what about your credit? Won't the bankruptcy destroy your credit for years to come? I'm glad you asked.

Credit After Bankruptcy

One of the most common reasons that people avoid bankruptcy is because they're afraid that it will destroy their credit for years to come. However, the reality is usually very different.

As we discussed with Chapter 13 bankruptcy, filing a Chapter 7 bankruptcy will very often improve your credit scores – usually substantially. Many of my clients are able – with some help from me – to have credit scores in the mid-600's within one year after their bankruptcy. This is usually much higher than when they filed the bankruptcy.

There are two primary reasons for this and both have to do with the way that credit scores are calculated. As we saw before, the most common credit scoring model is the "FICO" score developed by the Fair Isaac

Corporation. Under the most common model, 30% of the score is based on the "Amounts Owed" on your debts.

A large part of that calculation is based on the ratio of your balances to your credit lines. Ideally, that ratio should be less than 30%. So, for example, if you have credit card limits of $10,000, you should owe less than $3,000 on those credit cards to get the best FICO score.

Unfortunately, many of my clients have ratios that exceed 100% because the balances on their credit cards are higher than the credit limits on those credit cards. This will absolutely kill your credit score – even without late payments. (This is why someone who has never missed a payment on a debt can have a lower credit score than someone who has been late on payments.)

Once you receive your bankruptcy discharge, debts are supposed to be reclassified as "Included in Bankruptcy" on your credit report. If the creditor is properly updating the information, the credit account of someone in bankruptcy should report with a zero balance. This resets the ratios and helps to raise the credit score.

In addition, accounts included in a Chapter 7 case should not report as "late". Under the most common FICO score, 35% of the credit score is based on "Payment History" If you're late on your credit accounts when you file the Chapter 7, that information should be removed once you receive your discharge.

Having creditors update accounts that you included in your bankruptcy case as "Included in Bankruptcy" is the fastest way to improve your credit scores after you file. But, you should understand that creditors very often fail to properly update this information, even when they know that you filed the bankruptcy case.

A Creditor's failure to update accounts after a bankruptcy is unacceptable and potentially subjects the creditor to claims under the Fair Credit Reporting Act, the Fair Debt Collection Practices Act, and the Bankruptcy

Code. If a creditor refuses to update your account, immediately contact your attorney.

However, you should know that many bankruptcy attorneys don't really understand consumer laws like the FCRA and the FDCPA. I'm working to change this by teaching other attorneys about the interplay of the FCRA, the FDCPA and bankruptcy. But, it's a slow process. If your attorney can't help you, feel free to contact my office or an attorney that specializes in consumer laws like the FCRA and the FDCPA. I want you to get your fresh start, and it's really hard to do that if you can't increase your credit scores because the creditors won't follow the law!

Final Words on Chapter 7 Bankruptcy

So, bankruptcy really isn't the scary nightmare than many people say it is. In reality, it can be a wonderful tool to help you get our from under crushing debt and get your life back. The goal of the Chapter 7 bankruptcy process is to give you a fresh start. If it's appropriate for you, let it be your fresh start too!

SECTION 3

Credit After Foreclosure and Other Mortgage Problems

Chapter Eleven

Credit After Foreclosure and Other Mortgage Problems

I know that you may be in the middle of trying to save your home and keep everything together. So, your credit may be the last thing on your mind – right now. But, I urge you to step aside from your worries and start to think about your credit and how it will be affected by the actions you're taking to save or walk away from your home.

Like it or not, credit controls our lives. I want you to be able to take control of your credit situation and get back to having good credit again – soon.

So, I've decided to take you on a journey to restore your credit. If you're not ready for this step, just put this book aside and come back to it when you're ready.

But, if you're ready to get back on track, I'm ready to show you a complete system for repairing and restoring your credit. If you're ready, let's go!

I've talked about credit after bankruptcy, and how filing bankruptcy can actually improve your credit scores. But what if you don't file bankruptcy as part of your foreclosure/delinquent mortgage strategy? Is there hope for you, or are you doomed with bad credit for years to come?

As we discussed earlier, virtually any strategy that you pursue for addressing a delinquent mortgage will result in damaged credit and lower credit scores. This could prevent you from refinancing your current home or purchasing another home in the future.

Fortunately, I've got some good news for you. There are many ways that you can improve your credit after you've experienced problems with your mortgage. Therefore, you're not necessarily doomed to having late mortgage payments and foreclosure ruin your credit forever.

Although the entire system for restoring credit after foreclosure and other mortgage delinquencies is beyond the scope of this book, I want to give you a broad overview of the laws that regulate credit, the credit scoring system and some of the techniques for making this system work for you rather than against you.

Learn the Laws

To improve your credit after a foreclosure or other mortgage problem, you need to understand your rights under federal law. I have not included the full text of the various statutes that we'll discuss, because these statutes are VERY long and would take up too much of the space in this book. Instead, throughout the rest of this section, I'll give you the exact language from these various statutes whenever you really NEED it. However, with that said, you SHOULD read the full text of these statutes.

[If you want to see the full text of any of the statutes that I discuss throughout this book, make sure that you visit my website at www.SaveYourFloridaHomeNow.com. In addition to the full text of these statutes, you'll find many additional sample letters, forms, worksheets, and other resources to help you on your journey!]

Federal Laws

There are many federal laws that protect your various credit rights. For example, the Equal Credit Opportunity Act prohibits creditors from denying credit based on sex, race, marital status, religion, national origin, or age. The Truth in Lending Act requires that creditors provide written disclosures about the cost of credit and the terms of repayment before you enter into a credit transaction. And, the Fair Credit Billing Act establishes procedures for resolving billing errors on your credit card accounts.

However, there's really only three federal laws that you'll frequently use during your efforts to "repair" your credit. The first, and by far the most important, is the Fair Credit Reporting Act. The next federal law that you may find helpful in your quest for prosperity is the Fair Debt Collection Practices Act. This Act regulates collection agencies in the collection of debt. Portions of the Fair Debt Collection Practices Act that are extremely useful for credit repair after foreclosure or other mortgage problems. So, we'll look at these specific sections of the law and see how they can magically transform your credit reports and credit scores.

Finally, I want to introduce you to the Credit Repair Organizations Act. This federal law regulates people and companies that "repair" credit for profit – including me. You may find that you want assistance in your credit repair efforts. That's OK. But, you need to make sure that the lawyer or credit repair company you hire is competent, honest, and follows the Credit Repair Organizations Act. So, I'll tell you what this law requires from lawyers and credit repair companies and talk about whether you should hire someone to help you repair your credit.

The Fair Credit Reporting Act

The Fair Credit Reporting Act, 15 U.S.C. §§ 1681-1681x ("FCRA"), was passed by Congress in 1970, and became effective on April 25, 1971. At that time, there were many credit reporting companies spread throughout the country. As creditors increasingly used credit reports provided by these companies for their credit decisions, Congress realized that any errors in these credit reports could prevent consumers from obtaining goods or services that they truly deserved. So, the FCRA was Congress' attempt to protect consumers and regulate this growing industry.

Congress has amended the FCRA several times since it first became effective. The most recent major amendment was called the Fair and Accurate Credit Transactions Act of 2003 ("FACTA"). FACTA significantly amended the FCRA and added MANY new protections for consumers. Among other things, the new amendments provided by FACTA allow consumers to receive free annual credit reports, provide extensive protections for identity theft victims, allow consumers to access their credit scores, provide more safeguards for protecting the privacy of information, and preempt many states from enacting legislation that alter the provisions of the FCRA.

To give you an idea of the different rights and obligations provided by the FCRA, as amended by FACTA, let's quickly summarize the FCRA's major provisions. (But remember, you SHOULD read the entire text of the FCRA. Visit our website at www.SaveYourFloridaHomeNow.com to do this.)

1. You Have the Right to Know What's in Your Credit File

The FCRA allows you to obtain all of the information that the consumer reporting agencies ("credit bureaus") have about you in their files. You can receive free annual credit reports for this purpose. In addition, you are entitled to receive free credit reports for several other reasons. You can also pay the credit bureaus to receive this information.

2. You Have the Right to Dispute Incomplete or Inaccurate Information

We're going to spend a GREAT deal of time on this right. In almost every credit report that we see following a major credit problem like foreclosure or other mortgage delinquency, much of the credit information is incomplete and inaccurate. We will help you to use the FCRA to correct this information. This will help to "repair" your credit.

3. Credit Bureaus Must Correct or Delete Inaccurate, Incomplete, or Unverifiable Information

This is one of the ways that we'll use the FCRA to repair your credit. The credit bureaus have a legal obligation to correct or delete inaccurate, incomplete or unverifiable information. We'll make sure that they comply with this legal obligation.

4. Credit Bureaus Cannot Report Outdated Negative Information

This is the official method for removing bad credit information from your credit reports. The FCRA establishes maximum time limits for reporting most types of credit information. Once the specified time period has expired, the credit bureau must remove the information from your credit report.

5. You Have the Right to Access Your Credit Score

Credit scores have become perhaps the MOST important part of the credit-decision process. Until the FACTA amendments, you were not entitled to see the credit scores that your creditors used in deciding whether to grant your request for credit. This was a real problem for many consumers, especially those consumers with bad credit and foreclosures in their credit files. Now, however, you have the right to see the credit score and get a summary of the major factors used to calculate that score.

6. Access to Your Credit File is Limited

The FCRA limits access to your credit report. Only people or companies with a valid need to review your credit may do so. Generally, this list includes creditors, employers, insurers, and landlords.

7. You Must Provide Consent Before Most Employers Can Access Your Credit File

The FCRA requires that you consent before an employer, or potential employer, accesses your credit file. There are some minor exceptions to this, however.

8. You Must Receive Notice if Any Information in Your Credit File is Used Against You

The FCRA requires that you receive notice from anyone who uses any information contained in your credit reports to deny your application for credit, insurance, employment, or that takes any other adverse action against you. That entity must also give you the name, address, and telephone number of the credit bureau that provided the information to them.

9. You May Have the Right to Seek Damages from Violators

This MAY be an important right in your efforts to repair your credit and prosper after foreclosure or other mortgage problem. The FCRA allows you to file lawsuits against credit bureaus (and sometimes creditors) that fail to follow the FCRA's requirements. Filing a lawsuit CAN be a good thing sometimes, but not always. So, use this right wisely.

Final Thoughts on the FCRA

As you'll soon see, the FCRA will provide most of the tools that you'll need during your efforts to repair and correct your credit reports, and credit scores. By taking full advantage of all the protections and obligations set forth in the FCRA, your path to good credit can begin much sooner than you may ever have imagined. But, we have many tools in our tool belt, and we want to share all of them with you. So, let's take a quick look at the next major federal law that you may need to use in your credit repair efforts – the Fair Debt Collection Practices Act.

The Fair Debt Collection Practices Act

The Fair Debt Collection Practices Act, 15 U.S.C. §§ 1692 et seq. ("FDCPA"), was passed by Congress in 1977, and became effective on March 20, 1978. Congress created the FDCPA to combat "abusive, deceptive, and unfair debt collection practices by many debt collectors." In describing its reason for enacting the FDCPA, Congress said that "Abusive debt collection practices contribute to the number of personal bankruptcies, to marital instability, to the loss of jobs, and to invasions of individual privacy." I agree with this.

Many of my clients have suffered through extremely disturbing encounters with aggressive and unscrupulous collection agents. And, unfortunately, I have been forced to repeatedly battle collection agencies on behalf of many other clients, as well. So, I understand how you feel. I hope that you haven't had the "pleasure" of one of these encounters.

Fortunately, the FDCPA can be a VERY strong tool to combat those "bad apple" collection agencies that give the rest of the industry such a bad reputation. However, for our purposes in repairing your credit, we're really only going to use a very small portion of the FDCPA – the section that addresses "debt validation." In a moment, I'm going to explain this section in detail and show you a VERY powerful technique that uses this section to remove collection accounts from your credit report. So, we won't discuss it now.

The Credit Repair Organizations Act

The last major federal law that I want to talk about is the Credit Repair Organizations Act, §§ 1679 – 1679j ("CROA"). Congress passed the CROA in 1996 to prevent abuses in the growing "credit repair" industry. Many fly-by-night companies promised consumers that they could remove 100% of the negative information from their credit reports – for a fee. Unfortunately, this was never the case, and many consumers lost their money and never saw any improvement in their credit or their credit scores.

To combat this abuse, Congress included very specific provisions in the CROA that every company or individual involved in credit repair for a fee must follow. These provisions should protect you from unscrupulous credit repair companies – IF they follow the law. Therefore, IF you hire a credit repair company or professional, make sure that they're following the CROA.

To help you with this, let's look at a summary of the major provisions of the CROA. [But, as always, you should read the entire text of the CROA. You can find this text at www.SaveYourFloridaHomeNow.com.]

1. A Credit Repair Company Must Disclose Your Rights and a Description of Their Services

The CROA requires that credit repair companies provide you with two different disclosures. First, they must give you a disclosure called "Consumer Credit File Rights Under State and Federal Law". The text of this disclosure is provided in full within the CROA. This disclosure lets you know that you can obtain your own credit reports and repair your own credit – without help from the credit repair company. It also tells you that you have a right to cancel your contract with the credit repair company within 3 business days from the date that you signed it. Finally, this disclosure tells you that you have a right to sue the credit repair company for violating the CROA.

The second disclosure that you must receive is a written contract. In this contract, the credit repair company must include the terms and conditions of all payments for service, a full and detailed description of the services that the credit repair company will perform, the credit repair company's name and address, and a "conspicuous statement in bold face type" that you may cancel the contract within 3 business days after signing it.

2. A Credit Repair Company Cannot Charge For Services Until Performed

The CROA says that the credit repair company cannot charge or receive payment for services until the service is "fully performed". This was intended to prevent fly-by-night credit repair companies from taking all of their fees upfront and closing down.

3. A Credit Repair Company Cannot Engage in Prohibited Practices

The CROA specifies a number of practices that credit repair companies must avoid. For example, a credit repair company cannot "make any statement" or counsel another to make any statement that is untrue or misleading regarding your credit worthiness, credit standing, or credit capacity. And, a credit repair company can't make any statement or counsel another to make a statement that alters your identification. Finally, the CROA prohibits credit repair companies from making false claims about their services, or otherwise commit fraud.

Should You Hire An Attorney or Credit Repair Company?

OK. Now that you know some of the basic provisions of the CROA, let's talk about this basic question of credit repair. Should you handle your credit repair yourself, or should you hire an attorney or credit repair company to handle this for you? Well, it depends.

I used to advise my clients to avoid credit repair companies. Instead, I gave them all of the tools that they needed to repair their own credit – just as I'm doing with you in this book. I gave this advice because there weren't very many reputable credit repair companies at that time, and I thought that everyone enjoyed credit repair as much as I do!

But, things have changed a bit since then. First, several reputable credit repair companies have emerged over the years that really do a good job at repairing their clients' credit at a reasonable cost. In fact, I've trained hundreds of attorneys, mortgage brokers, CPA's, and other professionals across the country to repair their clients' credit. These professionals are competent and caring, and do a great job for their clients. So, as long as you find a GOOD credit repair company or professional, it's OK to let them help you with your credit repair efforts.

The second thing that changed my thinking about this issue is that I finally realized that not everyone shares my enthusiasm for credit repair. Many people equate this whole process with public speaking or public nudity – they just don't want to do it. I get that, finally. So, IF you can find a good credit repair company or professional to help you, and you REALLY don't want to do it yourself, then get the help that you need and deserve. (If you don't know where to find a reputable credit repair company or professional, call my office at 407-834-0090 or visit me on the web at www.cpricelawfirm.com. But, remember, you REALLY can do this on your own!)

Final Thoughts on Learning the Law

I don't expect you to become a lawyer and argue the fine points of the federal statutes in court. But, it is important that you understand the different rights that the federal and state statutes offer. Of course, I'll identify and explain the specific section of each statute that you'll need as we get deeper into our discussion of credit, credit scores, and credit reports. But, feel free to read the full text of the statutes if you get the urge to see the whole picture. (You know where to find them). But, for now, let's start looking at some specifics, starting with credit reports.

Chapter Twelve

Credit Reports – What They Are and How to Get Them

To really prosper after a foreclosure or other major mortgage problem, your creditors and future creditors must believe that you will repay any loans that they give you. The best tools that creditors have to make this determination are your credit reports and your credit scores. In this chapter, we'll talk about credit reports, and I'll tell you everything you need to get and read them. Then, in later sections, I'll tell you how to make your reports – and credit scores – appeal to any creditor.

What's a Credit Report?

OK. So let's start with the basics. What is a credit report? For our purposes, a credit report is a collection of information about you that attempts to explain your experience with different creditors. A credit report collects information from many, if not most, of your creditors about how you've handled your loans and debt. It will list which creditors you owe and how much you owe them. It will also show whether you made your payments on time, were sometimes late, or completely failed to repay the debt. And, your credit report may vary depending on which company you receive it from. Therefore, let's look at the companies that create the credit reports.

Consumer Reporting Agencies - We Call Them "Credit Bureaus"

You are the source of great interest, and profit, of many national companies. These companies, known as "consumer reporting agencies" under the Fair Credit Reporting Act, gather financial and other information about you and millions of other consumers across the country. They use this information to make a profit – that's right, they sell your information to make a buck.

These consumer reporting agencies sell your information to businesses and individuals with a "legitimate" need to know something about you. Most often, these businesses are creditors that want to lend you money or otherwise provide you with credit. But, the consumer reporting agencies have many customers that are eager for your information, including prospective employers, landlords, and insurance companies.

All of these businesses and individuals are trying to decide whether you're a "good risk" for whatever it is they're offering to you. If your credit report contains mostly "good" information, then you'll probably receive the loan or service. But, if your credit report contains mostly "bad" information, then you're probably not going to get the loan or service.

We're going to closely examine the information that's contained in your credit reports in a moment, and then we're going to talk about how to fix that information – because I guarantee that some of it is wrong. But for now, let's take a close look at the major consumer reporting agencies.

(As with the term "credit report," the term "credit bureau" never appears in the FCRA. All of the companies that we typically think of and call "credit bureaus" are in fact consumer reporting agencies. As with the term "credit report," a "credit bureau" is really a sub-set of consumer reporting agencies that primarily collect, maintain, and sell credit information to third parties, as opposed to information regarding medical or insurance claim histories, for example. For our purposes, I'll refer to the major consumer reporting agencies as "credit bureaus," because that is the generally accepted term for them.

The Big 3

There are currently three major credit bureaus (consumer reporting agencies) that collect, maintain and report general credit information regarding consumers– Equifax, based in Atlanta, Georgina; Experian (formerly TRW) based in Costa Mesa, California; and, Trans Union, based in Chicago, Illinois. These companies now each maintain credit information on more than 200 million consumers nation-wide.

Where the Information Comes From

Now that you know who creates the credit reports, let's talk about where the information comes from. Although the information may come from many places, it generally comes from three sources – you, your creditors, and public records. Let's look at each of these sources and the information that they provide.

You

Yes, you! You unknowingly supply a great deal of information to the credit bureaus. How? Generally this happens when you apply for credit.

When you apply for credit, you typically complete a credit application in which you supply your full name, Social Security Number, current and former addresses, and current and previous employment. And guess what your potential creditor does with the information you listed in the application? That's right. They send it all to the credit bureau. This information then becomes a part of your credit file. Therefore, it's important that you accurately complete this information on any credit applications that you complete.

Your Creditors

Your current and former creditors also provide information to the credit bureaus about you. These creditors tell the credit bureaus how you've paid your bills each month. But, not all of your creditors report all of your payment history to the credit bureaus.

Some creditors, sometimes called "automatic subscribers," report all of your payment history to the credit bureaus every month. Other creditors, sometimes called "limited subscribers" only report certain types of information – like delinquencies. Let's look at these different types of creditors.

Automatic Subscribers

Automatic Subscribers are creditors that regularly report information to the credit bureaus about your account with them. This information generally includes the date when this creditor opened the account, the total amount of the debt or credit limit, the current balance, and your payment history – good or bad.

There are many different types of automatic subscribers, including banks, credit unions, department stores, finance companies, and major credit card companies. But, just because a creditor is an automatic subscriber to one credit bureau, doesn't necessarily mean that the creditor will report to all of the major credit bureaus. That's one reason that the credit reports produced by different credit bureaus very often contain different information.

Limited Subscribers

Limited Subscribers are creditors that do NOT regularly report information to the credit bureaus. Instead, these creditors may only report certain types of information – like delinquencies or collection activities.

They generally do not report good credit information, usually just bad information.

There are many different types of limited subscribers, including apartment management companies, insurance companies, utility companies, medical providers, and collection agencies. As with automatic subscribers, many limited subscribers may only report information to one of the national credit bureaus. Therefore, bad information reported by a limited subscriber may only affect one of your credit reports.

Creditors That Do Not Reports to Any Credit Bureau

Finally, there are some creditors that do not report to the credit bureaus AT ALL. This means that any information – good or bad – will not show in any of your credit reports. Typically, these creditors include individuals, like landlords, or small companies. (When you're trying to improve your credit in later chapters, you need to be aware of creditors that do not report to the credit bureaus. These creditors will NOT help you to restore your credit. We'll talk about this later.)

Public Records

The last source of information for your credit report comes from public records. Public records are government records that anyone can access. All local, state, and federal courts maintain court files for each case in their court. These court files are available to the general public for review. (Foreclosure and bankruptcy records are public records, for example.)

Generally, public records that may appear in your credit reports include bankruptcies, judgments, foreclosures, and tax liens. Credit bureaus usually get this information from private companies that search public records for this information. (LexisNexis is a major player in this area after purchasing Dolan Information in 2003).

If your mortgage lender filed a foreclosure case against you, or you filed a bankruptcy case, someone discovered this information and reported it to the credit bureaus. That someone probably worked for a private company like LexisNexis.

You may find that the public information recorded in your credit report is wrong. Sometimes these employees make mistakes in recording the public records information. This can work to our advantage. We'll talk about checking the accuracy of your public record section in a moment, and then we'll talk about what to do about it in later chapters.

What's Included in Your Credit Reports

Identification and Employment Information

Every credit report starts with basic information about you. This information generally includes your full name, date of birth, current and previous addresses, Social Security number, current and previous employers and income. (Remember, you probably supplied most of this information to the credit bureau.)

Credit History

The credit history section is probably the most important section for our purposes. In this section, your creditors report information about your accounts with them. Depending on the type of creditor, this information could include the date you opened the account, the amount of your credit line, your current balance, and your payment history - good or bad.

Typically, a creditor reports your account information by listing how often you've made on-time payments and how often you've made late payments. When listing the late payments, a creditor will also show how late your payments were, typically in 30-day increments. Generally, if you're less than 30 days late on an account, the creditor will report that you were current on the account. (This isn't always true. Some creditors will report your account as delinquent even if you are ONE day late!) However, if you're more than 30 days late, the creditor will report this information as well.

In addition to your repayment history, the credit history section lists any serious problems with your account. For example, if you completely failed to repay a loan, your creditor will report this information to the credit bureau and it will appear in the credit history section. Also, your creditor will report any action it took against you if you to collect the loan from you, like sending your account to a collection agency.

Finally, the credit history section describes who is responsible for repaying the debt. Although there are several classifications, the credit history section basically divides loan responsibility into three groups. First, "individual liability" means that you are the only person responsible for repaying the debt. "Joint liability" means that you share responsibility for repaying debt with someone else. Finally, "authorized user" means that you can use another person's credit line, but that you aren't responsible for repaying the debt.

Credit Inquiries

The credit inquiries section lists every individual or company that has requested your credit history within the past 24 months. Potential creditors are interested in these credit inquiries because they may suggest that you have an increased and immediate need for credit. This could indicate a potential problem with your finances.

What's Not Included In Your Credit Reports

Contrary to popular belief, your credit report does not contain information about your checking or savings accounts, or your race, religion, gender, political affiliation, or personal lifestyle. Your credit report also does not contain medical history or criminal records.

Finally, your credit report may also not contain information from all of your creditors. As we talked about above, some of your creditors may not report to all of the credit bureaus, and some may not report to any credit bureau. Therefore, parts of your credit accounts and history may appear in different credit reports, or not at all.

How to Get Your Credit Reports

Because credit reports contain information about you, it only seems fair that you should have the opportunity to examine these reports for accuracy and truthfulness. Fortunately, Congress agrees with this. Therefore, the FCRA guarantees you access to the information contained within your credit reports. Credit reports aren't required to show you the actual report that they send to creditors, but they'll generally allow you access to most of the information.

How to Get Your Credit Reports For Free

There are several ways for you to get your credit reports for free. First, everyone is entitled to a free report from consumer reporting agencies every 12 months. In addition, you can get free credit reports if someone used the credit report to deny you something. Finally, you can get free credit reports pursuant to state law in several states. Let's look at each of these methods.

Get a Free Credit Report Every 12 Months

Among other things, the Fair and Accurate Credit Transaction Act of 2003 ("FACTA") requires consumer reporting agencies to provide a free consumer report to consumers every 12 months. This applies to all consumer reporting agencies, including the Big 3 and the specialty consumer reporting agencies.

To comply with FACTA, the Big 3 – Equifax, Experian, and Trans Union, set up one central web site, one toll-free number, and one mailing address through which you can order your free credit reports.

Order On-Line

The easiest way to get your free credit reports from the Big 3 is to order them online at the centralized web site – www.annualcreditreport.com. At this site, you can order one, two, or all three credit reports. You must provide your name, Social Security Number, and date of birth. In addition, for privacy purposes, each credit bureau will request identification information that only you would know, like the amount of your monthly mortgage payment or when you opened an account.

(www.annualcreditreport.com is the only web site authorized to provide free credit reports from the Big 3 pursuant to FACT. There are many web sites that have sprung up to take advantage of consumers seeking to get their free credit reports. These sites typically have similar sounding names, but then attempt to sell you reports or credit monitoring services. Don't get fooled by this!)

Order by Phone

You can also request your free credit reports by telephone, by calling 1-877-322-8228.

Order by Mail

Finally, you can order your free credit reports by mail. To do this, you must mail the "Annual Credit Report Request Form" to the following address:

Annual Credit Report Request Service
P.O. Box 105281
Atlanta, GA 30348-5281

Get a Credit Report for Free if You Were Denied Something

The FCRA provides that you are entitled to a free credit report if some "adverse action" was taken against you, based at least in part, on the credit report. This could include having a request for credit, insurance, employment or rental housing denied. It could also include a current creditor's action in raising your interest rate or lowering your credit limit.

Whoever took the adverse action against you must tell you why, and give you the name and address of the credit bureau that supplied the credit report. Then, you have 60 days to request a free credit report from that credit bureau.

In addition, you are entitled to a free credit report for the following reasons:

(1) You certify in writing that that you are unemployed but that you intend to apply for employment within the next 60 days;

(2) You are a recipient of public welfare assistance;

(3) You have reason to believe that your credit file contains inaccurate information due to fraud; or,

(4) You have received a notice from a debt collection agency affiliated with that credit bureau that your credit rating may be, or has been, adversely affected.

Get Additional Credit Reports for a Fee

If you've already received your free credit report under FACTA, and it's been less than 12 months since you received it, and you're not entitled to a free report for some other reason under FACTA, then you'll need to pay for additional reports. For the current fees, assuming that the web sites don't change, check these sites:

Equifax

On-Line

You can order your Equifax credit report online at the following address: www.equifax.com. For now, just order your "Equifax Credit Report." Don't order any of the other products – I'll tell you why in a later chapter.

If you're requesting a free or reduced fee credit report, you cannot order you're your report online. Equifax charges a $10.00 "service fee" for accessing your report online. Therefore, you'll need to order you report by phone or mail.

By Phone

You can order your Equifax credit report by phone by calling 1-800-685-1111.

By Mail

You can order your Equifax credit report by mail. Make sure you include with your request your full name, current address, Social Security Number, and most recent former address, and if applicable, a check made payable to "Equifax Information Services LLC", based on your state's fee. Send your request to:

Equifax Information Services LLC
P.O. Box 740241
Atlanta, GA 30374

Experian

On-Line

You can order your Experian credit report online at the following address: www.experian.com/reportaccess/. You CAN order a free or reduced fee credit report online. For now, don't order any other products, just your credit report.

By Phone

You can order your Experian credit report by phone by calling 1-888-EXPERIAN (1-888-397-3742).

By Mail

You can order your Experian credit report by mail. Make sure you include with your request your full name, current address, Social Security Number, and most recent and former addresses within the last two years. Experian also requests that you enclose with your request a government issued identification card, a driver's license, for example, and a copy of a recent utility bill. If applicable, send a check made payable to "Experian" based on your state's fee. Send your request to:

Experian
P.O. Box 2104
Allen, TX 75013

Trans Union

On-Line

You can order your Trans Union credit report online at the following address: www.transunion.com. You CAN order a free or reduced fee credit report online. For now, don't order any other products, just your credit report. (Of course, trying to order JUST your credit report, without other add-on products, is very difficult. Try these addresses if you have problems:

For a Free Report

http://annualcreditreport.transunion.com/tu/disclosure/disclosure.jsp?loc=1470

http://annualcreditreport.transunion.com/tu/disclosure/order.jsp?package=TransUnionPaidDisclosure

By Phone

You can order your Trans Union credit report by calling 1-800-888-4213.

By Mail

You can order your Trans Union credit report by mail. Make sure you include with your request your full name, current address, Social Security Number, most recent and former addresses within the last two years, date of birth, current employer, phone number, and signature. If applicable, send a check made payable to "TransUnion LLC" based on your state's fee. Send your request to:

TransUnion LLC
P.O. Box 1000
Chester, PA 19022

How to Read Your Credit Reports

Now that you have copies of your credit reports from all of the Big 3 Credit Bureaus (you have them, right?), it's time to take a look at them and see what the Credit Bureaus are reporting about you. In the past, you really needed an expert to help you interpret all of the codes and notations, and we'd need to spend a great deal of time on each section of the credit report.

Fortunately, however, the Credit Bureaus have done a good job over the last several years of making the credit reports very easy to read and understand. So, instead of going over a line-by-line analysis of each different credit report, we're just going to review the different sections that you'll find in each report. Then, in the next chapter, you'll have a chance to review each credit report – line-by-line – to find the mistakes in these reports.

Personal Information

Generally, most credit reports start with a Personal Information section. In this section, the credit reports list a variety of basic information about you. Typically, the Personal Information section includes your full name and any other names that you use or did use in the past, your social security number (or a portion of it), and your date of birth. It also usually includes your current and previous addresses and current and previous employment.

The information contained in this section does not affect your credit scores. However, it's vital that the credit bureaus accurately report all of your personal information. If not, the credit bureaus may be "mixing" your credit information with someone else. This happens most often with people who share similar names. But, I've seen credit file mixing with people who don't have similar names or social security numbers. You've got enough work to do on your own credit without worrying about repairing another person's credit too!

You may also find a "consumer statement" listed in this section. Under the FCRA, you are entitled, for various reasons, to include a statement in your credit report regarding your explanation for any bad credit information that appears in your credit report. In the past, this made some sense to do as a last resort. However, because creditors rarely see your credit report, I don't recommend this strategy to my clients.

Account Summary

The next section that you may find in your credit report is an Account Summary section. Not all credit reports include this section, and some credit report formats include it at the beginning of the Account History section. However, if this section is included in your credit report, you'll find that it can be a helpful way to quickly understand how the different credit bureaus are reporting all of your account information.

The Account Summary section typically includes summaries of your "Total Accounts", "Open Accounts", "Closed Accounts", "Delinquent Accounts", and "Derogatory Accounts". It also includes the total amount of debt that you owe for all accounts and your total monthly payment amount for all accounts. Finally, the Account Summary section will typically list the total number of Public Records listed in your credit report, and the total number of inquiries during the last two years.

As you review this section, remember that the different credit bureaus often contain different information about you. You know from our earlier discussion that some creditors only report information to one or two credit bureaus, while other creditors report to all three. In addition, the credit bureaus often fail to update their information in the same way. This means that even if an account is reported by all of the credit bureaus, the information that is reported may be completely different.

So, I guarantee that the summary of your accounts listed in the Account Summary section will be different for each credit bureau. That's OK. But, you want the differences between the credit information to be RIGHT. So, use this section as a guide. If one credit bureau is reporting 3 public records, and another is reporting only one, you need to look closely at the Public Record section of these reports. Or, if one credit bureau is reporting 2 collection accounts, but another credit bureau is listing five collection accounts, you need to look very closely at the account information in those reports. You get the idea.

Account History

The Account History section is probably the most important section of the credit report. In this section, the credit bureaus list detailed information regarding your different credit accounts. Because the Account History section is usually the section that contains most of the errors after a foreclosure and bankruptcy, we'll focus most of our credit "repair" efforts on this section.

Depending on the credit report format, the Account History section may be divided according to the type of account (real estate, installment, revolving, collection, etc.) or by "Potentially Negative" or "Accounts in Good Standing." However the section is divided, it will typically include the following information for each account.

Creditor Name

This section lists the name of the creditor that owns the account. This may often be different from the name that you are expecting. For example, MBNA manages "affinity" accounts for many different organizations. So, you may have a credit card account that features your alma mater or favorite cruise line. But, MBNA actually owns the account. Whenever you communicate with the credit bureau regarding the account, make sure that you refer to this official name in your communication.

Account Number

This section lists the account number that the creditor uses to identify your account. Well, actually, you'll probably only find a partial account number listed in this section. However, you only need the partial account number that is listed when you communicate with credit bureaus about this account.

Condition or Status

This section indicates whether your account is open or closed.

Balance

This section shows the amount that you currently owe on this account, according to the credit bureau's records. Because there is often a lag in reporting information to the credit bureaus, the balance listed in your credit report may not indicate your actual current balance.

You'll want to pay very close attention to this section of each account as you review your credit reports. One of the biggest problems with accounts that were involved in a foreclosure, short-sale or deed-in-lieu, or included in a bankruptcy is that they continue to incorrectly report the balance amount. This may go a long way towards allowing us to challenge the account under the FCRA. So, make sure you focus on the balance listed in each of your accounts.

Type of Account

This section lists the purpose of the account. For example, the account may be for a real estate loan, an automobile loan, a student loan, or a credit card account.

Payment Status

This section lists the current payment status, according to the creditor. For example, this section may report that the account is "Paid as Agreed" or "30-Days Late" or "Charged Off". This is another section that should closely examine for each of your accounts. This information is frequently incorrectly listed after a foreclosure, bankruptcy, or other mortgage-related deficiency.

Past Due Amount

This section lists how much of your payment amount is currently past due or delinquent. The Past Due Amount section is also frequently wrong after foreclosure, bankruptcy or other mortgage-related deficiency. This will affect your credit scores. So, look very closely at this section too.

High Balance

This section lists the highest amount that you ever owed on this account.

Terms

This section shows the number of payments that are scheduled with a particular creditor. For installment accounts, the Terms section will typically show the total number of payment due for the loan. For credit card and other revolving accounts, this section will typically show that the payments are due monthly.

Credit Limit

This section lists the maximum amount of credit for this account. You should always review this section for ALL of your accounts because this section can affect your credit scores. As we'll discuss in a moment, one of the major factors that affects a credit score is the proportion of your balances to your credit limits. As a result, your credit scores may be artificially low if the credit bureaus are understating your credit limits.

Payment Amount

This section lists the minimum payment amount due for the account balance each month.

Date Opened

This section lists the date the account was opened. If the Account History section includes collection accounts (some credit report formats have a separate section for collection accounts), CAREFULLY review the date opened for any collection accounts. As we'll discuss in a moment, collection agencies have a nasty habit of "re-aging" collection accounts.

This means that they report the account as opened on the day that they receive the account for collection. The problem with this practice is that the FCRA specifies the exact amount of time that account information can remain on your credit reports. By listing the date the collection agency received the account as the "Date Opened", the credit agencies can keep bad account information in your credit reports MUCH longer than necessary. So, DON'T let them do this!

Date Reported

This section lists the last date that any activity occurred in the account. This could include payment made, billings posted, collection activity started, or foreclosure or bankruptcy filed.

Account Owner or Responsibility

This section indicates your association with the account and your liability for repaying the account balance. The most common notations for this section are individual liability (you are the only one responsible for repaying the account), joint liability (you share responsibility for repayment of the account with another person), and authorized user (you have access to the account, but you are not contractually obligated to repay the balance).

Late Payment Summary

This section lists a summary of your 30, 60, and 90-day late payments (or worse) over several years. This is another section that is frequently wrong after foreclosure, bankruptcy, or other mortgage deficiency.

Remarks or Comments

This section contains additional comments about the status or condition of your account. This section could indicate that the account has been closed, or sold, etc.

Detailed Payment History

The Account History section also frequently includes a detailed payment history for each account that reflects as many a seven years of the account's history. You should carefully examine this section to make sure that any listed delinquencies are accurate.

Collection Accounts

Some credit report formats will have a separate section for Collection Accounts. Other credit reports will simply report this information in the general Account History section. Either way, make sure that you carefully review the information listed for collection accounts because it is frequently wrong. Let's quickly review the information that most credit bureaus include for collection accounts.

Agency Name

This section lists the official name of the collection agency that is currently collecting the debt. Generally, this is NOT the same entity that originally owned the debt. Instead, this is typically a third-party company that is collecting the debt on behalf of the original creditor or has purchased the debt from the original creditor and is collecting the debt on its own behalf. You'll want to use this name when communicating with the credit bureau about this debt.

You may find that there are SEVERAL collection agencies that report as collecting ONE original debt. We have seen credit reports that list FIVE different collection agencies for one original account. Just be aware of this as you review your credit reports.

Account Number

This section lists the account number that the collection agency has assigned to this collection account. This number is NOT the same number that your original creditor assigned to your original account. Therefore, you'll want to use the collection agency account number when communicating with the credit bureaus about this collection account.

Original Creditor

This section lists the name of the original creditor that owned the original account. (Sometimes, this section lists the name of a subsequent collection agency that purchased, and the re-sold, the account to another collection agency.) Because some creditors don't report their accounts to the credit bureaus, the original creditor may not otherwise appear in your credit report. In addition, for privacy reasons, medical accounts may be "masked" and not indicate the name of the creditor.

Account Owner or Responsibility

This section indicates your association with the account and your liability for repaying the account balance.

Current Status

This section lists the current status of the account – open, closed, paid, etc.

Current Balance

This section lists the current balance due on this account, according to the collection agency.

Original Balance

This section lists the original balance due on the account, before any of the additional fees and costs added by the collection agency.

Date of First Delinquency

This section lists the date that your payments first became delinquent in your original account. This date is VERY important under the FCRA, because it starts the clock ticking on the amount of time that the credit bureaus can report this account. In the past, there were many disputes between consumers and creditors regarding the "date of last activity" for the account, because that date controlled the time that credit bureaus could report collection account information. However, under the revised FCRA, credit bureaus can only report collection accounts for seven years and 180 days after the account first became delinquent. (I know that sounds confusing. I also know that it sounds like a LONG time to remain on your credit reports. Don't worry; I've got the answers to both of those concerns.)

Date Opened or Transferred

This section lists the date the account was transferred to the collection agency or the date that the collection agency opened the account. Remember, this date should be just that – the date that the COLLECTION AGENCY opened the account. It is NOT the date that the account originally went into default. We very often see collection agencies report the date opened or transferred to them as the date of original delinquency. This is WRONG, and will cause your collection accounts to remain on your credit reports much longer than necessary.

Date Reported

This section lists the date that the collection agency last updated the account information with the credit bureau.

Comments or Remarks

This section lists any notes about the account. For example, this section may indicate that the collection agency has been unable to locate you (which is usually untrue), or that the debt remains unpaid.

Public Record Information

The next section that you will find in your credit report is the Public Record Information section. This section lists any publicly available information that may affect your credit. For example, the public record section will list information about your foreclosure or bankruptcy case, including the date the case was filed and the case number, In addition, the public record section will list any judgments that creditors have obtained against you, and any state and federal tax liens that have been place against you.

With that said, let me warn you about the information contained in the Public Record Information section. This information is NOT necessarily accurate just because it was reported in some public record database. This information is frequently wrong. So, make sure that you review all of this information very carefully. As a result, it's frequently possible to remove foreclosure judgments and case information from your credit reports, possibly months after the foreclosure. (Really).

Inquiries

The next section that you will find in your credit report is the Inquiries section. This section lists the names of businesses and other entities that have requested your credit report during the last 24 months. Only "hard" inquiries are listed on credit reports that third parties request. (A hard inquiry is an inquiry made by a business or other entity in connection with your application for credit or some service. A soft inquiry is an inquiry made by you about your own credit report, a review of your credit by one of your existing creditors, or an inquiry from third parties who are prescreening your credit in hopes of offering you something – probably some form of credit.) If you request your own credit report, ALL inquiries – hard and soft – will appear in the Inquiries section of your credit report.

Hard inquiries CAN affect your credit score. So, you need to carefully review the hard inquiries that appear in your credit report to ensure that you actually authorized the inquiry. If you did not authorize the inquiry, you may be able to remove it from your credit report.

Creditor Contact Information

The final section that may appear in your credit report is the Credit Contact Information. (This information may also appear with the other account information in the Account History section.) This section lists the name and contact information for every creditor that appears in your credit report, and may also include contact information for creditors and other entities that have made inquiries. You will need this information to contact the creditors regarding any disputed you may have with that creditor.

Final Thoughts on Credit Reports

As I said earlier, credit reports have become much easier to read and understand. However, you MUST carefully review the information that each credit report includes. I guarantee that much of this information will be WRONG. This wrong information is probably lowering your credit scores and preventing you from receiving the best credit and services available. But that's going to stop now!

Chapter Thirteen

Credit Scores – The All-Important Numbers

Credit reports are important. But there's something that's even MORE important in your quest for good credit after foreclosure or other mortgage problem – your credit score. In the old days, I spent a great deal of time trying to make a client's credit report "look good" for a prospective creditor. That usually meant trying to add as much good credit as possible, and eliminate as much bad credit as possible. Then, if I couldn't get a particular bad credit entry removed, we'd write a statement that would appear in the credit report so that a prospective creditor would at least get to read the consumer's side of the story.

But today, creditors very often NEVER see a credit report. For many credit decisions, the sole basis for determining whether someone gets credit or not is the credit score. That's what allows companies to offer "instant" credit.

For most credit transactions, the score has become one of the most important factors in determining whether you qualify for a particular loan and the terms of that loan. Although a creditor MAY still actually look at a credit report, the score very often determines the parameters of the loan. For example, whether you get a loan or not may depend solely upon your credit score. If your score is too low, you don't get the loan. For many creditors, it's that simple.

Or, if your score is high enough to qualify for a loan, it may dictate your interest rate and other terms of the loan. Very small differences in your score can mean very big differences in the loan you get. That's why scores are so important.

So nowadays, although I still work on "cleaning up" my clients' credit reports, the focus has changed. Now, instead of trying to make a report "look nice" for a prospective creditor, I focus on how things in the credit reports affect the credit score. So, in many ways, the credit report is now only important to the extent that it affects the credit score. So, what is this credit score that has become so important?

What's a Credit Score?

A credit score is a number that attempts to predict your "credit-worthiness" at any given moment. Officially, it's supposed to predict how likely you are to become at least 90 days late on payments within the next twenty-four months. Credit scores are calculated using complex, secret formulas that are only known by the companies that produce them (although these companies have given us some general guidance on how they calculate credit scores.)

A company called Fair Isaac Corporation pioneered the use of credit scores in 1956, but they didn't become widely used by creditors until the 1980's. Then, in 1995, Fannie Mae and Freddie Mac recommended the use of credit scores in mortgage lending. From then on, credit scores became perhaps the single-most important tool for creditors when offering loans to consumers.

Now, credit scores are even used by insurance companies and other service providers in determining whether, and on what terms, they will offer their services to you. (Personally, I have real problems with the use of credit scores in the granting of insurance and other services. I have difficulty believing that someone doesn't deserve home or car insurance because they got sick and fell behind on their bills. Unfortunately, I don't get to set the rules. So, I just have to do everything I can to improve your credit scores so that you don't have problems with anyone - creditors or service providers!)

There are now many different types of credit scores, developed by different companies, for use in different industries. For example, there are credit scores that are used solely for automotive lenders, credit card issuers, or finance companies. (Some commentators have suggested that, between the different credit scoring companies, there are more than 1000 different credit scoring models currently in use.) But, the most widely used credit score, by far, is the score developed by the Fair Isaac Company, the pioneer of credit scores.

The credit score developed by Fair Isaac is known as a "FICO" score (from the "Fair Isaac Corporation"). To determine a FICO score for a consumer, Fair Isaac developed a formula based on nearly forty different "characteristics" that it claims predict the likelihood that the consumer will repay their debts.

Fair Isaac also groups different classes of consumers according to key "attributes" and then compares a given consumer's credit file to other consumers in that same group. For example, there may be a group of consumers who have filed for bankruptcy. There may be another group of consumers who have one late payment, and so on. Fair Isaac believes that separating consumers into groups of consumers with common key attributes makes the credit score even more predictive of credit worthiness. This system is called a "scorecard" system.

But guess what? There's more than one credit scoring model. Sure, there are other companies that have their own credit scoring system (we'll talk about that in a minute). But, even Fair Isaac has more than one credit scoring model. In fact, they have many different credit scoring models.

The most commonly used model is known as the "Classic" FICO scoring model. This model uses 10 "scorecards" or groups of people with similar key attributes. But, Fair Isaac has also developed another scoring model called "Next Generation" or "NextGen" that uses 18 scorecards or groups. Fair Isaac believes that the NextGen scoring model is even more advanced and predictive than the Classic model. In addition, Fair Isaac has developed enhancements to the Classic model.

So, why should you care about this? Well, it's a problem if you're applying for credit, because different creditors use different credit scoring models. Some may use the Classic FICO. Others may use the enhanced versions of the Classic FICO. Still others may use the NextGen FICO. And the result? Yes, that's right, different scores.

I may pull a credit score for a client, and get one score. But, if a lender uses a different credit reporting company for their credit report, it's very possible that the credit score will be different. So, while the client would qualify for a certain loan based on our credit report and score, the borrower may NOT qualify using the lender's credit report. This can be a real problem for loans that are teetering on the edge anyway.

Different Names for the FICO Score

The Big 3 Credit Bureaus all use a FICO scoring model when they issue credit reports to third parties - like creditors. But, each credit bureau has a slightly different scoring model and each has a different name for the resulting score that's produced using the information contained within their credit files. Equifax calls its version of the FICO score a "Beacon" score. Experian calls its version the "Experian/Fair Isaac" score. Trans Union calls its version of the FICO score the "FICO Risk Score, Classic" (formerly known as the "Empirica" score). So, even though these are all "FICO" scores, the different credit bureau's scores are almost always different from one another. The differences in scores result primarily because the information contained within each credit bureau's files are different, and because each bureau uses a slightly different FICO scoring model.

As a result, some creditors look at all three scores, the Beacon, Experian/Fair Isaac, and the FICO Risk Score, Classic (Actually, the lender could be looking at the NextGen scores, instead. These are called "Pinnacle" at Equifax, "Experian/Fair. Isaac Advanced Risk Score" at Experian, and "Precision" at Trans Union.) For example, almost all mortgage lenders review all three credit scores when a borrower applies for a mortgage.

Generally, mortgage lenders use the "middle" score to determine whether a borrower will receive the loan and on what terms. But, some creditors only look at one score. So, if you know in advance which score a particular lender or service provider uses for their credit decisions, you can focus on that score, or at least get an idea of whether you'll receive the offer.

Educational Credit Scores

But, different FICO scores are just the beginning. Adding to the confusion are "educational" credit scores that Experian and Trans Union offer to consumers through their web sites and through hundreds of affiliated companies.

If you've visited the web site for Experian or Trans Union, you probably found it hard to JUST order your credit report. On both sites, it takes some real investigative work to figure out how you can avoid ordering a credit score or credit monitoring service with your credit report. (That's why I listed the specific links in each web site to order just the credit report – I thought I'd save you the effort.)

But, you're probably asking, is that a bad thing? After all, I said that credit scores are more important than credit reports, right? Well, yes, that's true. But, you need the RIGHT credit scores. And the credit scores that Experian and Trans Union are pushing on their web sites are NOT the credit scores that they provide to third parties.

Experian's PLUS Score

On its web site, Experian offers the "PLUS Score." The PLUS Score is a proprietary score developed by Experian, and featured prominently in its web site. You really have to dig in the Experian web site to find out that the PLUS score is really an "educational" score. In its web site, Experian says that "the PLUS score is derived from information based on a credit report, using a similar formula to those used by lenders." Did you get that? The PLUS Score is a "similar" formula to those used by lenders. So, bottom line, it's NOT the score that lenders use.

It's supposed to be "easier to understand" than other credit scores (the FICO scores) and allows consumers to "see how changes to their credit habits can directly influence their credit rating." So again, it's not the score that creditors use in granting you credit. It's an educational tool to allow you to see how changes to your credit "habits" can affect your credit score. So, for "educational" purposes, the PLUS Score is OK.

Trans Union's TrueCredit Score

Like Experian, Trans Union has its own proprietary credit score that it offers on its web site – the TrueCredit score. And, like the PLUS Score, you have to dig deep to find an explanation that the TrueCredit score is not a FICO score. In its web site, Trans Union says "TrueCredit is not connected in any way with Fair, Isaac and Company; the credit score provided here is not a so-called FICO score. The credit scores of TransUnion may not be identical in every respect to any consumer credit scores produced by any other company." So, the TrueCredit score is another "educational" score that is NOT used by creditors in evaluating you for credit.

So What's the Problem with the PLUS Score and the TrueCredit Score?

What's wrong with looking at the PLUS Score and the TrueCredit score? After all, they're educational, right? Well, yes, but.... If you want to spend your money, then go ahead. But, if you really want to see the scores that your lenders are going to see, then you need to stick with the FICO scores.

Your lender will never see your PLUS Score or your TrueCredit score. And, in my experience, these scores are almost always considerably higher than the FICO scores based on the Experian and TransUnion credit information – the Experian/Fair Isaac and the FICO Risk Score, Classic. I've seen differences of more than 50 points between these "educational" credit scores and the FICO scores.

(This usually comes up when a borrower starts complaining that the scores they got online were much higher than the scores received by a mortgage broker who pulled their credit. They usually think that the mortgage broker is trying to trick them in order to justify a higher rate. Although I have no doubt that this happens, generally the difference in scores is really the difference between the FICO scores and the educational scores.)

So, bottom line – make sure that you review and work on improving your FICO scores. It MAY help to pull the PLUS Score and TrueCredit Score and play with the simulators that Trans Union and Experian offer with these scores. But, to REALLY improve the credit scores that your lenders will use, you need to understand the FICO scoring system. Let's do that now.

How Are Credit Scores Calculated?

OK. Now that we have an idea of what a credit score is, and which scores we really need to focus on, let's look at how the FICO scores are calculated. Yes, I know that I said that the formula is a secret. But, fortunately, Fair Isaac has given us a general idea of how they calculate the FICO scores. Their description is detailed enough so that we can use the information to increase your credit scores as much as possible.

Although Fair Isaac uses a lot of different information in your credit file, there are five main categories of information that determine your score, and each category has a different level of "importance". The five categories that determine your score, in order of importance, are: (1) Payment History; (2) Amounts Owed; (3) Length of Credit History; (4) New Credit; and, (5) Types of Credit Used. Let's look at each of these categories and how they affect your score.

Payment History – 35% of the Total Score

Payment History makes up 35% of your score. This probably makes sense, because this is the section that documents how you've repaid your debts in the past. According to Fair Isaac, the Payment History section looks at:

- Account payment information on specific types of accounts (credit cards, retail accounts, installment loans, finance company accounts, mortgage, etc.). This speaks for itself. How are you paying your debts?

- Presence of adverse public records (bankruptcy, judgments, suits, liens, wage attachments, etc.). These public record accounts have a major impact on scores. However, older items with smaller amounts have a smaller impact on your score than more recent items or those with larger amounts.

- Severity of delinquency (how long was the account past due?). A 60-day late payment does not impact your score as much as a 90-day late payment. However, the recency of delinquency may affect this.

- Amount past due on delinquent accounts or collection items. How much is still owed? This will be a major focus of our efforts.

- Time since any delinquencies, public records, or collection items. Generally, the older the event, the less impact it has on your score. See the chart below.

- Number of past-due items on file. The fewer past due items, the better.

- Number of accounts paid as agreed. This is the opposite of the previous factor. Here, the more accounts that you pay on-time, the better.

OK. Let's summarize and look at some major points for this section. Generally, the fewer accounts that show on your credit report with late payments, the better. Also, the older the delinquency, the better.

Remember, the FICO score is attempting to predict whether you'll become 90 days delinquent on a payment in the next twenty-four months. If you have a current delinquency, it seems more likely that you're in the middle of some financial crisis and may very well fall behind on your payments to creditors. But, it it's been two years since you had any delinquency, it seems likely that you have gotten over the financial problem, and are unlikely to have another late payment.

The risk of a future 90-day delinquency is highest when the most recent major delinquency was less than 12 months ago. As a result, the "recency" of a credit problem becomes a major component of the credit score. This can mean that a recent 30-day late payment on a credit card may have a greater impact on your credit score than major credit problem, like a foreclosure or bankruptcy, from six years ago.

That's why it's VERY important that you not have ANY recent late payments after your foreclosure or mortgage delinquency. (I can give you many sad examples of this principal in action. Several of my clients forgot this important lesson on recent delinquencies, and paid the price. In each case, I was in the process of refinancing their current mortgage to pay off their ongoing Chapter 13 case. In each case, the client had a very minor delinquency on something – in one case it was a 30-day late on a $30 credit card payment, in another it was a late cell phone payment – that caused their credit scores to plummet. In each case, their credit scores dropped by more than 40 points!) So, do whatever it takes to stay current on your bills.

This can become a problem when you pay an old collection account. Many clients have told me that their previous lender or mortgage broker advised them to pay off their old collection accounts to increase their score. Unfortunately, the effect is exactly the opposite. Paying off an old collection account makes it a recent event, and actually LOWERS your score!

Although payment history makes up the largest percentage of your credit score, it only makes up 35% of the score. Other factors make up 65% of the score. So, just because you have a bad payment history with some of your creditors, or even a foreclosure or bankruptcy, this does NOT mean that you will necessarily have a bad credit score. This is one of the big myths about credit scores.

Amounts Owed – 30% of the Total Score

The next category - Amounts Owed - tracks how much you owe on each account, and makes up 30% of your score. According to Fair Isaac, the Amounts Owed category looks at:

- Amount owing on all accounts. Do you owe too much? Of course, it's hard to say what "too much" is. Fair Isaac would say that it depends on the overall credit picture.

- Amount owing on specific types of accounts. The score considers the amount you owe on different types of accounts, like credit card and installment accounts.

- Lack of a specific type of balance, in some cases. Some "experts" say that you should pay off your credit cards in full each month. However, this may actually hurt your score. It's good to have some credit, and pay it back on time.

- Number of accounts with balances. Too many accounts with balances can indicate that you're over-extended. Again, what's too many accounts? Only Fair Isaac knows for sure.

- Proportion of credit lines used (proportion of balances to total credit limits on certain types of revolving accounts). If you're credit line is "maxed out," you're more likely to have trouble making future payments.

- Proportion of installment loan amounts still owing (proportion of balance to original loan amount on certain types of installment loans). It's good to have some installment accounts. It's not good to have them with high balances.

In my experience, the most important information in this section is the proportion of balances to total credit limits. This is one of my favorite areas to work on when I'm trying to raise the score of someone who has had a major credit problem. In general, you should try to keep this ratio below 50%. It's even better to keep it below 30%, if possible. You can immediately increase your credit scores by lowering this ratio.

Length of Credit History – 15% of the Total Score

The next category – Length of Credit History – tracks how long you have used credit, and accounts for 15% of your credit score. According to Fair Isaac, this section looks at:

- Time since accounts opened. The credit score factors the age of your oldest account, the age of your newest account, and an average age of all your accounts. You'll get a higher credit score with a longer credit history.

- Time since accounts opened, by specific type of account. In general, the credit score prefers that you have certain types of accounts – major bank cards versus finance company accounts. This factors how long you've had the different types of debt.

- Time since account activity. In general, it's better to have on-going recent credit activity in your accounts.

For this section, the longer you've had open credit accounts, the better. (That's why the common advice to close credit accounts before applying for a loan is crazy. By closing accounts, you DECREASE your length of credit history and lower your score.)

The risk that you'll default in the future is greatly increased if your credit history is less than 24 months long. By the way, this is another of my favorite areas to work on when I'm trying to improve credit scores. I have a super-secret method for increasing credit scores that works, in part, by increasing the length of credit history. Yes, I promise, we're going to tell you that one too. For now, I'm just trying to whet your appetite.

New Credit – 10% of the Total Score

The next category – New Credit – tracks your attempts to open new credit, and accounts for 10% of your credit score. According to Fair Isaac, this section looks at:

- Number of recently opened accounts, and proportion of accounts that are recently opened, by type of account. In general, opening new credit accounts will lower your score. And, if you have several new accounts, this may lower your score even more.

- Number of recent credit inquiries. Credit inquiries can lower your score. However, only "hard" inquiries lower your score, and sometimes even these inquiries have little, if any impact to the score.

- Time since recent account opening(s), by type of account. How long has it been since you opened a new account? The longer, the better.

- Time since credit inquiry(s). How long has it been since an inquiry was made? The longer, the better. But, an inquiry only affects your score for 12 months, even though the credit bureaus report them for 24 months.

- Re-establishment of positive credit history following past payment problems. Yes, new credit can lower your score. But, getting new credit after foreclosure or other major credit problem will greatly improve your scores in the long-run. That's why you need to do it.

The risk that you'll default in the future is greatly increased if you have multiple inquiries for your credit report. Therefore, you need to be somewhat selective when applying for credit. In general, you want to be pretty sure that you'll receive the credit when you apply. Otherwise, you're just needlessly adding inquiries that lower your score.

However, with that said, you MUST add new credit to your credit report after a foreclosure or other major credit problem. This means that you'll have to suffer through an initial hit to your credit score to improve it in the long run. So, be prepared for your credit scores to drop, at least initially, as you apply for new credit. But, your efforts WILL be rewarded with a higher credit score in the end – I promise!

There's probably one more thing that we should talk about here – the difference between a "Hard" inquiry and a "Soft" inquiry. Yes, it's true that an inquiry will probably lower your score a bit. However, that inquiry must be from a third party, like a creditor, with your permission. This is called a "hard" inquiry. And, if you have many recent inquiries, your score will drop more than if you have one recent inquiry.

A "Soft" inquiry is an inquiry made by you about your own credit report, a review of your credit by one of your existing creditors, an inquiry from a prospective employer, or an inquiry from third parties who are pre-screening your credit in the hope of offering you something – probably some form of credit. A soft inquiry will NOT affect your score. In fact, a soft inquiry will not even appear on credit reports ordered by third parties. So, you can pull your credit as often as you like, and it will not lower your score.

Types of Credit Used – 10% of the Total Credit Score

The final category – Types of Credit Used – tracks the "mix" of different creditors you have, and accounts for the final 10% of your credit score. According to Fair Isaac, this section looks at:

- Number of (presence, prevalence, and recent information on) various types of accounts (credit cards, retail accounts, installment loans, mortgage, consumer finance accounts, etc.). The credit score considers your "mix" of credit cards, retail accounts, installment loans, finance company accounts and mortgage loans. Do you have experience with revolving and installment debt, or only one type? Do you have high-interest rate finance loans? Do you have too few, or too many revolving accounts?

This final category really focuses on the types of creditors you have. Are you only receiving credit from high-interest rate finance companies? Or are you also getting credit from major banks and credit card companies. The difference in the "mix" of these different types of creditors will affect your score. "Better" creditors will get you a better score.

What is Not Considered in Determining Your Credit Score

In addition to the confusion about what does affect your score, there is great confusion about what does NOT affect your score. For example, I've reviewed many books on "credit repair" where the author sets forth a chart of "points" that creditors supposedly use in creating the credit score. These points usually include the type of employment, income, and length of residence. Although many lenders use these factors in deciding whether to grant you a loan, they DO NOT affect your FICO scores.

According to Fair Isaac, credit scores do not consider:

- Your race, color, religion, national origin, sex and marital status
- Your age
- Your salary, occupation, title, employer, date employed or employment history
- Where you live
- Any interest rate being charged on a particular credit card or other account
- Any items reported as child/family support obligations or rental agreements
- Certain types of inquiries (requests for your credit report)
- Any information not found in your credit report
- Any information that is not proven to be predictive of future credit performance
- Whether you are participating in credit counseling of any kind

What's a Good Score?

Now that we've looked at all of the factors that do, and do not, affect your credit score, let's look at the actual scores. What's the range of scores, and what's a good score?

The range for FICO scores is generally between 300 and 850, with 850 being the best. Fair Isaac divides the scoring range into five risk categories:

- 780 – 850 – Low Risk
- 740 – 780 – Medium Low Risk
- 690 – 740 – Medium Risk
- 620 – 690 – Medium High Risk
- 620 and Below – High Risk

In my practice, I generally see credit scores between 450 and 680. And, between those levels, there's a tremendous range in the loans, interest rates and other terms that those people may receive. So, the point is that higher is better, no matter what score you have.

Why Are Credit Scores Important?

So why have we spent so much time on credit scores? Because, as I said at the beginning of this chapter, the credit score is the MOST important thing in determining whether you will get most loans and many services – more important, really, than your credit report. And, if you do qualify for a certain loan or service, you may pay much more for that loan or service than someone who has a higher score than you.

How to Get Your Credit Scores

OK. So now that you know all about credit scores, how do you get your genuine FICO credit scores? The best place to get your FICO scores is from Fair Isaac through their "myFICO" website: www.myfico.com. You can get two of the three FICO scores on-line. – Equifax and Trans Union. (Experian ended its agreement with MyFico to provide its scores and no longer offers the real FICO score to consumers.) At this time, the cost is $15.95 for each credit report and score. At this time, you can only order the three FICO reports from www.myfico.com on-line. They do not accept phone or mail orders.

At this time, I don't have a good answer on how you can obtain your Experian FICO score. Lenders can still access the actual FICO score from Experian, but consumers may not be able to do this. You may need to have a lender pull your Experian credit score for you. Visit www.SaveMyFloridaHomeNow.com for updates on this issue.)

The VantageScore - A New Credit Score to Worry About?

As if the different FICO scores weren't confusing enough, now there may be another credit score to worry about – the VantageScore. The VantageScore was introduced on March 14, 2006 by the Big 3 credit bureaus, Equifax, Experian, and Trans Union. It seems to be their attempt to provide an alternative scoring model to the FICO Score, and perhaps break free from Fair Isaac. The Big 3 are currently attempting to get creditors to accept the VantageScore in place of the FICO score.

The VantageScore differs from the FICO scores in several ways. First, for some reason, the Big 3 thought it was a good idea to change the score range on the VantageScore. Now, instead of a range from 300 to 850, the VantageScore has a range from 501 to 990 according to the following chart:

A: 901 – 990 (Super Prime)

B: 801 – 900 (Prime Plus)

C: 701 – 800 (Prime)

D: 601 – 700 (Non-Prime)

F: 501 – 600 (High Risk)

As you can see from the chart, VantageScore also assigns a letter grade to different ranges of scores. Supposedly, this is to make the scores easier for consumers to understand. Personally, I think this "grading" system and the altered score range is going to confuse consumers even more than they are now. It really seems unnecessary to do this.

So, why did the Big 3 create the VantageScore? Well, it seems like the primary purpose is to compete with Fair Isaac. The credit bureaus refer to Fair Isaac as "the competition" when they talk about VantageScore.

In addition, their stated purpose is to bring consistency to the credit scores between the Big 3 credit bureaus. The VantageScore uses one scoring model to calculate the score for each credit bureau. As you recall, each credit bureau uses a separate FICO model to calculate their individual FICO score. So, even though they're using a FICO model, they're using slightly different models. Therefore, even if the information were the same at each bureau (it's not), the resulting score would be different at each credit bureau. The VantageScore, however, uses only one scoring model, so it's supposed to be more consistent between the credit bureaus.

However, using one scoring model doesn't address the basic problem with the different credit bureaus – they all have different information. So, even though VantageScore uses one scoring model, the scores from each credit bureau will STILL be different. So, will the VantageScore really aid consistency? We'll see.

The real question with the VantageScore is whether any lenders will use it. There is significant cost involved in revising software for credit evaluation. The different scoring range offered by VantageScore will require significant changes to the creditors' credit evaluation tools. It's unclear at this point whether large numbers of creditors will switch to the new system. It's interesting to note that there were no creditors involved in the introduction of VantageScore.

So, who knows? Personally, I doubt that the VantageScore will be widely accepted anytime in the near future. But, you should keep a close eye on it anyway. This MAY affect some of the advice in this book. (For example, the VantageScore does NOT count authorized user accounts in the score calculation. This would prevent us from using one of my favorite techniques for quickly raising credit scores.)

Chapter Fourteen

Repairing Your Credit – For Fun and Profit

OK. We've finally reached the chapters that you've been waiting for – the ones that tell you how to "repair" your credit. I'm going to show you, step-by-step, how to improve your credit reports and raise your credit scores.

To do this, I'm going to teach you a complete credit repair system. I call it the "RACE" system – Remove, Add, Correct, Explain. By following the steps of this system, you'll remove any bad information from your credit reports, add new positive information, correct any remaining bad information, and explain the rest. When you've completed the RACE system, your credit reports will be greatly improved, your credit scores will be increased, and you'll be "racing" to prosperity.

But first, I want to teach you an organized method that you can use to implement the RACE system. I call it the "WRTF" process – Write, Record, Track, Follow-Up. The WRTF process will help you to organize all of your communications with the credit bureaus and creditors and will greatly improve the results you receive from the RACE system. So, if you're ready, let's talk about the WRTF process.

The "WRTF" Process

The letters of WRTF process simply remind you of the steps that you should follow EVERY time that you communicate with a credit bureau or creditor – Write, Record, Track and Follow-Up. Now let's look at each of these steps.

Write

The first step of the WRTF process is to communicate with the credit bureau or creditor about whatever credit issue you have with them. The idea behind "Write" is to remind you that you should always put ALL of these communications in writing whenever possible. This means that you should avoid the temptation, and the credit bureaus' efforts, to communicate by telephone or over the internet.

I suggest that you do this for two reasons. First, because of the large volume of complaints that the credit bureaus and creditors receive from consumers, it is certainly possible that your communication will get lost in the shuffle. Yes, I know that's possible with written letters, too. But, written letters allow you to prove that you actually sent the communication.

With a written letter, you can prove that you sent your letter to the credit bureau and that the credit bureau actually received your letter. So, even if the credit bureaus lose your letter, you can prove that they DID receive it. And, as we'll soon discuss, the credit bureaus generally have only 30 days to investigate your complaint and attempt to verify it. If they can't, then the credit bureaus MUST remove the disputed credit information from your credit reports. That's why it's vital to your credit repair efforts to keep written records of your complaints.

However, I know that SOMETIMES there are reasons for communicating over the telephone or internet. I even do this occasionally if I need to quickly improve a client's credit scores. But, if you are forced to do this, you should STILL put the communication in writing. For example, you should send a letter that goes like this: "As we discussed during our April 30, 2010 conversation, you and I have agreed to the following ...."

OK. I think you get the point – PUT EVERYTHING IN WRITING! (Be sure to visit my website at www.SaveYourFloridaHomeNow.com to find many additional sample letters, forms, and worksheets that you can use in your journey to better credit!)

Record or Receipt

The second step of the WRTF process is to keep a record or receipt of every communication with the credit bureaus or creditors. You can use these records or receipts to prove that you sent dispute letters and that the credit bureaus and creditors received those dispute letters.

Therefore, you should always do two things when you send your written letters. First, make copies of EVERYTHING you send to the credit bureaus or creditors. Remember, letters have a way of disappearing. If the credit bureaus or creditors lose your dispute letters, you'll still have a copy. In addition, it will be much easier for you to keep track of the specific complaints you make to each credit bureau or creditor if you keep copies of all the dispute letters.

The second thing you should always do is send your dispute letters by Certified Mail – Return Receipt Requested. (You can also send your letters by overnight delivery services like Federal Express, United Parcel Service, or Express Mail from the U.S. Postal Service. Any of these services will provide you with a delivery confirmation. The only reason that we suggest that you use Certified Mail is because it's much cheaper than the overnight services.)

To send a letter by Certified Mail, take the letter to the post office, and complete the two Certified Mail forms. This service will cost a little more than normal first class delivery, but the benefits are well worth the extra expense.

There are two reasons that you should send all of your letters with a delivery confirmation and receipt (like Certified Mail – Return Receipt Requested). First, an employee at the credit bureau or creditor will have to sign the receipt. This proves that the credit bureau or creditor DID receive your dispute letter.

Second, this receipt will show WHEN the credit bureau or creditor received your dispute letter. Remember, the Fair Credit Reporting Act has time limits within which the creditors must respond. If the credit bureaus fail to respond to your dispute within 30 days, they must delete the credit information from your report. That's why it's so important to know when the credit bureau or creditor received the dispute letter. Then, if they fail to respond within 30 days, you win! But, before you can win, you need to make sure that you track all of your disputes, so that you know how long each credit bureau and creditor has to respond. So, let's talk about that process.

Track Your Disputes

The third part of the WRTF process is to TRACK your disputes with the credit bureaus and creditors. This means that you must have some organized way to keep track of all of your disputes. I've created a form called "The Dispute Tracker" that can help you to do this. You can download it at www.SaveYourFloridaHomeNow.com.

You don't need to use The Dispute Tracker to track your disputes. But, you MUST use SOME system that allows you to track your disputes and the dates that the credit bureaus received the disputes and when they responded. This is ESSENTIAL in your efforts to your credit repair efforts. With that said, let's look at the final step of the WRTF process.

Follow Up on Your Disputes

The last part of the WRTF process is to FOLLOW-UP on your disputes. It's VERY likely that the credit bureaus or creditors will not respond to your initial communications. Yes, they're supposed to do this, but sometimes they just don't. (That's why you need to keep copies of your letters and the Return Receipts).

Therefore, you're going to need to be persistent – don't let the credit bureaus or creditors ignore you into everlasting bad credit. You MUST send follow-up letters to the credit bureaus and creditors if they fail to respond to you. At the very least, this may get them to reply. And, if you ultimately need to bring court action to enforce your rights, it will be very helpful to show that the credit bureaus and creditors ignored several of your letters. For now, let me give you an overview of this process.

First, you send your written dispute letter by Certified Mail. If the credit bureaus fail to respond to your letter within 30 days, you'll send them another letter by Certified Mail with PROOF of the date they received the first letter. In this letter, you'll remind them of their legal obligations – and liability – under the FCRA and other laws. If they fail to respond to this second letter, you can either send notice to the FTC or sue them. That's the WRTF process in a nutshell!

You should use this step-by-step process EVERY time that you communicate with a credit bureau or creditor. If you do, you'll avoid many problems, and should win your disputes. (And that's a good feeling!)

Now that you know the system for communicating with the credit bureaus and creditors, it's time to learn about the stuff that's going to go into your communications. To do this, I'm going to teach you some of the basics from my complete credit repair system – the RACE system. So, it you're ready, let's fix your credit!

Chapter Fifteen

Removing and Correcting Bad Information

The RACE System of Credit Repair

The RACE system of credit repair is really a collection of basic and advanced credit repair techniques rolled into four easy-to-remember steps – Remove, Add, Correct, and Explain. To some extent, these steps follow the importance that I place on each set of techniques. However, I recommend that you do ALL of the steps at the same time, if possible.

For example, although you certainly want to force the credit bureaus to accurately report all of your credit information, your ultimate goal should be to completely remove all bad information from your credit reports. So, you'll be working to correct and remove bad credit information at the same time. In fact, because these two steps are so closely related, we're going to explain them at the same time.

And, you need to IMMEDIATELY start to add good credit information to your credit reports. Although you may not qualify for some types of credit until your credit scores improve, there are many types of good credit accounts that you can add to your credit reports NOW. So, I don't want you to think that you must wait until your credit is perfect again to seek out new credit.

Therefore, in the next several sections, I'm going to introduce you to all four steps of the RACE credit repair system. But, remember, I want you to work on ALL of the steps at the same time. OK? Great, then let's go!

Remove Bad Credit Information, and Correct It if You Must

The first step of the RACE system is to REMOVE bad credit information from your credit reports. I made this the first step of the RACE system because your primary goal with any bad credit information should be to remove that information from your credit reports, rather than simply correcting it. Sure, we want to get the credit bureaus to accurately report your credit information. But, unless you're able to get the credit bureaus or creditors to change bad credit information into good credit information (you can), simply correcting the incorrect bad information into correct bad information isn't good enough.

Of course, the third step of the RACE system is to correct bad credit information. And for some of your bad credit, correcting that information may be the best that you can do. But, whenever possible, you should try to get the bad information completely removed from your credit reports – even if that information is essentially correct. In this chapter, I'm going to show you many ways to do this.

However, because you will probably not be able to get the credit bureaus or your creditors to remove all of your bad information from your credit reports, I'm also going to explain how to CORRECT and improve that information in this chapter. Again, our goal is to completely remove all of your bad credit information. But, you can still significantly increase your credit scores by correcting inaccurate information in your credit reports, even if you can't get that information completely removed.

So, even though our goal is to remove bad information (have I said that enough?) I'm first going to show you the process for correcting bad information in your credit reports. I'll tell you about the most common mistakes that you'll probably find on your credit reports, and show you exactly how to correct these mistakes.

Then, I'm going to show you several ways to get the credit bureaus to completely remove the bad information from your credit reports. Most of these techniques rely on the Fair Credit Reporting Act. However, I'm also going to show you one of my favorite and most powerful techniques. This technique combines the Fair Debt Collection Practices Act and the Fair Credit Reporting Act into one extremely advanced credit repair technique.

And finally, I'll show how to FORCE collection agencies to remove collection accounts from your credit reports. But first, let's talk about correcting your bad credit information.

Correct the Bad Information in Your Credit Reports

In this section, you're finally going to get to see some benefit to the work I had you do in earlier chapters. If you carefully reviewed your credit reports, I can almost guarantee that you found mistakes in them – probably a lot of mistakes. This is very common for people who have had credit issues.

Why are there Mistakes in Credit Reports?

The main reason that there are so many mistakes in credit reports is because creditors don't do what they're supposed to do. I know that you probably find that hard to believe. But, almost all of the inaccurate information in credit reports is caused by creditors' failure to properly update that information with the credit bureaus.

You see, the credit reporting system relies almost completely on creditors. Except for public record information, your creditors supply most of the information in your credit reports to the credit bureaus. And, creditors supply most of that information to the credit bureaus electronically, using a system called Metro 2.

The Metro 2 Format

The Metro 2 format is a standardized credit reporting software that all of the major credit bureaus use to receive and update credit information. Using the Metro 2 format, creditors can electronically transmit credit information about their customers to the credit bureaus. But, as with any software, the standard rule applies – garbage in, garbage out.

If the creditor's employees fail to accurately enter their customer's credit information into the proper fields of the Metro 2 software, the credit bureaus will incorrectly report that information in these customers' credit reports. And, that's exactly what happens, every day!

File Mixing is Another Cause of Incorrect Credit Information

Another major cause of incorrect credit information is "file mixing". File mixing occurs when information from another person's credit report gets mixed into your credit report. It may surprise you to learn how this happens.

Although most people think that the credit bureaus keep electronic records of your credit file, that's not exactly how the process works. Instead, the credit bureaus keep all of the credit information for all consumers in their databases. Then, when someone requests a credit report, the credit bureaus use formulas, called algorithms, to find that information about the consumer.

To do this, the algorithms search for identifying information, like first name, last name, Social Security number, addresses, etc. Believe it or not, the credit bureaus do not need an exact match of your Social Security Number to pull your credit report. In fact, some consumer attorneys report that at least one credit bureau only requires that five of the nine digits in the Social Security number match, if other identifying information is similar.

Unfortunately, this means that people with similar names or similar Social Security numbers may end up "sharing" their credit information. I see this most often with family members, like fathers and sons with the same name. But, I've also seen this happen between people with very different names.

This is why you must closely review your identification information in your credit reports. If any incorrect information is reporting here, you MUST get it corrected. You don't want to spend a great deal of time and effort improving your credit reports, only to have them sullied again by someone else's bad credit!

But, I have a word of caution here. Sometimes, YOU won't be able to see file mixing in action with the credit reports that you receive from the credit bureaus, but your CREDITORS will see it. This happens because the credit bureaus require extensive documentation of your identity before they will send you your credit report. You've probably already seen this. They want your full name, Social Security number, current and former addresses, etc.

But, creditors can supply minimal information to the credit bureau and still receive your credit report. This means that the likelihood for file mixing is greater in a credit report that a creditor receives, than in a credit report that you receive directly from the credit bureau. Therefore, if possible, it would be good if one of your creditors will allow you to see a copy of the credit report that they received from the credit bureau.

The Process for Correcting Inaccurate Credit Information

Now that you know some of the reasons that incorrect credit information appears in your credit reports (there are more), let's talk about fixing these problems. You should use this general process whenever you dispute any credit information with the credit bureaus.

(But, as I've said once or twice before, even though you will dispute certain information regarding your incorrect credit, your ultimate goal should be to have credit bureaus completely remove that information.)

1. Identify the Incorrect Information

You should have already identified the incorrect information in your credit reports. Now it's time to take that information and draft a complaint letter.

2. Draft a Dispute Letter

Remember, writing is the first part of the WRTF system. So, unless it's an emergency, DO NOT use the credit bureau's online process to dispute your inaccurate credit. I say this for two reasons.

First, under the FCRA, credit bureaus must remove any credit information from your credit report if they fail to verify the disputed information within 30 to 45 days. But, unless you have proof of the date that you disputed this information, you cannot enforce your rights.

Second, I personally feel that the credit bureaus limit too severely the potential disputes that you can raise. When you write your own letter, you can dispute anything that's wrong with the credit information. This provides you with many more opportunities for the credit bureaus to simply remove the credit information from your file.

OK. So you know to write the letter. But, how should you dispute the credit information in that letter?

Well, the answer depends on the type of credit information and the problems with that information. But, in general, you want to dispute ANYTHING that's wrong with the account information. For example, here's a list of potential disputes:

1. Incorrect Balance;
2. Incorrect Past Due Balance;
3. Incorrect Credit Limit;
4. Incorrect Status;
5. Incorrect Charge-Off Date;
6. I Wasn't Late;
7. Not My Account;
8. Wrong Account Number

There are many more potential problems with credit entries, but this will give you an idea. Hopefully, you'll find MORE than one problem with your bad accounts. I like to dispute three or four items for each account. I do this because the credit bureaus' dispute system (E-OSCAR) only has room for transmitting two disputes to the creditor. If the credit bureau only transmits two disputes to the creditor, and I've disputed three, it sets up a violation of the FCRA – and a reason to have the account permanently deleted from the credit report!

Now, I'm NOT suggesting that you create disputes when there isn't any incorrect information. This may subject you to the "frivolous dispute" defense from the credit bureaus and make it much harder for you to object to legitimate problems in the future.

But, you certainly have a right to object to ANY incorrect information in your credit reports. And you should.

Make Sure that You Dispute the "Right" Information

While you're objecting to all of that incorrect information, remember to keep your eye on the ultimate goal of credit repair - raising your credit scores. You don't want to force the credit bureaus to correct an account and actually lower your credit scores.

For example, if the credit bureaus are incorrectly reporting a credit limit as HIGHER than it actually is, you DON'T want to object to this credit limit. Why? Think back to our discussion of credit scores.

One of the primary factors in the "Amounts Owed" section of your credit score is the balance-to-credit-line ratio. If you dispute a HIGH credit line, and the credit bureau responds to your dispute by lowering the credit line, then your credit score is likely to drop, because you've increased the balance-to-credit-line ratio. So, make sure that you dispute the "right" information.

3. Send the Dispute Letter by Certified Mail - Return Receipt Requested

As you recall, the second step of the WRTF system is to document all of your communication with the credit bureaus. This means that you should send your dispute letters to the credit bureaus by Certified Mail – Return Receipt Requested.

When you send your letter using this service, a credit bureau employee must sign for the letter, and provide the date they received the letter on the Return Receipt. Then, the Postal Service will send you the Return Receipt for your records. Now, you have proof that the credit bureau received your letter. You also know the starting date for the 30 or 45 –day countdown. But, you're not finished. You need to track your disputes.

4. Track Your Disputes

The third step of the WRTF system is to Track your disputes. Remember, you'll probably have at least three letters out at any one time (maybe more), all of which dispute one or more credit problems. If you don't use some type of organized system for your disputes, you're likely to lose track of which information you've disputed with which credit bureau and when. So, make sure you enter all of your disputes.

5. Follow Up

The final step of the WRTF system is to follow up with the credit bureaus. Remember, the FCRA allows the credit bureaus 30 to 45 days to verify the information you've disputed or remove it. So, don't let them ignore you. Instead, follow up with the credit bureaus after the time has run on your disputes. How you follow up depends on the response – or lack thereof – that you receive from the credit bureaus.

If You Receive a Preliminary Response Requesting Additional Information

The first response that you're likely to receive from a credit bureaus or creditor is a preliminary response requesting additional information. Sometimes this is just a stalling tactic. Then again, sometimes it's a legitimate request that will aid them in verifying the disputed information. So, assuming that the request is reasonable, just send them whatever information they request.

Under section 611(a)(1)(B) of the FCRA (15 U.S.C. §1681i(a)(1)(B)), the credit bureaus get a 15-day extension if they request additional information from you. The extension is NOT 15 days from the date the credit bureaus receive the additional information from you – it's a maximum of 15 days beyond the normal 30-day limit.

If the Credit Bureaus or Creditors Correct the Mistakes

Under section 611(a)(1)(A) of the FCRA (15 U.S.C. §1681i(a)(1)(A)), the credit bureaus have 30 days to investigate your dispute, and then must either correct the mistake, delete the information, or tell you why they think the information is accurate. Of course, the response that we HOPE to get from the credit bureaus is that they have corrected or removed the information from your credit report. Congratulate yourself if you receive this response from the credit bureau, because you've just "repaired" your credit!

If so, just move on to the next bad account and start again. But, more often than not, the credit bureaus will respond that the information is "verified" and will refuse to correct or delete it.

If the Credit Bureaus Do Not Correct the Mistakes

Don't be too surprised if the credit bureaus refuse to correct the disputed information. More often than not, the credit bureau will respond to your dispute by claiming that your creditor has "verified" that the information is accurate. If this happens, and it will, don't get discouraged. You just have some more work to do.

In this section, I'm going to tell you how the credit bureaus and creditors are supposed to investigate disputed credit information. Then, I'm going to tell you how this process really works. When you understand the flaws with this system, I'll show you how to take advantage of these flaws and force the credit bureaus to correct this "verified" information.

The Reinvestigation Process - The Way It's Supposed to Work

The FCRA provides the process that the credit bureaus and creditors are supposed to follow when a consumer disputes credit information. As you know, under section 611(a)(1)(A) of the FCRA (15 U.S.C. §1681i(a)(1)(A)), the credit bureaus have 30 days to "reinvestigate" the disputed information once they receive your dispute.

Under section 611(a)(2)(A)(1) of the FCRA (15 U.S.C. §1681i(a)(2)(A)(1)), the credit bureaus must notify the creditor about the dispute within 5 days and forward to that creditor all relevant information about the dispute that the credit bureau has received. If the credit bureau subsequently receives additional information from the consumer, the credit bureau is supposed to send that additional information to the creditor as well.

Under section 623(a)(2)(B) of the FCRA (15 U.S.C. §1681s-2(a)(2)), once the creditor receives notice of the dispute from the credit bureau, the creditor is supposed to conduct an investigation to determine whether the information is accurate and complete. The creditor must then notify the credit bureau about the results of the investigation, so that the credit bureau can notify the consumer.

Then, under section 611(a)(6) of the FCRA (15 U.S.C. §1681i(a)(6)), the credit bureau is supposed to provide written notice regarding the results of the reinvestigation and a copy of the updated credit report. This is how the reinvestigation process is supposed to work. Unfortunately, in practice, the credit bureaus and creditors have their own interpretation of this process.

How the Reinvestigation Process Really Works

Now that you know how this process is supposed to work, let's see how it works in the real world. Because the credit bureaus receive so many credit disputes (as many as 50,000 per week), they developed an automated on-line reinvestigation processing system called E-OSCAR (It stands for "Online Solution for Complete and Accurate Reporting"). E-OSCAR is a web-based system that allows the credit bureaus to notify creditors about disputes and for creditors to report the results of their "investigation".

Unfortunately, there are some real problems with the E-OSCAR system. First, your creditors don't receive the dispute letter that you send to the credit bureau. Instead, a credit bureau employee tries to determine the reason for your dispute and turns that dispute into one of 26 two-digit codes. This code is then transmitted to the creditor as part of an Automated Consumer Dispute Verification through the E-OSCAR system. As a result, several paragraphs of explanation about the problems with one of your accounts becomes a two-digit code for "not my account" or "not late".

In addition, under the E-OSCAR system, your creditors NEVER see any supporting documentation that you might have included in your dispute letters. Who knows what the credit bureaus do with these documents. What we do know is that credit bureaus don't send this information to creditors. So, at best, the only information your creditors receive about your dispute is a two-digit code based on a credit bureau employee's best guess about the dispute.

Even creditors complain that the E-OSCAR system makes it difficult for them to fully investigate credit disputes from their customers. Unfortunately, the credit bureaus require that ALL creditors use the E-OSCAR system for addressing credit disputes. As a result, EVERY dispute regarding any creditor that you send to the credit bureau is subject to the flaws of the E-OSCAR system.

And, although creditors complain about this process, we know that they aren't really innocent parties in all of this. As you recall, it's really the creditors that create the problems in the first place. If they accurately reported your credit information to the credit bureaus, there wouldn't be any need for you to complain about that information.

Unfortunately, creditors also aren't much help during the reinvestigation process either. As we mentioned before, the FCRA requires that creditors investigate any consumer disputes and ensure that the information is complete and accurate. If not, they must make the necessary changes and notify the credit bureau.

The FCRA doesn't specify what steps a creditor must take to ensure that this information is complete and accurate. However, the courts have ruled that creditors must conduct a "reasonable investigation". The FTC has ruled that at a minimum, this means that the creditor should review the original account records for this investigation, and conduct some form of investigation.

Unfortunately, evidence from many court cases suggests that creditors do NOT conduct any form of investigation, apart from confirming the information that they are currently reporting to the credit bureau. This means that, in reality, many creditors are just verifying the inaccurate information that they're already reporting to the credit bureau.

So, let's look at this reinvestigation process. The credit bureaus DON'T send your dispute letter to the creditor and DON'T send any evidence that you sent to prove your dispute. Then, a credit bureau employee tries to cram your dispute into a two-digit code and transmits this code to the creditor. The creditor then reviews the inaccurate information that they're reporting to the credit bureau, and doesn't have any other information to prove that that information is wrong.

So, is it any wonder that the credit bureaus won't correct inaccurate information in your credit report? In fact, I'm always a bit surprised when the credit bureaus DO correct the information.

Request the Method of Verification - A Very Powerful Credit Repair Tool!

If a credit bureau responds to a VALID dispute by claiming that the creditor has "verified" that the information is accurate, you need to ask the credit bureau to tell you HOW it verified the information. Under section 611(a)(7) of the FCRA (15 U.S.C. §1681i(a)(7)), the credit bureau must send you "a description of the procedure used to determine the accuracy and completeness of the information" within 15 days after you request this information. This description must also include the name, address, and telephone number of the furnisher of information that the credit bureau contacted to verify the information.

I have found this to be a very powerful technique to correct and remove bad information from credit reports. Remember, most creditors do NOT conduct any form of investigation following a dispute.

Very often, a credit bureau will simply remove the disputed information once I send a letter requesting the procedure they used to verify the information. Why? Because they don't want to tell you what procedure – if any – they used. They would rather just correct or remove the disputed information.

Watch Out for Deleted Information that Gets Reinserted

One of the most frustrating problems with credit repair is having deleted information return to a credit report. One of the most common reasons for this is that creditors fail to update their internal Metro 2 records, and "dump" the old bad information to the credit bureaus. (The credit bureaus can also cause this problem if they fail to permanently remove disputed information from their files. Occasionally, credit bureaus will "suppress" or "cloak" disputed credit information pending the outcome of the investigation. This is called a "soft delete". Unfortunately, unless the credit bureaus actually delete the information from their files, suppressed or cloaked information will typically reappear in your credit report.)

In the old days, the credit bureaus reinserted deleted information all the time. Back then, all that I could do about it was to send another dispute letter and start the process all over again.

Apparently, this practice frustrated a lot of people because Congress amended the FCRA in 1996, and again in 2004, to prevent this deleted information from returning. Now, under section 611(a)(5)(C) of the FCRA (15 U.S.C. §1681i(a)(5)(C)), the credit bureaus must maintain reasonable procedures to prevent the reappearance of deleted information. In addition, under section 611(a)(5)(B)(i) of the FCRA (15 U.S.C. §1681i(a)(5)(B)(i)), a credit bureau can only reinsert deleted information if the creditor "certifies that the information is complete and accurate." And, under section 611(a)(5)(B)(ii) of the FCRA (15 U.S.C. §1681i(a)(5)(B)(ii)), the credit bureau must notify you in writing within 5 business days if it reinserts deleted information into your credit report. Failure to follow these rules and procedures subjects the credit bureau to liability under the FCRA.

In addition, the 2004 amendments also require that creditors take steps to prevent this information from returning. Under section 623(b)(1)(E) of the FCRA (15 U.S.C. §1681s-2(b)(1)(E)), creditors must modify, delete, or permanently block any inaccurate or unverifiable information in its files. Failure to do this subjects the creditor to liability under the FCRA.

So, at least legally, deleted information is not supposed to get reinserted into your credit reports. Nevertheless, you should always watch out for this problem. If deleted information DOES get reinserted into your credit reports, you should immediately send a dispute letter to the credit bureau and the creditor and threaten legal action.

Final Words on Correcting Information

OK. That's the process for correcting mistakes in your credit reports. I know that I took some twists and turns during that process and included a lot of explanation. So, let's summarize the procedure.

1. Identify the Incorrect Information;

2. Draft the Dispute Letters;

3. Send the Dispute Letter by Certified Mail – Return Receipt Requested;

4. Track Your Disputes with the Dispute Tracker;

5. Follow-Up Based on the Response You Receive

6. Start on the Next Problem

If you follow this procedure, you WILL correct most of the mistakes in your credit reports. As a result, your credit scores should improve. But, remember, we ultimately want to try to REMOVE all of the bad credit information from your credit reports. I'm going to show you many ways to do this in a moment.

Removing Bad Information from Your Credit Reports

Now let's talk about the real goal of credit repair – to remove bad credit information from your credit reports. First, we're going to talk about the "official" way to remove bad information.

Under the FCRA, most bad credit information can only appear on your credit reports for a certain amount of time. After that, the information becomes "obsolete" and must be deleted from your reports. The credit bureaus want you to believe that this is the ONLY way that you can remove bad information from your credit reports.

But, that's just not true! In fact, to show you just how wrong this is, I'm going to follow up our discussion of obsolete information with MANY different techniques that you can use to remove bad credit information from your credit reports. Sound good? OK. Let's go!

Remove Obsolete Information from Your Credit Reports

So, let's start with the official way to remove bad credit information from your credit reports. Under Section 605 of the Fair Credit Reporting Act (15 U.S.C. §1681c), credit bureaus can only report most credit information for a certain amount of time. After that time expires, the FCRA says that the information is "obsolete" and credit bureaus CANNOT report this information in your credit reports. (In legal terms, this section is called a statute of limitations, because it limits the amount of time that something can happen – in this case, how long the credit bureaus can report bad information.)

This means that the credit bureaus MUST remove bad information from your credit reports once that information becomes obsolete. Of course, they don't always do this. Therefore, you must help the credit bureaus identify obsolete information in your credit reports and remind them of their legal obligation to remove that information.

But, to do that, YOU need to understand the different statutory time limits for the different types of credit information. Then, you'll be ready to battle the credit bureaus. So, if you're ready, let's look at these time limits.

Statutory Time Limits for Reporting Credit Information

As a general rule, MOST types of bad credit information become obsolete after seven years. However, the FCRA specifies five exceptions to this seven-year rule – bankruptcies, civil suits and judgments, paid tax liens, collection and charge-off accounts, and records relating to arrest. In addition, the Higher Education Act of 1965 gives additional exceptions to the seven year rule for student loans. To give you an idea of how these time periods work, let's look at the general rule, and then each of the exceptions to the general rule.

General Bad Credit Information

Let's start with the general rule. Under section 605(a)(5) of the FCRA (15 U.S.C. §1681c(a)(5)), most of your bad credit information becomes obsolete after SEVEN years. This section is the catch-all section for most types of credit. This means that ANY credit information that is NOT listed as an exception to the general rule becomes obsolete after seven years. For this type of credit information, the seven year "statute of limitation" starts to run from the date of the last scheduled payment prior to default.

Therefore, if the last payment that you made on one of your credit cards was credited to the June 15, 2003 payment, the credit bureaus can only report the delinquency until June 14, 2010. (In practice, they probably won't report the information after May 2010.)

Remember, this is the general rule for most types of credit information, other than the six specific exceptions. This seven year period does NOT change even if you included this account in the bankruptcy that you filed on September 30, 2003. I don't know why, but many people think that credit bureaus can report the accounts associated with a bankruptcy filing for TEN years. However, this is simply not true.

So now you know all about the general catch-all seven-year rule for credit reporting. But, for now, let's see how the six exceptions to the seven-year reporting rule affect you.

Bankruptcies

Under section 605(a)(1) of the FCRA (15 U.S.C. §1681c(a)(1)), credit bureaus can report information about all types of bankruptcy cases for 10 years after the date of filing. This includes Chapter 7, Chapter 11, and Chapter 13 cases. (However, the credit bureaus have voluntarily agreed to remove information about DISCHARGED Chapter 13 cases after seven years).

Civil Suits and Judgments

Under section 605(a)(2) of the FCRA (15 U.S.C. §1681c(a)(2)), the credit bureaus can report information about civil suits and judgments for seven years from the "date of entry" or until the governing statute of limitations has expired, whichever is longer. For a civil suit, the date of entry is the date the suit was filed. For judgments, the date of entry is the date that the judgment was entered.

For lawsuits, this generally means that the credit bureaus can only report information for seven years after the suit is filed. (There is some disagreement about how the statute of limitations might affect this. But, in general, the credit bureaus can probably only report this information for seven years).

But, this section can dramatically increase the amount of time that credit bureaus can report information on judgments. Why? Because in many jurisdictions, the "governing statute of limitations" for judgments can be much longer than seven years. In fact, in some jurisdictions, the statute of limitations can be as long as 20 years! That means that the credit bureaus could report this information for up to 20 years!

How does this section apply if you've been through foreclosure? If you've been through foreclosure, and a "Judgment of Foreclosure" was entered in your case, this should only remain on your credit report for seven years. However, if the creditor received a "Deficiency Judgment", the deficiency judgment could theoretically remain on your credit report for 20 years! (This is another good reason to consider filing a bankruptcy case to eliminate any potential deficiency judgments or claims).

The only good news about this is that the FTC has determined that PAID judgments can only be reported for seven years after the judgment was entered. The reason behind this is that payment of the judgment eliminates the need for a statute of limitations relating to the collection of the judgment.

Of course, there are MANY ways to resolve your credit problems. Don't worry if you have an unpaid judgment on your credit reports. I'm going to tell you about some techniques that you can use to have this judgment removed from your credit reports, even if the information isn't officially obsolete.

Paid Tax Liens

Under section 605(a)(3) of the FCRA (15 U.S.C. §1681c(a)(3)), the credit bureaus can report information about paid tax liens for seven years after the date of PAYMENT. This means that the credit bureaus could report information about the tax liens for more than seven years after they were first filed.

Because the FCRA specifically excludes PAID tax liens from the seven-year general rule, it should follow that UNPAID tax liens should be subject to the seven-year general rule. However, the FTC has taken the position that the credit bureaus can report unpaid tax liens for as long as they remain filed and effective.

Collection and Charge-Off Accounts

Accounts sent to collection and charged to profit and loss are subject to a slightly different seven-year rule than other types of credit accounts. Under section 605(a)(4) of the FCRA (15 U.S.C. §1681c(a)(4)), these accounts are still generally subject to a seven year limitations period. However, unlike other types of accounts, the time limit starts to run approximately 180 days after the first delinquency that caused the creditor to place the account for collection or charge it off. So, as a practical matter, the time period for collection and charge-off accounts is six months longer than for other credit accounts.

Congress added this section to the FCRA in 1996 to address some of the confusion in determining when a creditor actually placed an account into collection or charged it off. Now, it's a simple calculation. But, just to make sure, let's look at an example.

Let's say that you defaulted on one of your credit card accounts during January 2003. After several months, your creditor sent your account to a collection agency. If this account was NOT a collection account, the credit bureaus could report the delinquency on your credit reports for seven years, or until December 2009. However, because this IS a collection account, you should add six months to this date, or until June 2010.

Watch Out for Re-Aging

While we're talking about collection accounts, I want to make an important point about a common practice called re-aging. In almost every credit report I see, collection agencies incorrectly list the date of delinquency as the date that they RECEIVED the account from the original creditor or another collection agency.

Let me give you an example of this. As in the previous example, let's say that you defaulted on one of your credit card accounts during January 2003. After several months, your creditor sent your account to a collection agency. Under the FCRA, the credit bureaus could report this information for six months after the actual default plus seven years. Therefore, the information about this collection account would become obsolete after June 2010.

But, let's say that after unsuccessfully trying to collect payment from you for some time, that collection agency transferred or assigned your account to another collection agency. And, after some time, that collection agency transferred your account to another collection agency, and then another, and then another.

Finally, in July 2010, ABC Collection Agency received your account. They immediately reported the account to all of the credit bureaus, with a date of delinquency as July 2010 – seven years and six months after the actual default date. By this date, the information about this account would have been obsolete under the FCRA, and the credit bureaus would be forced to remove it.

But, because the new collection agency listed the date of delinquency as July 2006, they "re-aged" the account and started the seven-year period all over again. Of course, this is illegal. But, it happens all the time.

Also, another common re-aging scam (I mean "mistake") with collection accounts is that collection agencies act as if payment on the account restarts the time period for credit reporting. Although payment may be a problem in other ways (for example, this may lower your credit scores, and may restart the time limit for the statute of limitation that allows the creditor to sue you), this will NOT restart the statute of limitations for credit reporting purposes. So, as with other re-aging scams, you should make sure that collection agencies don't list the date of delinquency as the date of any recent payment to them!

Student Loans

Student loans are NOT one of the exceptions set forth in the FCRA for credit reporting time limits. So, you would think that they would be subject to the same seven-year rule as everything else. But, guess what. Student loans have their own credit reporting time limits.

You won't find these time limits in the FCRA. Instead, you'll find them in another set of statutes called the Higher Education Act of 1965. Under the Higher Education Act of 1965, there are two sets of rules for credit reporting, depending on whether the student loan is a loan provided under the Federal Family Education Loan Program or whether it's a Perkins Loan. Let's start with the Federal Family Education Loan Program.

Federal Family Education Loan Program

The Federal Family Education Loan Program ("FFELP") provides three types of loans for students – the Stafford Loan, the Federal PLUS

Loan (for parents) and the Federal Consolidation Loan. These types of loans are generally made to a student or parent by a lending institution and guaranteed by a guarantee agency and reinsured by the United States.

Pursuant to section 430A(f) of the Higher Education Act of 1965 (20 U.S.C. §1080a(f)), credit bureaus may report defaults on FFELP loans for seven years from the latest of three dates. The first date is when the Secretary of Education or the guaranty agency pays a claim to the loan holder on the guaranty. The second date is when the Secretary of Education, guaranty agency, or lender first reported the account to the credit bureau. The third date occurs when a borrower enters into a repayment agreement and then subsequently defaults. In this case, the seven-year period would start from the date of the last default.

So, for FFELP loans, it's very possible that the credit bureaus will report a default much longer than seven years from the actual default. For example, using the first date, it may take years for the Secretary of Education or guaranty agency to pay a claim on the defaulted loan. So, if it takes three years for this to happen, the default information will remain on the credit reports for ten years. But, it could be worse – if you default on a Perkins Loan.

Perkins Loan Program

Unlike the FFELP loans, a Perkins loan is a loan made directly to the student by the student's school acting as a lender. Upon default, the loan can be assigned to the United States for collection.

Under section 463(c)(3) of the Higher Education Act of 1965 (20 U.S.C. §187cc(c)(3)), credit bureaus can report information about Perkins loans until "the loan is paid in full." This means that if you've defaulted on a Perkins loan, and you still owe money on that loan, the credit bureaus can report the default FOREVER! Therefore, you should probably give priority to repaying Perkins loans if you have already defaulted in your payments.

Removing Bad Information that is Not Obsolete

As you know, the credit bureaus want you to believe that the ONLY way that you can remove bad information from your credit reports is when that information becomes obsolete. Fortunately for us, that's not really true.

In fact, there are many ways to legally remove bad credit information from your credit reports, even if that information isn't obsolete. In this section, I'm going to show you several of these techniques, including one of my favorite techniques for removing collection accounts from your reports.

The first technique is one that we've already talked about. This technique uses the procedural safeguards that Congress built into the FCRA. As we talked about before, section 611(a)(1)(A) of the FCRA (15 U.S.C. §1681i(a)(1)(A)) requires the credit bureaus to investigate your dispute within 30 days. Here's the actual language from the statute:

> Subject to subsection (f), if the completeness or accuracy of any item of information contained in a consumer's file at a consumer reporting agency is disputed by the consumer and the consumer notifies the agency directly, or indirectly through a reseller, of such dispute, the agency shall, free of charge, conduct a reasonable reinvestigation to determine whether the disputed information is inaccurate and record the current status of the disputed information, or delete the item from the file in accordance with paragraph (5), before the end of the 30-day period beginning on the date on which the agency receives the notice of the dispute from the consumer or reseller. (emphasis added).

Now, to give you the whole picture, here's the text of paragraph (5):

(5) Treatment of Inaccurate or Unverifiable Information

(A) In general. If, after any reinvestigation under paragraph (1) of any information disputed by a consumer, an item of the information is found to be inaccurate or incomplete or cannot be verified, the consumer reporting agency shall–

(i) promptly delete that item of information from the file of the consumer, or modify that item of information, as appropriate, based on the results of the reinvestigation; and

(ii) promptly notify the furnisher of that information that the information has been modified or deleted from the file of the consumer. (emphasis added).

So, between these two paragraphs, we get the whole technique. If the creditor cannot verify the information, or fails to verify the disputed information within 30 days (45 days if you send the credit bureau additional information), the credit bureaus must "promptly delete the item of information from the file of the consumer."

I use this technique all of the time with my clients. And you know what? It actually works. It's certainly not 100% effective, but it does work.

So, if you're trying to get bad credit removed from your credit reports, you should try to find as many problems with each account as possible. I gave you a list of potential problems earlier. I don't recommend that you make up problems just to see if you can get the information removed. If you do this, you're likely to get the "frivolous dispute" defense from the credit bureaus and they will flag all of your future legitimate credit repair efforts, making it much more difficult for you to repair your credit.

Also, you should always be fairly specific about the reason for your dispute. Because credit repair companies are often disputing accurate information, they really don't have any real basis for the dispute. As a result, their dispute letters will say that the "account isn't mine" without any additional explanation.

Eventually, this type of dispute letter will draw the frivolous dispute defense and make future credit repair efforts difficult. So, don't do this. Try to be as specific as possible.

This is one of the areas where your efforts to correct and remove bad credit information overlap. This is because you can't really ask the credit bureaus to remove a bad account because the balance is not correct. Therefore, you must ask the credit bureaus to correct the balance, while hoping that the creditor can't actually verify the information or fails to verify it within the 30 or 45-day period.

To use this technique, follow the standard WRTF process. If the credit bureau does not respond within 5 days after the 30 or 45-day period, you should send them another letter. In that letter, attach a copy of the first letter and a copy of the Certified Mail Return Receipt, and demand that they comply with the FCRA and remove that information from your credit report.

Finally, if the credit bureaus fail to respond to your second letter, you should try sending one final letter. If this final letter doesn't work, you may need to notify the Federal Trade Commission or other authority, or consult with an attorney.

Remember, this technique is NOT 100% effective. But, ANY bad information that you can get removed from your credit reports is good. So, give this technique a shot.

Removing Collection Accounts from Your Credit Reports - The Debt Validation Technique

Now I'm going to tell you about one of my very favorite techniques for removing collection accounts from credit reports. It is extremely effective and not well known. I'm typically able to remove 50 to 75% of a client's collection accounts using this technique. It's called Debt Validation.

The Debt Validation technique combines the Fair Debt Collection Practices Act ("FDCPA") and the FCRA for maximum effectiveness. Under section 809(b) of the FDCPA (15 U.S.C. §1692g(b)), a consumer has a right to request a "verification" of a collection account from the collection agency. (I know that this is confusing. The statute is titled "Validation of debts" but the text of the statute talks about "verifying" the debt. We're not sure why Congress did this. It may just be a mistake). Here's the actual text of the statute:

> b) If the consumer notifies the debt collector in writing within the thirty-day period described in subsection (a) that the debt, or any portion thereof, is disputed, or that the consumer requests the name and address of the original creditor, the debt collector shall cease collection of the debt, or any disputed portion thereof, until the debt collector obtains verification of the debt or any copy of a judgment, or the name and address of the original creditor, and a copy of such verification or judgment, or name and address of the original creditor, is mailed to the consumer by the debt collector.

The thirty-day period mentioned in the statute is the time within which you must respond to a collection agency's first communication. However, collection agencies do not use certified mail to send this communication, and do not know when, or if, you actually received the notice. In fact, you may NOT have received the notice. Bottom line, it's OK to request the validation at any time.

The FDCPA does not define "verification" or what a collection agency must do to comply with the statute. However, court cases and FTC Informal Staff Letters provide some guidance.

According to these authorities, a debt collector must provide the consumer with the following pieces of information to validate or "verify" a debt:

(1) the agreement with the original creditor that grants the debt collector authority to collect the debt:

(2) the original credit agreement that bears the signature of the debtor; and,

(3) the complete payment history starting with the original creditor.

These authorities have also determined that a computer printout listing the bill is not sufficient to validate a debt.

Now, let me tell you why this technique is so effective. You have probably already seen that many of your accounts get passed between several collection agencies. Many of my clients have had six or seven collection accounts for one original creditor.

And, guess what happens while your accounts are being transferred from one debt collector to another? That's right. Your original account information gets lost.

Sure, the debt collector will have some information from the original creditor or the last debt collector. That information probably includes your current balance. But, what they probably DON'T have is the original records of your account.

When you ask for these records, the debt collector simply can't produce them. And, very often, the original creditor can't locate them either. As a result, the debt collector can't "verify" the debt, and they must STOP attempting to collect the debt.

But, let me tell you why you want to use this technique for credit repair. When the collection agency receives the validation/verification request, it must STOP reporting the account information to the credit bureau until it can provide the verification. In addition, the collection agency must notify the credit bureaus that the information is disputed. The failure to do either of these things makes the collection agency liable for damages and attorney fees under the FDCPA and the FCRA.

Because the debt collector can probably NOT verify the debt with the original account information, it must STOP reporting the collection account to the credit bureaus. But, in case it doesn't do this, I always add a second step to this process.

If the debt collector continues to report the collection account to the credit bureaus, you should send a dispute letter to the credit bureaus. In this letter, you should explain that you requested that the debt collector validate the debt, and that you had not received a response from the debt collector. You should also attach the letter that you sent to the debt collector requesting the validation of the debt and a copy of the Certified Mail Return Receipt.

Typically, this information will be enough to have the credit bureau remove the information. However, if the credit bureau follows the normal reinvestigation procedure and the debt collector verifies the debt, then they've both violated the FCRA. The debt collector has violated the FCRA and the FCDPA. Fortunately, you probably won't need to get that far. By this point, the collection account has probably been removed from your credit reports. Good job!

Bonus Technique for Debt Collectors – Question Their Registration or Licensing

Here's a bonus technique that I include in all of my letters to debt collectors if possible. Many states require that debt collectors become registered or licensed by the state before they can legally collect debts from the state's residents.

For example, in Florida, it's a misdemeanor - a crime – for a debt collector to attempt to collect a debt in Florida unless that debt collector is registered with the state. Non-registered debt collectors are also subject to administrative fines and penalties.

All that I have to do to determine whether a debt collector has registered with the state is run a quick search in Florida's debt collector database. More than 50% of the out-of-state debt collectors that report collection accounts on our clients' credit reports are NOT registered in Florida.

Therefore, I always include a paragraph in my letters to these debt collectors that let's them know that I know about their failure to register. I'm never fully sure whether the collection agencies remove the collection accounts because of their inability to validate the debt, or because they're concerned about their registration problem. But, it doesn't really matter to me. All that I care about is that they remove the collection account and go away. And, more often than not, that's exactly what happens. (It's also a lot of fun!)

This Technique Works for Paid Collection Accounts Too!

The FTC has determined that consumers have a right to request validation of accounts even if they have already paid them! This doesn't seem to make much sense initially, because it doesn't seem that someone would pay a debt that they didn't think they owed.

But, I can tell you from experience that many people really DO pay debts that they don't owe. This generally happens because it's sometimes hard to identify the original creditor for these debts. For example, I had one client who paid three different debt collectors for the same debt.

(This is a good example of why the debt validation statute is an important protection for consumers.)

So, use this to your advantage. If you have collection accounts on your credit reports that show "Paid" or "Settled", use the debt validation technique. And, don't forget to add the question about licensing or registration if appropriate. You may be pleasantly surprised by the results.

Removing Inquiries

Finally, I want to talk to you about credit inquiries. As we talked about earlier, "hard" credit inquiries will cause your scores to drop somewhat, but generally not as much as other credit problems. For most of my clients, it's more productive for me to focus on all of the other credit problems first. This will probably be true for you too.

But, once you've removed or corrected everything else, you should try to remove as many inquiries as possible. Here's how to do it.

First, figure out which inquiries are the "hard" inquiries. These are the only inquiries that will lower your credit score. Therefore, these are the only ones that we care about.

Next, draft a dispute letter to your CREDITOR asking them to explain why they pulled your credit. If the creditor fails to respond, send another letter to the creditor threatening legal action. You should also send a letter to the credit bureaus and attached a copy of both letters that you sent to the creditor. This will generally get the credit bureaus to remove the inquiry.

If the creditor responds with proof that you authorized the inquiry, you may want to explain why you didn't understand that the creditor was going to pull your credit. This happens all the time. Salesmen are sometimes hesitant to ask if they can pull your credit because they're afraid that you'll say no and they'll lose the sale. So, they just gloss over this technicality and pull your credit anyway.

If you really didn't authorize the inquiry, stick to your guns and force them to remove the inquiry. Creditors are usually much more willing to remove, or fail to verify, credit inquiries than they are with other types of credit information.

Handling Problems with the Credit Bureaus

OK. Now you know all about the FCRA and the obligations that it imposes on credit bureaus and creditors. But, what happens if the credit bureaus or creditors simply fail to comply with your requests?

If this happens, and it may, there are two things that you can do. First, you can complain to any agency that regulates the credit bureaus or creditors. Generally, this means that you'll lodge complaints with the Federal Trade Commission or any agency in your state that investigates unfair or illegal business practices.

Your second option is to sue. Under many portions of the FCRA, you have a private right to sue the credit bureaus for their failure to comply with the FCRA. Unfortunately, the FCRA severely restricts your right to sue creditors or other providers of information for violating the FCRA. In addition, you may be able to sue collection agencies for FDCPA violations as well.

Let's take a moment to very briefly review these two options.

Complaining About Creditor Bureaus and Creditors

Your first option when dealing with a stubborn credit bureau or creditor is to complain to the authority that is responsible for regulating the credit bureaus and creditors. This is generally the Federal Trade Commission ("FTC"). Under section 621 of the FCRA (15 U.S.C. § 1681s), the FTC is responsible for enforcing the requirements of the FCRA.

But, you should understand that the FTC generally does NOT respond to single complaints against a credit bureau or creditor. Usually, the FTC will only respond if there appears to be an ongoing and repeated violation of the FCRA. But, it doesn't hurt to try.

In addition, even though Congress added new obligations on furnishers of credit information (creditors) to the FCRA, the FTC's ability to enforce those duties is extremely limited. So, don't count on much help from the FTC when handling disputes with creditors.

If you do file a complaint with the FTC, make sure that you send a copy of the complaint to the credit bureau. This complaint MAY get the credit bureau to quickly correct the problem, just in case the FTC actually does investigate the complaint.

Once you've completed your complaint, send it to the FTC at the following address:

Federal Trade Commission
CRC-240
Washington, D.C. 20580

Alternatively, you can file a complaint on-line at: https://rn.ftc.gov/pls/dod/wsolcq$.startup?Z_ORG_CODE=PU01. (It's OK to do this on-line because we're not concerned with time periods or deadlines.)

Suing the Credit Bureaus and Creditors

The second option that you MAY want to consider if a credit bureau or creditor fails to comply with your disputes is to sue them. The FCRA DOES allow you to sue the credit bureaus for various reasons. In addition you may have additional rights under the FDCPA or state laws to pursue creditors in court. (One of my favorite techniques for removing foreclosure judgments involves suing the mortgage lender in state court and is very effective!)

However, before you get too excited about suing the credit bureaus or creditors, let's talk about some of the problems that you may encounter. First, if you're suing one of the Big 3 Credit Bureaus, or a major creditor, remember that they have extensive resources and can afford to fight your lawsuit.

You, on the other hand, probably do NOT have a great deal of money, or time, to spare for your battle. Therefore, you'll be forced to bring an action in small claims court – where you won't need an attorney – or find a lawyer who is willing to handle your case on a contingency basis (meaning that the lawyer only gets money if you win the case).

In addition, you might LOSE your case. Courts have ruled that truth is an absolute defense to any action brought under the FCRA. Therefore, you may not be able to recover any damages, even if the credit bureaus failed to comply with the FCRA.

Therefore, don't rush into a lawsuit against the credit bureaus or creditors. There's nothing wrong with threatening to do this (because you have the right to do it). But, as a general rule, you should exhaust all of your other options first.

If you really think that you're out of options, I suggest that you seek out the services of a competent attorney who handles consumer law cases. Many attorneys do not handle these cases. If you can't locate a local consumer law attorney, you can contact me at www.cpricelawfirm.com and I will attempt to steer you in the right direction.

Final Thoughts on Removing Bad Credit

OK. That's it for removing bad credit from your credit reports. Hopefully, you should be able to completely remove many of your bad accounts by using several of the techniques we just discussed. But remember, there's still more to the RACE system. In the next chapter, I'm going to tell you about the next part – Adding good credit to your credit reports.

Chapter Sixteen

Adding Good Information to Your Credit Reports

The next step in the RACE system is to ADD good credit information to your credit reports. In a way, this is really the whole point of the RACE system. You're trying to increase your credit scores so that you can rebuild your credit. But, to increase your credit scores, you have to rebuild your credit. This sounds like a chicken and egg problem. Which comes first? Higher credit scores or new credit?

Well, the answer is a little of both. To increase your credit scores, you MUST add new credit. With new positive credit in your credit report, your credit scores will start to rise.

But, that doesn't mean that you can apply for and receive any type of credit. Instead, you need to use the techniques that I'll show in this chapter to get new credit accounts. Then, as your credit scores start to increase from these new accounts and from your other credit repair efforts, you'll be able to apply for and receive other types of credit. In the process, you'll rebuild your credit.

So, in this chapter, I'm going to show you some sure-fire ways to get new credit that will be added to your credit reports. You can add these new credit accounts even if you just recently been through foreclosure or filed bankruptcy, and even if your credit scores are still low. So, don't be afraid to follow this step of the RACE system.

(But, I have one word of caution here. It's very possible that your credit scores will actually drop when you start to add new credit. This is OK because your scores will increase over time with the new credit. However, DO NOT apply for new credit if you're in the middle of some other large credit transaction, like buying a car or house. If you do, your scores may drop and you may not qualify for the purchase. In this case, you should wait until after you have completed this large transaction before you apply for additional credit.)

"Adding" Account You Already Have

The first technique to add good credit information to your credit reports is to make sure that all of the good accounts you currently have are reporting to all of the credit bureaus. When you reviewed your credit reports, you may have found accounts that one or two credit bureaus were reporting, but not all three.

As you recall, this happens because not all creditors report to all three credit bureaus. Although most large creditors do report credit information to all three credit bureaus, many creditors only report to one or two credit bureaus. Therefore, several of your accounts may only appear in one or two credit bureaus.

If these are good credit accounts, you want to try and get all of the credit bureaus to report them. This will increase your credit scores from the credit bureaus that are not currently reporting the information.

You'll have to take the initiative if you want to get these accounts added to all of your credit reports. The FCRA does not require credit bureaus to report credit information from all of your creditors. And, it's likely that the account won't be updated after the initial entry. Nevertheless, this is a quick and easy way to add good credit to your credit reports and immediately raise your credit scores.

Adding Accounts Using Another Person's Good Credit

Another way to add good credit to your credit reports is to use another person's good credit. There are two ways to do this – Authorized User Accounts and Co-Signed Accounts. Let's talk about these techniques.

Authorized User Accounts

This is one of my very favorite techniques for adding good credit and raising credit scores. By adding authorized user accounts to your credit reports, you can immediately increase your credit scores, and it doesn't cost you anything.

An authorized user account really isn't YOUR account – it's another person's account. That other person qualified for the account and is responsible for repaying the debt. You don't have any liability for the account and don't have to repay any of the debt. You're just authorized to use the account.

To become an authorized user of an account, the account holder must request that the creditor add you to the account as an authorized user. Then, you may, or may not, receive a credit card with your name on it.

The creditor will then report the account information in YOUR credit report, even though the account really isn't your account. But, the good news is that you've added good credit to your account.

And, it gets better. Even though an authorized user account really isn't your account, it WILL affect your credit score – hopefully for the better. You "inherit" the entire history of that account immediately.

That means that if the account has been open for twenty years, it adds twenty years of credit history to your credit report. This will increase your credit scores.

If the balance is $1,000, and the credit line is $10,000, your balance-to-credit line ratio is 10% for that account. This will balance out any other high ratio accounts that you have.

The benefits go on and on. For all practical purposes, an authorized user account IS your account for credit score purposes. But, this can work both ways.

If the account holder fails to pay the account on time, this bad payment information will get reported in your credit report too. If the credit line is "maxed out", your credit scores may actually decrease if you add this account to your credit reports. You get the idea.

If you want to use this technique – and you should – just make sure that you pick the right person and the right accounts. Only ask people who use credit responsibly. And, only ask these responsible people to add you to accounts that are in good standing and that have a balance-to-credit line ratio of less than 50%.

Let me warn you in advance about the response you may receive when try this technique. Many people are very hesitant about adding authorized users to their accounts. I run into this problem all the time when we're trying to get clients qualified for mortgages. Many of our client's mothers and fathers have initially refused to add their children to their accounts as authorized users.

However, they almost always consent when I explain what we're doing and why. It also helps to tell them that the authorized user doesn't need a credit card imprinted with their name, and that they will terminate their authorized user status after their scores have improved. You might want to suggest these same things if you run into resistance.

Co-Signed Accounts

Another way to add good credit to your credit reports by using another person's credit is co-signing. When another person co-signs a loan with you, they become jointly liable with you for the entire debt. This type of loan is most common with automobile financing.

With this type of account, the creditor qualifies you and your co-signor for the loan. If your co-signor has good credit, you are more likely to receive the loan than if you applied without the co-signor. However, because of your credit, the terms of the loan will probably not be as good as if the co-signor applied without you.

Creditors are more willing to lend to you if you have a co-signor because they can seek repayment from the co-signor if you don't make the loan payments. And, because your co-signor has good credit, the lender is reasonably sure that the co-signor will repay the loan if you don't.

To use this technique, locate a friend or family member with good credit that trusts you enough to be jointly liable for the debt. Then, approach a lender and explain that you want to apply for credit with your co-signor. Then, the lender will check both of your credit reports.

If your co-signor's credit scores are good enough, the creditor will give you the loan or credit line. Then, as you repay the loan, the creditor will report the account and payment history to the credit bureaus. This will add new good credit to your credit reports and increase your credit scores.

But, be careful with this technique. If you don't repay the loan, the creditor will look to your co-signor for repayment. If the co-signor doesn't have the funds available to repay the loan, their credit will suffer too. Many people have been forced to file bankruptcy cases because they co-signed for someone else who didn't repay their loan. When the creditor sought repayment from the co-signor, they didn't have the money for repayment and ended up in bankruptcy.

So, be careful with your co-signor's credit and trust. If you use this technique, make sure that you repay the loan!

Secured Credit

If you recall, we talked about collateral and secured credit in earlier chapters. Secured creditors are creditors that "back up" their loans with some asset that you own. If you don't repay the loan as agreed, the creditor takes the asset to repay the debt. An asset that you use to back up loans is called collateral.

Because the creditor can take the collateral to repay the loan, these loans are generally safe for creditors. Therefore, most creditors will give you a secured loan, even if your credit scores are low.

So, secured credit can be a powerful technique for adding new good credit to your credit reports. Now, let's look at two ways that you can use secured credit to increase your credit scores.

Secured Bank Cards

The first way to use secured credit is to open a secured VISA or MasterCard account. Most major banks and many other creditors offer secured VISA and MasterCard accounts.

Here's how they work. You open an account with the bank that issues the secured credit card. Then, the bank uses that account as collateral for the credit line.

Depending on the bank, the credit line could be as much as 150% of the balance of the account. However, it's usually 100% of the balance of the account.

So, if you send the bank $500, they'll issue you a VISA or MasterCard with a $500 credit line. If you don't repay the loan, the bank will seize your $500 account to repay the credit line.

Then, as you make payments on the credit card account, the bank reports this information to the credit bureaus, and your credit scores will increase. As always, you need to make sure that your payments are timely. And, you should try to keep your balance under 50% of the total credit line.

The real problem with secured VISA or MasterCard accounts is that they're expensive. Banks typically charge an application fee initially and an annual fee each year. In addition, the annual percentage rate on these cards is usually quite high.

However, even with these problems, you MUST get at least one VISA or MasterCard (you may be able to qualify for an unsecured bankcard. I'll tell you about this in the next section.) It's essential to your credit re-building efforts that you have a bankcard like VISA or MasterCard. After some time, most of the banks that issue secured bankcards will return your initial deposit money so that the credit card ultimately becomes an unsecured bankcard.

Passbook Loans

Another way to add new credit to your credit reports using collateral is with passbook loans. Passbook loans are similar to secured bankcards, but the fees and interest rates are generally much lower than with secured bankcards.

To apply for a passbook loan, you must deposit money with a bank or credit union. This could be in the form of a regular savings account, or a certificate of deposit. Then, ask the bank or credit union for a loan secured by the account. Most banks and credit unions call this a passbook loan.

But, BEFORE you do this, make sure that the bank or credit union re-ports passbook loans to the credit bureaus. Many do not. And remember, our goal here is to add good credit to your credit reports. So, it's not very helpful to go through this trouble if the loan isn't going to show up in your credit reports anyway.

Most banks and credit unions do not charge any fees for passbook loans. And, the interest rate on the loan is usually only 2 or 3% higher than the rate that the bank or credit union pays to you on the savings. So, these accounts can be a very good way to add positive credit information to your credit reports – IF the bank or credit union reports the loan to the credit bureaus!

Unsecured Credit

The final way to add new good credit to your credit reports is to open new unsecured credit accounts. It used to be that the ONLY credit you could receive after a major credit problem was secured credit, like secured bankcards or passbook loans. But, because so many people have been through foreclosure and filed for bankruptcy, and because of the increased competition between banks for your business, many banks now offer bankcards that are completely UNSECURED. This means that you don't need to send them any money to secure the credit line.

I generally advise my clients to wait until they receive solicitations from banks offering these bankcards. These solicitations are usually "pre-approved". This means that the bank knows about your bad credit and poor credit scores, but is willing to give you the bankcard anyway. (I suggest waiting for the banks to send the solicitation so that you don't waste an inquiry by applying for a credit card and not getting approved.)

As with secured bankcards, the real problem with these credit cards is that they have high fees and interest rates. But again, it's worth paying these ridiculous fees and interest rates to accomplish our ultimate goal of increasing your credit scores. As your scores improve, you will qualify for "better" bankcards with no fees and low interest rates. Then, you can stop using these high-fee/high interest rate bankcards. But for now, I suggest that you get at least two bankcards (unsecured if possible, secured if not).

My Favorite Source for Reestablishing Unsecured Credit

I have one additional source for reestablishing unsecured credit after foreclosure, bankruptcy or other major credit problem. This credit source is part of my overall plan for all of my credit repair clients. However, the creditor has asked that I not list the information in this book. Instead, you can get information about the program by calling 1-800-803-7390 or by visiting my website at www.SaveYourFloridaHomeNow.com.

By using this credit source, you can instantly add a $5,000 to $10,000 unsecured credit line to your credit report with minimal cost to you. I added this credit source to my own credit reports and saw an immediate increase in my credit scores. You can do this too!

Final Thoughts on Adding Credit

OK. That's it for adding new credit to your credit reports. But, remember two main things from this chapter. First, make sure that ALL of your good credit gets reported to ALL three credit bureaus, if possible.

Second, it doesn't make sense to apply for new credit if the creditor won't report the account information to the credit bureaus. So, always ask the creditor BEFORE you apply for the credit (and get an inquiry on your credit) whether the creditor will report the account information to the credit bureaus. If not, don't apply for the credit. Just find another creditor that WILL report your account to the credit bureaus and apply for credit with that creditor.

Chapter Seventeen

Explaining Bad Information In Your Credit Reports

The final part of the RACE system is to EXPLAIN your bad credit information. You'll only have to do this if you haven't been able to correct or remove your bad information using the other parts of the RACE system. And, you'll probably only need to do this if you're applying for a mortgage. But, it can sometimes help to have a well-written explanation just in case a creditor wants to see it.

Write a Personal Statement

The primary reason for preparing a statement about your foreclosure or bankruptcy is to prepare for mortgage financing. Many underwriters want an explanation letter regarding these problems before they will approve the loan. So, I want to tell you what these underwriters expect to find in an explanation letter.

First, they want to see that the foreclosure or bankruptcy wasn't really your fault. For example, they want to see that an unexpected illness, injury or job loss forced you to file the bankruptcy. They do NOT want to see that you took trips around the world and cleared out jewelry stores with your credit cards.

Second, they want to see that whatever forced you into the foreclosure or bankruptcy has stopped and that you have the ability to repay your debts. For example, it's not very persuasive to say that your foreclosure or bankruptcy was caused by your job loss – if you're still unemployed. And, it's not helpful to say that the foreclosure or bankruptcy was caused by your ex-spouse's failure to pay child support, if that's still a problem.

Instead, it's better to identify the unfortunate cause of your foreclosure or bankruptcy, and explain how it's been resolved and how you're able to pay your bills now. For example, you could explain how you were injured while at work, and had to survive on reduced pay for four months. This caused the problems. But now, you're much better and working full time with full pay. Do you see how much better this is from the creditor's perspective?

In fact, that's how you should write your letter. Think about it from the creditor's perspective. What would you want to see in a letter if someone were asking you to loan you money? Would you want them to tell you that they're addicted to shopping, but they're working on it? Probably not.

So, think like a creditor when you draft your letter. (I'm NOT telling you to lie in your letter. But, there's always a way to improve the way you present the truth.)

Write a Consumer Statement

I have VERY mixed emotions about presenting this information to you. I say that because I don't believe that Consumer Statements are helpful – AT ALL. But, let me tell you what a Consumer Statement is, and then you'll understand why I don't think that they're useful.

Under section 611(b) of the FCRA (15 U.S.C. §1681i(b)), a consumer has the right to place a statement regarding a disputed debt in their credit report. Then, anyone who reviews the credit report will see the statement.

For example, let's say that you bought a new plasma television on credit, but it didn't work when you took it home. You asked the dealer to give you another television, but the dealer refused.

So, you refused to pay the monthly payments for the television. As a result, the dealer sent your account to a collection agency, and you ended up with a collection account in your credit reports.

If this happened, you'd probably use the techniques that we discussed earlier to remove the collection account from your credit reports. But, let's say that none of that worked and you still have the collection account in your credit reports.

Under section 611(b) of the FCRA (15 U.S.C. § 1681i(b)), you could add a statement about your dispute to your credit reports. However, you can only do this if you already disputed the account with the credit bureaus and if the dispute failed to resolve the problem.

If these things have happened, you can add a statement of any length to your credit reports to explain your side of the story. (You're limited to 100 words if the credit bureau helps you write the statement.) Then, anyone who reviews your credit report will see your statement. This sounds like a good idea, right?

Well, it used to be a good idea. But that was when creditors actually saw your credit report. Now, creditors rarely see your credit report. Instead, they're only looking at the credit scores.

Because the Consumer Statement has NO effect on your credit score, it really doesn't help your credit repair efforts. So, in most cases, it doesn't help – AT ALL – to add a Consumer Statement to your credit reports.

Personally, I never bother with them. I'd rather use my time disputing credit information that will actually raise credit scores. But, if you're bored, the FCRA allows you to add your explanation of a dispute to your credit reports.

Final Thoughts on Explaining Credit

OK. That's it for the last part of the RACE system. And, it's also the end of the RACE system. So, I have one word for you.

Congratulations! You've officially completed the most difficult part of this book! And soon, if you use the RACE system, you'll also be finished with the most difficult parts of your life after foreclosure or other major credit problem.

Conclusion

It's only money.

That's right.

It's only money.

Receiving a summons feels horrible. Working with a lender to modify a loan feels horrible. Filing for bankruptcy feels horrible.

Talking to an attorney about what you see as personal failures – even though they are not – feels horrible.

I sympathize, but I also have three words for you:

Get over it. You're in a terrible position, but you do have options. You can make choices. You can take concrete steps to protect and exercise your legal rights. You can use the legal process – in a way that it was specifically designed by lawmakers, and for the purpose they designed – to buy time, improve your leverage, and make the best of a horrible situation. Sometimes I think that's what we as Americans do best: We take bad situations, apply creativity, persistence, and good old-fashioned know-how... and we turn those bad situations into something better.

It's only money. It's just stuff.

The important things in your life are your family, your friends, your relationships... those are the things that matter.

You will survive. Heck, you will prosper.

Do everything you can to make sure you survive the threat of foreclosure and live a great life after foreclosure.

I know you can do it. I did. If I did...I know you can, too.

Best wishes ----

-- *Charlie Price*

www.ingramcontent.com/pod-product-compliance
Lightning Source LLC
Chambersburg PA
CBHW060425200326
41518CB00009B/1487
* 9 7 8 0 6 1 5 3 8 1 3 6 7 *